UNLOCK THE SECRETS OF THE NEW AGE

We have entered a new age. A time of new awareness. One that has been at our fingertips for a millennium. We can tap into the universe. We are only now rediscovering our untapped resources and ready to explore another reality that gives our lives depth and meaning, one that goes beyond time and space.

This manual is a spiritual first-aid handbook. Its main purpose is to acquaint you with spiritual understanding, connect it to your day-to-day life, and teach you about energy fields and how to improve your life by using them with people, places, and things you come in contact with. If you follow the teachings in this book, you can be your own practitioner, your own medium.

THE
UNSEEN
WORLD

*A Clairvoyant's Guide to
the Astonishing Power of
Your Mind and Spirit*

BARBARA STABINER

BANTAM BOOKS
TORONTO · NEW YORK · LONDON · SYDNEY · AUCKLAND

THE UNSEEN WORLD
A Bantam Book / January 1989

ISBN 0-553-27858-4

Published simultaneously in the United States and Canada

Bantam Books are published by Bantam Books, a division of Bantam
Doubleday Dell Publishing Group, Inc. Its trademark, consisting of the
words "Bantam Books" and the portrayal of a rooster, is Registered in
U.S. Patent and Trademark Office and in other countries. Marca
Registrada, Bantam Books, 666 Fifth Avenue, New York, New York
10103.

PRINTED IN THE UNITED STATES OF AMERICA

O   0 9 8 7 6 5 4 3 2 1

*For my husband Marty, my inspiration, who shares all of his
rainbows with me*

*For my daughters Lauren, Elissa, and Keri, who are but the
aspects of my soul*

*For Betty, my sister in past lives who did her thinking while
typing*

*For my parents, Miriam and Morris, who taught me
love*

I am a woman who seeks to make some contribution on this planet through spiritual guidance, healing, and teaching. I am a Clairvoyant.

I am often asked the same questions by those beginning to wet their feet in new ways of thinking, new ways of seeing.

For this reason I decided to gather those questions and answer them from my own understanding and experience.

Thus, I humbly offer this little book. May it become a useful companion on your personal journey, and a springboard to a fresh and broadening vision.

CONTENTS

Introduction
by Marty Davis

Marty Davis is a former network radio and television journalist. She has a master's degree in journalism from the American University in Washington, D.C., and is married to Robert W. Davis, a Republican congressman from Michigan.

> **Human history becomes more and more a race between education and catastrophe.**
>
> —H.G. WELLS, 1920

Who among us can forget the catastrophe of January 28, 1986? On that day, the space shuttle *Challenger* exploded, killing all seven crew members, including America's first teacher in space. To paraphrase William Shakespeare, my wounded heart and soul felt slashed to bits by razor blades. Barbara Stabiner—the author of this book—and I knew the shuttle was doomed the *day before* the tragedy.

On the morning of January 27—the day before the explosion—I called Barbara.

"I feel terrible," she moaned. "I got it last night."

"Got what?" I asked.

"Disaster. I feel disaster," she said. "It feels like a giant explosion. I see America in mourning."

"What is it?"

"I don't know, but I see an *S*—a word that begins with the letter *S*."

The letter *S*. What could that mean? Her words gnawed at me all day. Dear God, what was it?

I was watching the *CBS Evening News* when it hit me. A picture of the space shuttle flashed on the TV screen. "That's it!" I shouted to my husband, Bob. "That's it!" I pointed to the screen. "It's the space shuttle! It begins with the letter *S*."

I already had told Bob what Barbara had said earlier in the day. He didn't say much. He's grown accustomed to my unexplainable feelings.

"You're crazy," he replied. "Every time the shuttle goes up, people think something is going to happen."

"Bob, I know you don't believe me, but I just know it's the shuttle. It's going to explode tomorrow. I don't know how I know it, but I do. I have to call Barbara."

It was 7:30 P.M.—sixteen hours until the launch.

Barbara picked up the phone. I could tell she was still feeling bad. "Barbara." I hesitated. "It's the space shuttle."

There was a pause. I could hear her breathing. "Oh my God," Barbara said quietly.

"What are we going to do?" My hands were cold and I was sweating, that chilly nervous sweat I always get before I go on camera.

"I don't know. I'll think about it and call you back in a couple of hours."

I turned to Bob. "Maybe we should call NASA."

"Forget it, Marty. They're not going to believe you. They probably get hundreds of crank calls."

I knew he was right. So I waited for Barbara to call me back.

At nine-thirty the phone rang.

"Did you pick up on anything else?" I said.

"I'm seeing a fire and explosion, someone of Polish descent, the initials J.A.—does that mean anything to you?" she asked.

"No."

"The dates October twenty-eighth—something about a crash on October twenty-eighth—and January twenty-eight. Marty, do you know if there is anyone who is Polish—do you have the names of the crew?"

I knew there were seven, but I could remember only a couple.

"Hang on. I'm going downstairs to look for the newspaper in the garbage."

I ran downstairs and frantically ripped open garbage bags. I rummaged through several before finding a newspaper story which listed the names of the crew. No J.A. No one with a Polish-sounding name. And only one astronaut with a foreign last name: Ellison Onizuka.

"There's a J.A.—Judith A. Resnik," I reported. "There's a guy named Onizuka, but that's not Polish."

"I'm going to light some candles," Barbara said wearily. "Maybe that'll keep it from going up tomorrow. Good night. I'll talk to you in the morning."

At 9:30 A.M. I was in the bathroom reading *The Washington Post*. Exhausted after a terrible night's sleep, I picked up the phone in my bathroom and called Barbara.

"Thank God," she said. "The thing didn't go off."

I was surprised. "Why not?"

"The weather, too."

I hung up, relieved. But then I looked at my newspaper and saw a photo of schoolteacher Christa McAuliffe in her space suit. As I was staring at it, the feelings that had been tugging at me for the past twenty-four hours returned. *That poor woman*, I thought to myself.

I took a shower and started to get ready for a lunch date I had with a prominent Washington journalist and a CBS News correspondent. I was putting on my makeup when the phone rang. It was 11:45 A.M.

It was Barbara.

"Turn on the TV," she ordered.

I did. There was Dan Rather—a solemn Dan Rather—reporting, "The space shuttle *Challenger* exploded just after launch. . . ."

I froze. An eerie chill consumed my body and I began to shake and sob. I watched, fascinated and horrified, as CBS replayed the tape of the doomed launch. I saw the explosion and somehow I felt disconnected from reality.

"Oh no, oh no," I cried. "I can't believe it. Why, Barbara, why did this happen? We knew about it. We could have done something." I was sobbing uncontrollably.

Barbara was incredibly calm. "This has happened to me before. It's destiny. There was nothing you could have done. If you're going to go on [developing psychic abilities], you've got to learn how to handle it."

I got another call then. I told Barbara to hold while I took the call. It was Bob, obviously shaken. "Did you see it?" he said in a hushed voice.

I started to cry again. "Yeah, I'm talking to Barbara now."

He hung up. I knew he was having a hard time dealing with what had happened.

"Call me later this afternoon," Barbara said. "We must do something to help these people. They died so fast, they're still earthbound."

Foggily I made my way to the refrigerator. I was in a slow-motion dream. I poured myself a glass of wine and lighted a cigarette. *Dear God,* I thought. *Why did this have to happen? And how did I know it would?*

That evening Barbara wanted to perform a spiritual ritual to get the seven dead crew members away from the Earth Plane. She said it had happened so fast that their souls were confused— they didn't know what had hit them.

Okay, I told her. I'd try, but I was a little drunk. She told me to light a white candle. All I had was a birthday candle. That was fine, she said. We repeated The Lord's Prayer three times in unison while gazing into the flickering flame. She told me to imagine a golden staircase. "Can you see the seven astronauts," she said. "They are standing at the bottom."

Yes, I could. I was mesmerized by the flame. By God, I *could* see them!

One by one she called off each name: Christa McAuliffe, Francis (Dick) Scobee, Judith Resnik, Gregory Jarvis, Ellison Onizuka, Ron McNair, and Michael Smith, and persuaded them to walk up the golden staircase to free their souls from the Earth Plane.

"Can you see them?" she asked. "What are they doing?"

I told her what I saw.

"Good," she said.

Later Barbara revealed that she wanted to make sure I was seeing the same events she was.

I watched each one go up the staircase. Some were afraid. Barbara told them not to be. Some didn't want to go. It was all so real. I could see them so clearly. At last they were all up the staircase. I saw them waving good-bye to Earth. Barbara closed with a prayer.

I didn't sleep well for a long time after the shuttle tragedy. My mind was churning. I kept replaying the events and knew that my life would never be the same. Somehow I felt that this was the turning point in what had been an existence of self-canceling chaos. I began to feel that I was here on earth for some pure, lofty purpose and that it had probably been that way from the beginning, but I just wasn't aware of what fate had in store for me.

I remembered the old *Mission: Impossible* TV series, and the voice on the self-destructing tape droning, "Your mission, should you choose to accept it . . ." I finally had my mission and the choice was clear.

In 1901, author H. G. Wells observed, "The past is but the beginning of a beginning, and all that is and has been is but the twilight of the dawn."

It is the dawn of my odyssey of spiritual evolvement and I am not afraid. I have Barbara Stabiner to thank for patiently honing my heretofore latent psychic ability.

I have found power in the mysteries of thought,
exaltation in the chanting of the Muses;
I have been versed in the reasonings of men;
but Fate is stronger than anything I have known.

—EURIPIDES, 438 B.C., GREEK PHILOSOPHER

—MARTY DAVIS
MARCH 14, 1986
WASHINGTON, D.C.

PART ONE

—

IN THE
BEGINNING . . .

**Most of the Saints were never too
educated . . . What a blessing!**

TARA SINGH

1

The Art of Existence

I believe there is no wall between science, spirituality, and religion. As science explains more of the intriguing mysteries of life and the Universe, it reaches into those areas which previously were accepted only by the minority who understand these mysteries through psychic understanding, or who accept them solely on faith. We are becoming increasingly aware of the crumbling walls that once separated tangible science from elusive spirit. The more that science attempts to explain, the more it finds that logic is not the answer to everything.

All of us are multidimensional in character. Man is not just a self-enclosed, psycho-physical entity. He is also made of the social, spiritual/religious aspects of his being, which complete the complex structure of his existence. As a social being, he cannot find happiness through mere preoccupation with his own individual pleasure. Concern for social welfare is a vital factor of his well-being. By virtue of his religious aspect, he cannot live without some faith. He needs an ideal for which he can live and to preserve that for which he would be willing to die.

The human condition is multifaceted. Man is no longer satisfied with the answers provided by the "rational world." He needs a standard by which he can live, a dream toward which he can strive.

Every experience we have, physical or spiritual, fits together into a pattern that is part of the whole Universe. Man is the observer of the Universe, the experimenter, the searcher for truth, but he is not a spectator alone. He is a participant in the continuing process of creation.

It is through total commitment to a positive set of values that our lives become meaningful. Each individual must find the answers to his or her basic issues of existence; each of us must discover our own truth, ingrained in the depths of our own being, in the context of our own living experience. This discovery is part of our own personal evolution. This discovery is, indeed, our own salvation.

This is the Art of Existence. It is swimming in the stream of life. It is the ability to cross and recross the flux of time by boat if available, by swimming if necessary, and by both when the boat springs a leak and sinks before going the distance. Our existence depends upon our stabilizing the various aspects of ourselves. Once we balance the physical, psychological, spiritual, and religious aspects inside us, our lives fall into a peaceful pattern.

A decision was made before incarnation, in spirit worlds, to pick the time of our birth, place, and family to work out our Karma and destiny. We picked this trip and chose this life, and now we must begin to learn how to live it. We are charged with learning to explore the possibility of a separate reality, a reality we are finding to be valid. This is unlike the reality of our childhood teachings. Now our understanding has to link old-generation thinking with some conditioning for a new, progressive era.

The nature of this separate reality I speak of goes beyond the logical and reasoning mind of man. During this Age of Aquarius we are beginning to recognize a new electrified energy system affecting the way we think and perceive. We are now living in a Golden Age of positive change for our very own orbital sphere of a planet, learning that everything is *energy*. It inhabits everything. Energy *is*, energy is *forever*, and energy is always pure.

Man's evolutionary process is ready to advance now. Evolved souls, which some people call ghosts or spirits, have chosen this Aquarian Age to incarnate to help mankind discover an enlightened spiritual path. This book is going to explore the purposes and reasons we are here now, explaining the how-to's of being our own Gods, our own creators working in conjunction with all our "God sources" in the cosmos to realize our desires and dreams.

The time has come to take the *occult* (meaning "hidden knowledge"), the psychism out of the "booga-booga" tearooms. Let's open the windows to let in fresh air and light. We can explore this extraordinary part of nature just as we are. We can learn to understand where it all fits in to each part of our lives. We can also learn the laws of reincarnation. It's something like a charade, but the cast of players changes with each incarnation, and new scenes and places also come to exist. But the purpose of exploring our soul's growth never changes on any planet.

Have you ever attended a party or conference and looked around at the faces and into the eyes of some of the people there? You probably felt that some of them were vaguely familiar. Perhaps you wondered, What school did I attend with them? How did I know them—were they in my class? The class before mine? Well, it may be that the class you attended was in Egypt, Peru, or perhaps Atlantis, the school of the soul's experience.

We have entered a new age, a time of new awareness. One that has been at our fingertips for a millennium. We *can* tap in to the Universe. We are only now rediscovering our untapped resources and ready to explore another reality that gives our lives depth and meaning, one that goes beyond time and space. Knowledge easily learned is old, but knowledge that is new cannot come about without effort on our parts. When that feeling of despair comes and the ailing spirit can no longer be soothed, where can one go?

People may not get the answers that they need or may not always be satisfied with these answers the "rational world" provides. When new thoughts, insight, and positive feelings are awakened, ask yourself: Do you want to search for truth and light? New ideas, ideals, and a new perspective on which to base your future actions? The planet Earth is undergoing changes. The vibrations of the planet are speeding up, not only in the field of electronic communication, but an internal quickening. Nothing holds together as it once did.

Confusion prevails! If you are willing to work hard, change the old conditioning, and look to find the truth and what it is that is going on around you, you will find that all that you think you may *see* is not the case, but what you *feel* is. Once you understand this, a change will start to occur within you. Your life will be enhanced.

How we use our new knowledge determines its effect inside us and on the world around us. We are creators. What we create in our feelings, whether good or bad, is very important, for it is part of our personal world. We come from a source, a creative one, so we must create and exist as reflections of our own creation here in this time span. We are creating as we are learning and experiencing life. Therefore, everything in the Universe is intended for our learning, and life and death are just part of our tools. They are transitions from one dimension to another.

All energy is created in order to give polarity so that our souls can be shaped by two opposing forces. Each of us must find the answer to our own basic issues of existence, all of which can be found in the depths of our own being, within the context of our own living experience. It is vital to explore further and to pull in new sources of information to broaden our lives' scope.

Our spirits are such that they are constantly reaching and searching for fulfillment. We look first to the material things of the world, but they bring only temporary satisfaction. Then we look to organized religion with great hope and expectation, but still we do not find the answer to the real question: What is the meaning of my *life?*

Books on the occult and psychism have been around for many ages, but the time wasn't right for most people to gravitate to them. Up to this point many people have not been able to listen to, hear, or learn those teachings. We seem to be ready now.

This manual is a spiritual first-aid handbook. Its main purpose is to acquaint you with spiritual understanding, connect it to your day-to-day life, and teach you about energy fields and how to improve your life by using them with people, places, and things you come in contact with.

If you follow the teachings in this book, you can be your own practitioner, your own medium. I've also tried to embellish your understanding of how spiritual cleansing works, and how our health and vitality can be restored. Some rituals in this manual can be used to lift your emotions and help you feel renewed inner strength. Rarely do people understand all the rituals connected with religious practices, but the common denominator among the religions I teach is that all rituals and prayers are designed to keep us on track, so that we feel better once we have participated and cleansed our spirits.

For the "spiritual practitioner," these at-home formulas for change and transition are growth-oriented. Some of what is taught here has been communicated by spirit guides or entities, other material comes from my higher self or mind, so that I may teach you how these energy transfers can achieve positive results with those of you who are ready for these teachings.

All the procedures in this book are simple, safe, and effective. They have been utilized and positively work if they are followed as set down here. The beginner will have no difficulty in their application, but students already on the path of alchemy will receive hidden messages on how to transform a passage or two into their own contexts so that they can apply them to their own healings. When I am telling the novice how to use visualization concepts, more experienced seekers should read carefully between the lines to get help in their self-development and self-awakenings.

I have included my sources for many of these formulas in the bibliography. I have also channeled my concepts very effectively through meditation and such various tools of enlightenment as the I Ching, astrology, and the Tarot. Let me not forget to add, most important of all, that my connections with other worlds of spirit entities have guided me and have been my mainspring source. Their telepathic brain wave messages certainly did help. I have attempted to give you all these views in the book: what my entities have provided on a conscious level and for practical use.

This is not fantasy. These formulas have worked for those of my clients who have been ready for their spiritual trek. Each day can be a learning experience as we rid ourselves of the bugaboos of fear, and stay on the "straight path," which is a spiritual one. Faith and hope play a part.

Robert Milliken, the Nobel Prize winner in physics, has said, "We have come from somewhere and are going somewhere. The great architect of the Universe never built a stairway that leads nowhere." I believe this says it all.

2

Besides Myself . . .
How I Got There

My daughter Elissa was nudging me to get up. It was 7:00 A.M. and reluctantly I was adjusting my focus to see where I was. There have been so many mornings like this, when I wondered what reality I was now in. I felt as if I'd missed it again. Those out-of-body experiences were just as real as my dream states . . . only, which of them were real and which were dreams? I had to lie there for a few moments more, in order to collect all the information I'd gathered while asleep, to sort it out and write it down. It wasn't always like this.

Over the last three years, some things in my life were beginning to form a pattern. The sense of it was, my life belonged to the Universe. It was comforting to know that more and more people were becoming aware, learning the how-to's of the spiritual truths that were coming more and more out into the open. I never felt they were the province of gypsy tearooms.

In my nightgown I sat at the kitchen counter and poured a cup of coffee, hoping that life would push aside the deathlike feeling I felt. I grabbed for the newspaper and saw the last three words of a headline: GOOD RIDDANCE 1985!! Was that ever the truth! It had been the foulest year I could remember since 1972, when I truly began my spiritual trek in earnest. Since then I've had to function on several different levels at once.

When my brother Stuart died in 1972 as well as my cousin Jeff—both in their early twenties—I had to begin my work in earnest. No more supposings and musing about supernatural

8

things would do. Pain is one sure way to change a person's life. I simply chose to find out if there was such a thing as eternal life, if our spirits lived past death and inhabited other dimensions in the cosmos. Both young men had died tragically in the prime of their youth. I had to know if it was destined to be that way. Soon after their passings I began to see that they weren't at all far away. Both of them were seen, as apparitions, by my two daughters—Elissa (we say she is the truly grounded one) and Lauren—and by me. My youngest, Keri, who was too young to talk then, today thinks "Kool and the Gang" are her guides and doesn't get out of shape when a spirit or two passes her by.

I first learned about my own abilities when my husband, Marty, was playing baseball for the Brooklyn Dodgers organization, during the winter season in Caracas, Venezuela. I began working with clients, helping them to grow healthy, long fingernails by the use of special herbs. In the off season at home I continued to do this professionally. As my following grew, I soon learned that I could feel the energy vibrations of my clients, and discovered that while holding their palms, I could see into the future. I began to reschedule their nail appointments as psychic reading sessions. I felt I had to make a choice. But how could I tell people my truth, read them the scripts I saw, and accept the responsibility for perhaps causing problems in their lives? Besides, where did I get my credentials? Should I say that God gave them to me? Well, I decided to go on, and that story forms the basis for this book. I made the commitment and began preparing for the coming changes this Age has promised. I had enough information given to me by my spirit guides to last to the year 2000.

I dutifully recorded many things in my journal to see for myself if all the information coming in was real. In looking back over it recently, so many predictions on world issues, weather conditions, and insights for various people had come true. I could no longer doubt the preciseness and truth of my unseen forces. What an incredible feeling it was to know that it was all for real, but now how was I to tell others my truth without interfering with theirs? "Have faith" was what I heard inside, the promise that spirit entities would work side by side with me and guide me.

We, as humans, often have to experience emotional and physical pain, as it strengthens us, and only by going these changes is there growth, as great new things are born. Since the turn of the century, there have been predictions and prophecies that said that the human race is about to enter into a great change. The year 1984 was the ending of a cycle followed by a new beginning, where the breakthrough in world consciousness would be clear. Feeling and caring for others was a part of it. I like to think of it as "group" or "mass therapy." By the end of the 1980s and 1990s, I believe that the prophecies about the human race achieving fulfillment can come to fruition. A time when we are likely to see beyond the planet of our birth and reach for the knowledge and guidance of the Universe is as yet inconceivable to many of us. But the time is coming when we can shift our understanding into other dimensions, to other solar systems, to be guided from our ancient paths to new ways. The potential is there!

When January 1986 began, I was ready to let go of all my burdens, tensions, and frustrations. But by January 22 I began to feel the hairs stick up on the back of my neck. Something was in the wind. On that day a personal family tragedy occurred, however, and I thought that was the end of that. But as I shifted into the next five days, the feeling of impending doom was back. What now? By Sunday, January 26, I could no longer ignore what my body was telling me. Throughout that week, the people in closest contact with me asked what was wrong, as I didn't sound the same as I usually did. I told them something major was about to occur. Many of them replied, "I thought it was me." However, when Marty Davis, the wife of Michigan Republican congressman Robert Davis called, I could no longer ignore those inner promptings. Marty Davis had been learning her lessons well. It goes that way with "Star People." (Star People are entities who have come to Earth, on the starships, from other planets to live a life in service. They do not have Karma to fulfill but volunteer for a life on Earth to reach and guide mankind to adjust to the new spiritual vibrations of great change.) I said to Marty, we both know something's up but I want to finish my day's work and deal with it later. I suggested she hold off telling Bob or trying to inform NASA, as they might not believe her and I had to be sure first. I kept hearing the word *space* inside my head. But I was confused. Was it the space shuttle scheduled to launch tomorrow? I hung up the phone after telling Marty to have faith and say prayers and leave the rest to the higher forces. The day went on, but it was as if I was having a waking nightmare—different from other times I'd sensed things, where I could be detached. What I had experienced this time was a direct hit—the approximate time of the impending disaster. I was sure it had something to do with an air-bound vehicle. I put it out of my mind until the evening, when I made a connection with my higher guidance. What Marty didn't know was that I had not opened a newspaper for a week, since my family was in mourning for a relative. I had not even heard on radio or television that a space launch was scheduled. Hearing from her that morning only sharpened my senses and helped piece together the puzzle of my feelings.

I sat down at 9:00 P.M. that evening, lit three white candles, turned the dimmer switch to low, and proceeded to take my transformational breaths of energy. This was necessary to tune me in to my channels. I turned on the tape-recorder and in minutes went into a level for communication. No words were necessary from my source. I saw a picture in my mind of what was to be the front page headline of the following day: SHUTTLE DISASTER. The date: January 28, 1986.

I had to tell someone, to share the strain of the turmoil within me. But when I offhandedly mentioned what was in store to my husband, he answered, "Oh, here we go again!"

The next morning I called Marty Davis. She wasn't surprised when I gave her my findings. What can we do? she asked me. We leave it to God, I replied. Sometimes destiny has a way of taking over. By 10.00 A.M. I'd finished with my first appointment and called Marty back. While I was speaking with her, all the anxiety and despair disappeared. I was myself again. I told her there had been a switch in plans, a cancellation due to the weather conditions. I felt relief warming my insides. I was ready for my next appointment; my fears had ceased. I then had an early lunch, and while eating I found myself gravitating to the TV set, intent on relaxing for a while. I could not believe my eyes: the shuttle was launching. The rest we know. I immediately reached for the telephone and called Marty in Washington. I waited while she sobbed uncontrollably. Then I told her that some things on heaven and earth cannot be explained. It's simply the free will of man that makes them happen. Adversity has a positive side; we do learn and change our course into a more positive direction. I taught Marty how to connect with the other side to give the seven on the shuttle prayer, understanding, and perhaps direction. Thus we experienced what every one of them went through. We saw them enter into a vortex of light and watched as they went through a light of great power. We were done.

A writing came through, and I picked up my pen as I felt my hand shake, and wrote:

> *A bullet of light*
> *Shot through the Universe*
> *A thought, an action, no need of deed*
> *Embracing a fullness of great power*
> *Brought forth by the trigger of a united soul*
> *One mind—to weep for the needy and encompassing a Universe—so vast—*
> *Full of potential*
> *Swept up into the night, to fill up again and go forth and merge within the stars*
> *Then, blacked out by oblivion . . .*

I had come so far in my journey. My hopes, thinking patterns, and beliefs held me together. I was taught by spirits, but at the same time I followed my instincts and manifested them. Ego never entered my mind. I like to base myself in the present. As I write this, I don't really know except for a few key points here and there what I am going to achieve during my life. Actually, I don't intend to change doing what I have been led to do. My soul craves growth and to see beauty in all things. My mind seeks new pathways to explore. I chose the route while in spirit. By choosing my birthday I chose to experience a calling I felt while in spirit worlds to finish up my Karma and any residue. It's too bad we forget that when we are finally here and born again. Getting back on the track and opening ourselves up to all of it is what the trek is all about.

Now I have found what I have been searching for—I found that it's me! When I leave this earth plane I shall merely be done for now.

May my laughter never cease to be.

3

Glossary for the New Age (A Learning in Itself . . . Please Study)

Some glossaries are boring, arranged like dictionaries and merely a collection of information on words and their meanings. After a word or two has been defined, the seeker then closes the book: end of subject!

This glossary incorporates specialized information necessary for the would-be "metaphysician" to know, a not so abstract study of what is outside objective experience. It will come together as you study it. I have placed it at the beginning so you can prepare for the journey beyond that we will share.

AKASHIC RECORDS ("soul history")—All of our physical as well as nonphysical forms are recorded in the Akasha, which is a hall of records and exists on a plane where all past soul records are kept of past lives' occurrences. These records can be read by those whose soul faculties are developed from Earth (they are called past life readers).

ALCHEMY—A medieval chemical science and speculative philosophy aiming to achieve the transmutation of the base metals into gold. Also, the study of a Universal cure for disease and for a discovery of a means of indefinitely prolonging life. A power or process of transforming something common into something special. An inexplicable or mysterious transmuting.

13

ALPHA WAVES OR ALPHA RHYTHM—A mode of electrical activity detectable on the surface of the brain, with frequencies of about eight to twelve waves per second, that generally predominates when an individual is in a quiet waking state or in meditation.

ALTERED STATE OF CONSCIOUSNESS (ASC)—A mental condition in which modes of perception and mental functioning are qualitatively different from those of the normal waking state.

ANGEL—A being from celestial realms (Angel worlds). An energy being who does not have a corporeal body and has risen above the human being. The Angel may dwell either in the atmospheres of the Earth, which are called the Astral worlds, or may dwell in the Etheric worlds of other systems. They are beings set apart from the evolutions of mankind by their purity of devotion to the Godhead and to the beings they serve. Their function is to concentrate, intensify, and amplify the energies of God on behalf of the entire creation. They also minister to the needs of mankind by giving them hope, faith, and clarity of mind. They are pure light (therefore an energy) or rods and cones of consciousness that can come in to be diverted into action when called for and when there is a need, or invoked into service. There are many types and orders of Angels who perform specific services in the cosmic hierarchy.

ARCHANGEL—An order of Angels (Chief Angel). One who is a well-advanced Angel, having passed tests of certain initiations qualifying him or her to be a leader of others.

APPARITION—A realistic visual hallucination, usually a person, which in many cases involves paranormal communication. An unexpected sight. (See "Hallucination.")

AQUARIAN AGE—A period of approximately two thousand years following the Piscean Age. The cycle during which the solar system moves through the area of cosmic space known as Aquarius. A time designated for changing and upgrading man's thinking in the New Age.

ASCENDED MASTER—One who has mastered the planes of time and space. Has already mastered, too, the process of self. He has already achieved the balance of most of his Karma and fulfilled his Divine plan. Now he works with the God force on the higher planes of spirit or heaven.

ASTRAL—Refers to the seven atmospheres that surround the Earth, which are also called the Seven Heavens of the Earth or the Seven Planes of the Earth. A frequency beyond the physical and yet below the mental. It corresponds with the emotional body of man. It can be used in the negative concept of that which is impure or psychic. (See "Emotional body.")

ASTRAL BODY—One of the seven bodies of man pertaining to Earth Plane life. Appearance similar to physical body. Upon transition called death, it becomes the operative body for the consciousness in the Astral realms.

ASTRAL PROJECTION—When the mind or the spirit of a person or of an animal is separated from the physical body and travels to another place or to another state of being.

ASTROLOGY—The psychic science that believes that the planetary bodies influence and give direction and motivation to the Karma of the soul by means of charting out a map and using the Zodiac: planets and stars involved with us in human affairs. Can also map out terrestrial events by their positions and aspects.

ATTUNED—The harmonious communication between two living things when they are tuned in to the same thought or idea.

AURA—The electrical life energy that surrounds living things and is represented by the different colors of the spectrum of that particular thing, a luminous form. It surrounds the four lower bodies on which the thoughts, impressions, feelings, words, and actions are registered. It surrounds the physical body, can be seen by some, and comes from within.

AUTOMATIC WRITING—Writing done while the writer is in a dissociated state and unconscious of the writing. *Channeled* communication by one from another realm, written via control of the subconscious of the channel or of instrument over the hands. May be handwritten or typed.

AVATAR—A spiritual leader or master who aids the Earth and all of mankind for a certain period of time on Earth or elsewhere.

AWARENESS—The state of consciousness or the ability to understand a concept or an environment or state of being.

BILOCATION—Being in more than one place at the same time.

BIOFEEDBACK—A technique by which one may learn to control an unconscious bodily function, such as heart rate, by observing information fed back by an instrument that is monitoring the function of physical, mental, and emotional tension.

BIORHYTHM—An inherent rhythm that appears to control or initiate various biological processes.

CAUSE AND EFFECT (Law of)—As you sow, so shall you reap.

CENTERING—Refers to being one with one's own self. A state of balance by which all things are in their proper perspective.

CHAKRAS—A center of energy focus, generally located around the seven major endocrine glands, but which penetrates the other more subtle bodies.

These spiritual centers as represented by the vertebrae of the spine. The Indian people believe that the vertebrae of the spine are the spiritual centers of man, which must be worked on to progress to a higher state. It is a Sanskrit word for wheel, disc, circle. Denotes the centers of light anchored in the Etheric body and governs the flow of energy and the four lower bodies of man. There are seven major Chakras corresponding to the Seven Rays.

CHANCE—The result that would be expected over the long run, according to the laws of probability, in the absence of any systematic influence.

CHANNEL—The ability to attune oneself to hearing on another plane of existence. A level of awareness brought forth from spirit dimensions to direct energy into our physical dimension.

CHRIST—A title indicating achievement of the spiritual consciousness of a son of God. Also refers to the entire race of man operating in that level of consciousness.

CHRIST, ANTI—One who does not accept brotherhood and equality of all men as sons of God.

CHRIST CONSCIOUSNESS—Achievement of some degree of understanding and use of spiritual powers and talents.

CHRIST SELF—The superconscious, I Am, higher self, oversoul level of consciousness.

CLAIRAUDIENT—The ability to hear with the inner ear or to hear voices or sounds or to have communication within the inner hearing.

CLAIRVOYANCE—Seeing via the third eye. A spiritual talent. Extrasensory perception of objects or events. ESP via visual impression.

COLOR RAYS—The light that emanates from the Godhead. The Seven Rays of the white light whose energies reach through the prism of the Christ consciousness to make the rainbow.
1. Blue
2. Yellow
3. Pink
4. White
5. Green
6. Purple and gold
7. Violet

CONSCIOUSNESS—A state of awareness of things and conditions as a whole in the environment.

CONTROL—The personality, ostensibly a disembodied spirit, that regularly displaces the normal personality of a trance medium and mediates between sitters and spirit communicators. (See "Medium.")

COSMIC BEING—An ascended master who has attained the awareness of the energies of the many worlds and systems of worlds in this galaxy and beyond to others.

COSMIC CONSCIOUSNESS—Man's awareness of himself and the God energies that work through him both in this world and others and fully understands the self-fulfilling cycles here (in this plane and in cosmic dimensions). In regard also to personal consciousness, where a soul has achieved many initiations leading to self-understanding.

COSMIC LAW—The law that governs all manifestation through the cosmos on the planes of both spirit and matter.

COSMOS—The Universe or world regarded as an orderly, harmonious system. It includes the planes of matter known and unknown. All that exists in time and space is the cosmos. There also exists a spiritual cosmos, which includes the counterpart of the material cosmos and beyond.

DEATH—Transition from physical life or expression on Earth to another realm, such as physical incarnation on some other planet or expression on Astral or Etheric realms.

DESTINY—A predetermined cause of events often held to be an irresistible power.

DEVIC—One of God's creations and kingdom of entities. Concerns the elemental or nature kingdom.

DISCARNATE SPIRITS—Existing apart from a physical body, a condition attributed to spirits of the dead and some other entities.

DEHAUNT—To cleanse from top to bottom unseen forces and entities, usually within a physical structure.

DISCIPLE—One who accepts and assists in spreading the doctrines of another. A messenger of light.

DIVINE PLAN—The plan of God for the individual soul that was started in the beginning of the present incarnation when in spirit form. The Divine plan determines the limits of the individual expression of freewill. What the potential of that soul is, is known by God and can be released by the individual through manifestation of the plan when in physical embodiment.

DOWSING—Searching for something hidden, generally underground, by noticing movements of a forked stick or other hand-held device held over the place of concealment.

ELOHEIM—One or more of the seven Eloheim in the Godhead, heading the Seven Rays of life creators of manifestation for spirit. Plural for the official office of the hierarchy. More than one in a council or group. (See "Hierarchy.")

EMOTIONAL BODY—One of four bodies of man. It exists as a body within the physical, made up of desires and feelings. It is also called the Astral body or desire body, which brings forth the feeling energy (lower body).

ENTITIES—A conceptual reality. An independent, separate, or self-contained existence. (See "Spirits.")

ESP—See "Extrasensory perception."

ETHERIC BODY—Part of one of man's four bodies. It is intertwined with the feelings of the soul. Also called the memory body.

EVIL—Misused energy. The veil of misqualified field energy that man imposes upon the world of matter through his misuse of the sacred fire. (See "Sacred fire.")

EXORCISE—The process of driving out negative thoughts or negative patterns from the mind of the individual. These patterns or thoughts may be outside entities that have possessed the mind of the individual or may be past life memories that have possessed the individual.

EXTRASENSORY PERCEPTION (ESP)—The obtaining of information that is not accessible by means of any known sense.

EYE (THIRD)—The spiritual sight or vision. Spiritual focus of light in center of forehead.

FALLEN ANGELS—Those who followed the negative aspects of consciousness and fell to the lower levels of awareness whereby Universal Law has cast them out of the higher planes. Then they were put on Earth, where some may still be in spirit and others as reincarnated human beings.

FATE—An inevitable and irresistible power supposedly controlling human destiny. Final outcome of a decision or development. The end result of your life and the goals you are to achieve.

FLYING SAUCER (UFO)—Unidentified flying object. Common term on Earth for interplanetary and interdimensional spacecraft from other planes and planets.

FOCUS—The tuning in upon an object, a place, or a thing whereby the sharpest amount of concentration enables the individual to make contact with the meaning of the object of focus.

FOUR LOWER BODIES—See "Physical body," "Mental body," "Emotional body," "Etheric body."

FREE WILL—The freedom to create, option to choose the right- or left-hand path, life or death, positive or negative spirals of consciousness. A soul may choose a path of good or negativity in a plane where both polarities of time and space are relative. A soul may also accept or reject the Divine plan.

FREQUENCY—Relates to the different vibration of identity that is involved in the identity of a person, place, or thing.

GHOSTS—Thought forms or emotional projections that exist in their former habitat and continue to exert an influence or a pressure upon that environment. In many cases the ghosts are merely fragments of the original soul that are fixations, whereas the soul has long since incarnated into another body. Apparition of nonliving individual. (See "Apparition.")

GOD CONSCIOUSNESS—The conscious self-awareness of you, the creator, on Earth. The awareness of the I AM—THAT I AM or I AM presence. Man's awareness of himself fulfilling the cycles of the cosmic with the attainment of initiations leading to a cosmic awareness of selfhood. (See "Cosmic consciousness.")

GOLDEN AGE—The cycle of enlightenment, peace, harmony, and balance. Known also as the Age of Aquarius. It follows the two-thousand-year cycle of the Piscean Age, which heralded in Jesus Christ. It fulfills the prophecy of the "Divine plan," as above, so below, through "thy kingdom come, on earth as it is in heaven."

GREAT WHITE BROTHERHOOD—The fraternity of saints, sages, and ascended masters of all ages who come from every nation, race, and religion and have reunited with the spirit of the living God. The term *white* refers to the halo of white light that surrounds their forms.

GUARDIAN ANGELS—The Angels in charge of working with the individual soul in order to guide and to teach it and to assist the soul in working out its karmic curriculum.

GUIDES—Higher-plane teachers for one still on the Earth plane. They are also Angels or spirit life, assigned to individual souls to teach certain specific lessons that the soul has a need to learn.

GURU—The Indian term for a teacher who has an Earth body and who aids and assists the individual to work out his Karma.

HALLUCINATION—The apparent realistic experiencing of sensations without any physical basis for the sensations.

HAUNTING—A paranormal phenomenon that is manifested repeatedly at a particular place, usually a house.

HEALING—When a mental fixation or an emotional fixation exists in a person, place, or thing by which the perpetrator. has a need to maintain or to continue or to set in motion an influence upon the physical world.

HEAVEN—An attitude and atmosphere of man's expression, wherever he is. No specific place except to denote the Etheric realms.

HELL—An attitude of man's expression. No specific plane. Referring to lower consciousness.

HIERARCHICAL BOARD—Spiritual government in the solar system working down through the individual planetary departments. Headquarters is on Saturn.

HIERARCHY—The Universal chain of individual beings who fulfill the work of God. They send down to Earth a light of the energies of God consciousness and fill the ethers of time and space with their love. Spiritual government in solar system working down through the individual planetary departments.

ILLUSION—A misinterpretation of sensory information.

INDEPENDENT VOICE—A term used in spiritualism to indicate that the medium has been taken over by a spirit entity who speaks through the medium and sometimes apart from the medium in order to communicate from one world to another.

INITIATE—A being that has been instructed or is adept in some special field of expertise.

INITIATION—Instructions investing knowledge for some experience through rites or ceremonies.

INTUITION—Subjective conviction or insight attained without conscious justification.

JESUS—An ascended master. An avatar of the Piscean Age. He brought in the Christ Conscious Age and he fulfilled the abilities of working with God and the self. He reincarnated on Earth to give the world the understanding of the Father. He holds the office in the Hierarchy as the World Teacher.

KARMA—Karma is the Law of Consequences, Merits, and Demerits. The force that molds our physical destiny in this world and regulates our period of misery or happiness in the world to come. A Sanskrit word for action or deed. There is a Universal Law in the heavens, that man determines his fate by his thinking, actions, deeds, words, and feelings. It refers to the plan of the Universe as if it is the master plan of the entire Universe having many parts, having many separate sections, being similar to a weaving of the Universe that must be unraveled thread by thread and pattern by pattern to understand its workings.

KARMIC DEBT—That which one owes payment for, due to action in this or prior lifetimes. Must be paid off at some time in a spiritually proper manner.

KIRLIAN PHOTOGRAPHY—A photographic film recording of the electric field pattern around an object placed in the field.

KUNDALINI—Spiritual force that rises through the spine in the process of awakening the mental personality to the spiritual consciousness and powers. Kundalini fire begins in the lower spine or sex center Chakra, then rises gradually until reaching the head or Crown Chakra.

LAMA—A priest of Tibet who secludes himself in a monastery high up in the Himalayan Mountains to learn of his inner power by isolation.

LEVITATION—Alleged lifting or elevation of an object without known physical means.

LIGHT—An energy of God.

LIGHT BODY—A fourth-dimensional body of man; his Etheric or Christ body; one of seven bodies related to Earth living.

LORDS OF KARMA—Ascended beings who make up this great karmic board or panel. There are seven ascended masters who determine whether a soul has the right to be free from the wheel of Karma (or take another round with rebirth), the Laws of God, and live in the consciousness of love.

MAGNETISM—Refers to an electrical energy or a life energy that has the power to attract either tangible or intangible material to itself.

MAN—The male and female images and manifestations of God.

MANTRAS—Chants or vocalizations used by the people of India and Tibet in order to tune themselves up to a state of meditation using the sound of their voices as the energy.

MASTER—One who has mastered something powerful spiritually.

MATERIALIZATION—The principle of alchemy, whereby mind or energy can be condensed or contracted and dropped down to a lower frequency to become tangible as a state of matter or of visible observable material. (See "Alchemy.")

MEDITATION—A state of tuning in to one's own self—getting inside yourself.

MEDIUM—A sensitive, or one who is a psychic conductor or go-between who acts as the conductor or telephone between two worlds or two states of being.

MENTAL TELEPATHY—The process of establishing a communication between two minds using a focus to establish a connection.

MESSENGER—One who has had training by an ascended master, who learns major concepts of God's plan and teachings. Messengers deliver the laws to the people, the prophecies at this time of the Aquarian Age.

METAPHYSICS—The study that lies beyond the physical. Basic spiritual laws of the Universe.

MYSTICISM—A system of belief that relies upon certain intuitive experiences for spiritual development and insight into the nature of the world.

NEOPHYTE—Newly converted, a beginner.

NUMEROLOGY—The psychic science of numbers whereby numbers have a meaning. This is a form of translation similar to astrology. Astrology uses the influence of planets upon the lives of people, whereas numerology uses the influence of numbers upon the lives of people.

OBJECT PSYCHOMETRY—The technique of tuning in to an object in order to read the vibration and the meaning of the person who was in contact with this object or sometimes of the environment of the object itself.

OCCULT—The hidden mysteries of life, opened to the seeker of knowledge and wisdom.

OM—AUM—A designation for God, means "power."

OUT-OF-BODY EXPERIENCE (OBE or OOBE)—An experience in which people feel they are seeing the world from some specific place outside their physical bodies.

PARAPSYCHOLOGY—The scientific study of situations in which a human or other organism acquires information from its environment or exerts physical influence upon it independently of its sense or motor mechanism.

PATH—The straight way of life. A path of initiation where a being pursues the Christ consciousness.

PHOTO ANALYSIS—The technique of analyzing the vibration of a person, place, or thing from a photograph.

PHYSICAL BODY—One of the four bodies of man. The outer covering that corresponds to the material vehicle where we can manifest energies and bring our lives into a form. (See "Etheric body," "Mental body," and "Emotional body.")

PINEAL—Crown Chakra or highest spiritual center in the body. When the pineal gland is opened and the spark between it and the pituitary (third eye center) is ignited, Christ consciousness occurs.

PITUITARY—The master gland for the physical body, spiritually known as the third eye. The Kundalini fire must be raised to the pituitary center before the pineal can be united for awakening the soul to Christ consciousness.

PK—See "Psychokinesis."

PLANE or REALM—A dimension, a realm, a level of expression.

POLTERGEIST PHENOMENA—German word meaning "noisy ghost." Spontaneously occurring paranormal sounds, movements of objects, and other effects. Usually in the vicinity of a specific person.

POSSESSION—When an entity, or a spirit, or a memory, takes control of the mind of a person or a living creature and controls and dominates this subject.

PRAYER—A form of desire expressed in a focused manner. This is also similar to a form of meditation to accomplish a direct result.

PRECOGNITION—Extrasensory perception of future events. (See "Extrasensory perception.")

PROPHESY—By Divine inspiration. To predict with assurance or on the basis of mystic knowledge; to give instruction.

PSI—A term used by parapsychologists to refer to the unknown factor(s) responsible for those interactions between organisms and their environments that do not appear to conform to the known Laws of Science; the subject matter of parapsychology. (See "Parapsychology.")

PSYCHIC—Also called a Clairvoyant, medium, sensitive, or telepathic. Someone who has developed the natural state of ESP to accomplish a desired result. Deals with Earth and Astral energies of man. Also deals with the probing of dimensions in time and space beyond the Physical Plane. A psychic is one who has the power and developed ability to penetrate the lower and upper Astral Plane. He or she also has the ability to raise spiritual energies to exceed beyond these planes to go into the higher octaves of spirit or God.

PSYCHIC CENTERS—Centers of magnetic influence that motivate the psychic ability of the individual. The third eye, the solar core, and the Chakras are all considered psychic centers. (See "Chakras.")

PSYCHIC HEALING—Healing by laying on of hands, directed mental activity, or other paranormal means.

PSYCHIC SURGERY—Alleged paranormal cutting and healing of incisions to remove or repair abnormal tissue.

PSYCHOKINESIS (PK)—Paranormal influence upon a physical object or situation by mental effort or intention.

PSYCHOMETRY—The ability to analyze an object or a thing by having contact or visual contact with object or thing.

RAPID EYE MOVEMENT (REM)—Characteristic eye movements that occur when a person is dreaming.

RAYS—Light beams or radiant energy. When invoked by using the name of God or in the name of Christ, a healing ray comes out of the third eye.

RECEIVER—In a telepathy test, the person who is trying to obtain information that is in the mind of the sender.

REINCARNATION—The doctrine that some element of a personality survives death and is reborn in the body of an infant. It is the process within Karma whereby a soul is incarnated into many bodies and many lives in order to learn lessons.

ROOT RACE—A group of souls who have a unique pattern for the "Divine plan" as they came into this incarnation to fulfill a mission on Earth. Some are of positive inclination for the Earth's upgrading, some the negative aspect.

SACRED FIRE—God has a life force of its own, its power, "all there is." He comes forth with the element of fire. Fire is either a purifier of energy or a destroyer. The sacred fire comes from the hierarchical ███ that work through the God force. It is a baptism ██ ██ purification or for alchemy and transmutation. It alway ███ turns to the supreme source of the I AM THAT I AM.

SAGE—A profound philosopher, pe ███ of judgment, wisdom, and knowledge.

SEANCE—Literally, a sitting. A meeting of several people, usually with a medium, for spirit communication or the production of psychokinetic effects.

SENDER—In a telepathy test, the person who is trying to send information to the subject.

SENSITIVE—A channel, prophet, instrument or medium. Someone who shows evidence of exceptional PSI ability, particularly ESP; a psychic.

SEVEN RAYS OF LIFE—The seven major groupings of aspects of God; the Seven Flames.

FIRST: Will and power (blue)
SECOND: Intelligence and wisdom (yellow)
THIRD: Personal love and feeling (pink)
FOURTH: Crystalization (colorless crystal clear)

FIFTH: Unity, integration, healing balance (green)
SIXTH: Transmutation, cleansing, purification (violet)
SEVENTH: Divine love, peace, rest (gold and white)

SEVENTH ROOT RACE—Souls that have evolved, are sent forth in the Aquarian Age, and come in through the Seventh Ray (violet ray). This is through the birth process.

SHAMAN—A holy man or psychically aware individual who goes from place to place or person to person giving inspired messages.

SIN—Free will that has been utilized for negative purposes; going against the cosmic or Universal Law.

SOLAR CORE—A psychic center near the belly button or the middle of the abdomen of a person.

SOUL—The spiritual principle embodied in human beings. A moving spirit; man's moral and emotional nature. Accumulation of an individual's experiences in his or her eternal living.

SOUL MATES—Individual souls who have shared favorable close and loving associations within one or more lifetimes. Each person can have many soul mates, though they do not necessarily incarnate with or come into contact with them during any one lifetime.

SOUL TWIN—Each person has a twin soul. Twin souls are two separate individualities at all times. This does not mean one soul has been split to gain experiences. Spirit guides guide your twin soul along the same path, perhaps in different regions in consciousness. Has the same complements, backgrounds, and abilities.

SPIRITS—Discarnate entities who are out of the body.

SPIRITUALISM—A religion based upon the belief that spirits of the dead can communicate with the living through psychically sensitive people called mediums.

STAR CHILD—Star People are entities who chose to be born on this planet in the normal way and who come from other galaxies or starships. They are born on Earth and qualified to give a life of service to teach and give humanity a higher understanding on Earth.

SYMBOLOGY—The picture language of the higher worlds and of the mind.

TAROT CARDS—A deck of cards believed to be derived from ancient Egypt and used for fortune-telling or divining.

TEACHER (spiritual)—One who teaches spiritual matters. May be on this or higher plane.

TELEPATHY—Extrasensory perception of information that exists only in the mind of another person.

TELEPORTATION—The process whereby an object, person or thing is transported from place to place or from world to world, via dematerialization and materialization.

THIRD EYE—A psychic center at the apex of the two eyes above the eyebrows and in the forehead region.

TRANCE—An altered state of consciousness, self-induced or induced by hypnosis or other means that involve modification or cessation of normal consciousness and emergence of ordinarily inaccessible mental information or processes.

TRANSFIGURATION—A change of one's own features, or of entire body, caused by overshadowing by one's Christ self or by an ascended master.

TRANSITION—Term of denoting death of an individual on one plane so as to begin a new life on another plane. Generally speaking, it means making a change.

TRANSMUTATION—Purifying one's mortal consciousness and body so as to permit raising into fourth dimension, physically as concerns Christ consciousness.

TUNING IN—Refers to the focusing upon a person or object in order to make contact with the essence of that person or object.

VIBRATIONS—Refers to emanations or electrical energy coming from living things or from anything that echoes the vibrational frequency of that thing.

WALK-INS—A walk-in occurs when a soul or entity of a higher vibration makes an agreement with a soul of a lower vibration, in spirit dimensions, that the lower conscious soul will have to go through a pregnancy in the mother's womb as she can only hold those vibrations for the gestation period of the lower entity. At an agreed upon time, a switch will be made and take place in a fraction of a second of the higher conscious entity to take on the body of the other soul. Often, no noticeable change is determined by the family or those close to the child. Either they will have total recall of their early childhood or virtually none. It usually occurs at the ages of five to twelve but some cases have been reported in later years. Especially, if the soul has given up and is tired but needs more time to finish its destiny to the aid of mankind. This is not always usual!

WHITE BROTHERHOOD—The group of spiritual teachers, guides, and masters who, having discovered God's truth and having learned to demonstrate spiritual powers, are guiding those who have not into that same level of Christ understanding. Pertains to this solar system. Also called the White Lodge or Ascended Masters Council.

WHITE LIGHT—A seal of protection. An iridescent light that you place around yourself or other objects from head to toe. This will seal off any negative energy coming at you, as this energy cannot pass through this light. Also opens up and attracts all good energy.

WITCH—A psychic person who has knowledge of the ancient religion of Wicca and is capable of performing magic either for good by using nature and natural means or for evil by using black magic arts.

YANG—The Masculine active principle in nature, exhibited in light.

YIN—The Feminine passive principle in nature, exhibited in darkness.

YIN/YANG—Means the mastering of both energies in a human being.

4

Tips From a Clairvoyant's Eye

Choose and stand—for truth is in the eyes
    of the beholder
Nasty business this is—deciding what is to be
    or not to be
To be noble is not the question
To see beyond is—
Be retentive and ready as spiritual warfare
    has begun
The sides are gathering and its quicksand
Make way for the change

DESTINY . . . PROPHECY . . .
FREE WILL

Become a Cosmic Person
You chose it. Now do it!

Maintain my own inner divine center, dear Lord
Make it a house of peace, so I can give
and share with others

I do not believe that Clairvoyants can foretell the future exactly
the way it is going to be. What they can tell their clients is, to
my understanding, that in predicting the future, what matters is
the unfolding of two elements.

Destiny: That which is predetermined and linked to your Karma, and *prophecy*, that which is our free-will expression. They're not the same!

Everyone has to account for his or her daily living experiences. Each day we are faced with decisions, some small, some large, and we must account for each choice, whether it turns out to be right or wrong. We even have opportunities to find out if the decisions were incorrect and to reconcile these decisions or correct our mistakes. Certainly, important issues do take more of our time to work out. These instances might even become the best time to think out our problems and to motivate new opportunities for our growth. These times of change and growth help us choose the avenues that will enhance our lives.

The route to each individual's goals must be made under his or her own guidelines. So much depends on what gift to humanity you feel you have to give. And it is up to each of us to decide how much time and energy we want to give to other people and how much we want to leave ourselves to achieve our future goals.

Some individuals come into a lifetime to divide their time between home and family while doing their chosen work or by providing some service for others. We have been born here with help and advance preparation, and have been conditioned before arriving for whatever responsibilities we need to take on. We decide this before birth, to fulfill karmic obligations. Perhaps we forgot our responsibilities to others and are born again into a different body in order to retrace actions that we didn't complete in the last incarnation. The soul or conscience helps us to remember, and our inner feelings guide us. We carry over Karma from a previous existence; put another way, what man has done, he can undo. That is when we use our free will. Karma is not a hard rule, as it is changeable. This is according to man's attitude and his desire. We do get the opportunity to change if we understand our needs and lay the foundation for progress with our convictions and strengths. That is where free will stops. It concerns the right choices and, consequentially, correct actions. It is the soul's journey that keeps us on track and helps us choose what task we will tackle first. What wins out may be our destiny.

Often our priorities get away from us, but we have to measure them by who and what we are. Some think, *I'll weed out the needless things, selfishly, so I can get to my destiny faster. Why not take the shortest route to get where I have to go?* Some who need the learning and experience take a longer road. So therefore we must accept the best conditions of these times with the right attitude. Some of the control may be out of your hands and rest with other people. In the meantime, can you deny yourself the opportunity to grow? By constantly exercising our free will, we can will the good of humanity. Wait patiently for these new opportunities to present themselves. Chances are, they will.

Free will is determined by priorities. It is meted out by the conditions and influences of our situations and surroundings. These conditions limit the availability of choices to select from. Free will is determined personally, if one chooses to accept freely and openly what opportunity is offered. Someone who does not have opportunities perhaps did not create any friction for growth in his or her lifetime. We create friction by putting two different forces together, in either positive or negative situations. Friction enables us to make our many choices and prevents our being too set in our ways. Getting "stuck" gives us no options, no room for growth and change.

Some of humanity live on the basis of the Law of Accident. This means that things "just happen" to them, rather than being *created* by them. They say then that they are the victims. They may even find alibis for troubled world situations and personally release themselves from action or responsibility. They blame it on Karma, but this is not always the case. Some also assume that nothing is their affair, that everything will work itself out, so why bother doing anything? They are willing to let someone else do what's necessary. These acts help bring evil and havoc into the world, and allow anything just to happen, bringing about negative Karma. When people do not want to struggle for freedom, as a result, they may be left out of the gains of freedom in their own lives. Only through free will and the will to do good can we actively end present conflicts. Responsibility for the good of one another and oneself can bring about a positive state, subject to the Law of Destiny. Some people may need help in deciding to open up to their options. Whatever path you decide for yourself is your ultimate path, subject to the Law of Consequence.

When you decide what feels right, based in part on the gifts your spirit guides provide for you, your life will then move from the Law of Accident to the Law of Destiny. When human beings just allow the tide to wash over them and control their lives, they cannot be masters of their own ships, and the map of destiny charts a different course for them. In order to move to a state of free will, a person has to have faith and trust in his inner guides and teachers until results of his actions reward that faith. To participate in our lives makes us become free; by trusting our need to learn and building an increased awareness of our responsibilities, we can be motivated. Because we have contacted the still, small voice within, faith in our choices will grow as we begin to trust the guidance to a greater extent. *Prophecy* is based on the Law of Accident. Most prophecies can be changed if the person assumes the role of humble student. From the role of humble student, the person can progress, in time, to be in touch with his own inner voice. Though God is not known to those who are subject to the Law of Accident, He becomes increasingly known when a person's actions move him from accident to destiny.

When a soul is ready to evolve further on *this* Earth Plane, in *this* life span, it is important to maintain faith and to make a commitment. Each soul has returned to develop character. Since world conditions and technologies are in constant flux, when a soul reincarnates it has to adapt to a new world. The circumstances under which a soul returns are carefully selected by the Lords of Karma, but all entities, including God, have to act within the Laws of Nature of the galaxy. No one, not even our spirit guides, can predict how a soul will act, react, or progress under certain conditions. This is why we reincarnate. The goal is not always the learning but the experience we acquire along the way. How we respond to these challenges affects a soul's destiny. This is where free will or choice comes in. Our lives begin as a road map, astrologically, with signs and guideposts. It is up to each individual to decide which road or avenue of life to follow. Although our souls may feel weary, as perhaps we have repeated old lessons, we must keep our faith and move on to express our needs until our lives feel right.

When one is evolved there is no free will on a destined path, since our lessons have already been learned. You still have the right, however, to make choices. There is no free will involved where karmic debts must be paid, past life carryovers. Free will can go either way, helping you to make a positive or a negative choice from your soul. But the strength of that will to follow your heart's desire depends on how genuinely free you are to express yourself. If the will is weak and cannot overcome negativity, your desires will occur on a negative level, and you will have others leading you. Clearly, you did not take on that responsibility to yourself. If it was part of your destiny, you would have positively committed yourself. There is a difference between a karmic function and a destined function. A soul function operates between them and is the connecting factor.

Free will is a teaching tool for people who cannot make decisions. It can be light and mundane, as simple as deciding if you want coffee or tea. No one can judge another's free-will choice, as no one can understand any other being's circumstances, karmic, destined, or otherwise. A person must choose if he wants to take on a "do-gooder" role in this life. Many souls do not have to make major decisions or function in a spiritual way. Some come into a lifetime to rest and to play; other souls have come to work. Therefore, there are different levels of free will. No one can judge what another soul must do. Since you are reading this, perhaps you are ready to change your old, set ways or conflicts. You recognize the need to change in order to express your needs and realize your cosmic and spiritual potential, as well as self-understanding. When you find this potential, it transforms your inner knowing into positive manifesting. And even though we may find that our destinies are set prior to our coming into this life, and no matter how tough the sledding may be, we go forth. Faith is both a spiritual gift and the fruit of our labor.

Concentrating on the word *love* will open you to becoming a cosmic person. If you choose it, then do it! Fulfilling our commitments is the basis for our destinies. The soul decides the role it will fulfill; thus, one's destiny involves what the soul does in this life. If your Karma enables you to be born at one level and you then find you can rise above it and do more than you expected to do in this lifetime, you have understood that growth has much to do with your needs and what you feel you want to accomplish here. The age of your soul does help in working along with your natural cycles. The synchronicity of various energies available to you at a given time—those whom you know, environmental influences, and so on—also plays a part. If you feel you have a task you must complete before you die, it means you have a destiny. But your fate is still shaped by your decisions!

Survival on this Earth Plane is rather difficult. Certainly we have to support ourselves and eat. But we do not necessarily have to forget our dreams or desires. The retiree is a good example. He says, "I've worked all my life, reared my family, built my nest egg, so now I can do as I choose, change my life, and earn my rest. I don't have to do anything else but enjoy myself before I die." He is saying that he worked so hard at doing his chores and taking care of his responsibilities that now he can make the time to do whatever he couldn't do before. The question arises: What can he do to fulfill that cycle of his life, broadening his vision and sharing his joy with others rather than recalling the "good old days" and doing nothing? Entering this new life cycle unfortunately means that many retirees vegetate, and the will and body wither away as well. Must we forget our dreams and desires as we worry about survival, rather than use our creativity? The choice is ours, to overcome life's pressures and work them through.

Astrology can be a helpful tool to aid and benefit your decisions at the times when the road is bumpy. By charting your astrological plan, you gain understanding for your growth and life. It can help you to evaluate your decisions based on your personal boundaries, and help you to contemplate your interaction with the Universe as well. It can also show you under what conditions you were born. Astrology helps us gain knowledge about the physical nature of the Universe as well as explaining the metaphysical aspects of it. The occult sciences teach the Universal Laws and patterns of man, and astrology is one of them. Certain planets have been said to affect the energies—mental, physical, and emotional—of people on Earth. A competent astrologer can help anyone who is ready for this helpful tool. By having a personal life chart done that shows what planets will affect you, you can learn to evaluate and understand various aspects of your soul. The key words I have listed after each sign of the Zodiac aid in decision-making and show how to utilize the energies of each sun sign.

KEY WORD*		VIRTUE
ARIES	I am	PATIENCE
TAURUS	I have	ENDURANCE
GEMINI	I think	ONENESS
CANCER	I feel	MERCY
LEO	I will	PRIDE
VIRGO	I analyze	PERFECTION
LIBRA	I balance	FAIRNESS
SCORPIO	I desire	HONESTY
SAGITTARIUS	I perceive	RIGHTEOUS JUDGMENT
CAPRICORN	I use	PRINCIPLED
AQUARIUS	I know	HUMILITY
PISCES	I believe	UNDERSTANDING

*These key words explain aspects of the soul.

To achieve your destiny is your graduation day. Prophecy what is predicted—is merely a state in between to see if we can commit ourselves enough to fulfill our destiny. Prophecy merely implies that anything *could* happen. Ultimately, the soul will do only what it is destined to do. The soul has made the bargain prior to incarnation, and must take full responsibility for its choices. That pact was made in another lifetime, however, so it is not up to the person living in this time.

A Clairvoyant can estimate the outcome of a person's destiny. But he or she is governed by the individual's guidelines (or God-lines) by reading the individual maturity of that soul in order to decide which path he will ultimately choose. Remember, your destiny is in your hands and therefore is up to you—depending on the choices you make while you're here on Earth.

WHO ARE GOD'S TEACHERS?
OR HOW TO PICK YOUR GURU

The dictionary explains democracy as a government that is run by the people who live under it; a country, state, or community having such a government; a treatment of others as one's equals.

Democracy gives people the maximum amount of freedom to think, to move about, and to satisfy their emotional and physical needs. It provides freedom and opportunities as we open ourselves to criticism as well as praise. Its aim is giving us the freedom to express ourselves and make choices, whether another person agrees or disagrees. It is up to us whether we work as individuals toward our own goals without concern about anyone else, or choose team work with others, pooling our resources and moving in the direction of God or our spiritual source of power.

Correct judgment is a result of experience, when our intuition says, *not now, later*. Understand it is our inner voice that tells us right from wrong, which instinct should be followed to keep us in the flow. Flow is simply the life energy we always take with us when we need that inner wisdom or strength.

Knowing how to choose your spiritual teacher springs from these instincts as they will guide you to the ultimate path of truth. You will hear the truth of your teacher in his or her words, if you are open to truth—not what you *wish* to hear, but what you *feel* as truth from the core of your inner self.

The question then arises: How can another mere mortal advise you or give you the right direction? If you have already decided on a path to find truth, you know that others may live in a world of verbal and emotional confusion. Many teachers teach solely to convince themselves of where they are not. Some teach nothing but despair and death, but I believe God chooses his true teachers to teach his lessons of joy and hope.

We live in a world of materialism and sin and are deluged by untruths. The self-deceiving must deceive; therefore, they must teach deception. They force it on others. Who are they? How are they chosen? What do they do? How do they work out their own salvation and the salvation of the world? And so then we look for God's teachers. But just let us define God. Leave nothing to chance. God cannot send us anything but perfect good; it is not his nature. If you think God sent us difficulty, you are giving power to your troubles. He has a plan for every one of us. Your task is to find what is good.

A teacher of God is anyone who chooses to be one. These teachers have made a deliberate choice to work toward their beliefs and help others to benefit from what they've learned. They have also learned how to separate their own life decisions from those of everyone else they meet.

The teacher's road is established, teachings of his own truth enforced, sure of his path in line with his own direction from a clear source or channel. It is a channel whose light has entered the darkness of confusion. He comes to bring salvation to every corner of the world, giving to others where he wishes the dark-

ness of doubt and confusion of this material world not to enter.
He can be a teacher of God even if he isn't sure there is a God,
or if he comes from all religions or from no religion. His calling
is the Universe. His function is to save time and his ways are
limited.

He has already mastered time and space, humility, patience,
and the ability to respond at any given time if God demands it.
While he has also mastered divine wisdom, he is ever ready for
the next set of lessons as if he hadn't mastered anything at all.
He listens and hears.

Our weariness and pain come from our inability to handle or
accomplish the things we hold in our sights, to make our lives
what we wish them to be. Some think, *Is there ever to be an
outcome for what I wish for myself and others? Can I find the
answers within myself to effect a change? Is there hope? Do all
things end with the fear of our death, or is there a plan, a
resurrection of our continual hopes to change the course of this
life's darkness?* I believe this resurrection, which we call a
rebirth, can be explained as a new cycle of faith, when we
become able to put forth our desires in a new direction.

Who, then, are God's pupils? Certain pupils have been assigned to each of God's teachers; these pupils begin to look for
their teachers as soon as they have answered the call in their
hearts. Each teacher has his or her own special understanding, in
order to help those on that level of understanding reach for the
next phase of their lives.

A teacher has chosen to fulfill this role in his life's plan, a
promise made while in spirit form before being born again on
this plane. Although many people do not believe they have
reached any level—beginner, intermediate, or advanced—as metaphysical students of life, they have—and there are always teachers there to help and guide them. Finding the right one will
soothe an ailing spirit and turn understanding into helping each
of us be the director of our lives. Sometimes simply a different
approach, a fresh idea, a new thought on how to proceed, helps.

When the true teacher and pupil come together, a teaching and
learning situation truly begins. The pupil learns, the teacher
learns, and if we keep in mind that we don't know enough, we
can continue searching for and understanding other ways to
reshape our world lovingly and effectively. It is truly an Aquarian
Age concept to reach toward giving and receiving. Those who

share one interest and goal go from being the learners to the
teachers. Each of us reaches out for others who have the same
interests as our own.

The teachers of God have no set teaching level. Everyone has
his own understanding and level of growth that is likened to
one's own set of fingerprints. The true teacher finds there is no
one from whom he cannot learn, so there is no one whom he
cannot teach. It may have been designated from the higher
worlds that a teacher is the one from whom a person must learn.
From a practical point of view, a teacher cannot meet everyone,
nor can everyone find him. Therefore, there is a Divine plan:
there *is* a teacher who can teach each one of us. There are no
accidents in finding your salvation if you are on a path of light
and truth. The potential exists, of course, of finding who you
think is the right teacher, but who is not. Still, you will be off
the path for only a little while.

Meeting your real teacher, for the first time often seems to
start with a casual encounter. *Example:* Oh, I just met someone
at a party who just *happened* to be speaking of Clairvoyants, or a
Tarot Reader, or Astrologers, etc. Or, I just *happened* to bump
into someone at a store, on a street corner or in an elevator. . . .
But if you "happen" to hear someone's name at least three times
from different sources, maybe it is just a coincidence—or maybe
some unknown force is guiding you. Nothing is by accident.
Believe that your salvation has come.

You might find that after spending many years under the
guidance of one teacher for your life's direction, suddenly it is
not working anymore. Maybe you have risen above this teacher
and are ready for the next . . . or perhaps it is time for you to
become one. Teachers do not sit in front of classrooms or at
desks. Maybe, then, you are to be your own director of traffic
and to instruct those who come your way to help them find their
own truths. Maybe, by being truthful and kind with words of
love, you have already given what someone needed.

Sometimes a relationship with pupil and teacher may last for a
long duration and then they need to separate for a while, possibly
coming back together later at a different level of communication.
There are no wrongs when we need to find the rights. The true
teacher is accepting of all and opens the door when the time is
right. But the highest level of all teaching and learning situations
is when each person separately and individually does his own

work. Then each one living within his own set of guidelines and beliefs can form a permanent lifelong relationship. These are few but do exist when the student and teacher have reached a state of harmony and balance in their relationship, with unlimited potential for shared learning.

In that type of unity there is strength and enough potent energy to meet the masters of love together. True love is what we call it, the ultimate of sharing of life in all its forms. Here on this planet is where we express it all.

Can these, God's teachers, guide us and show us the Trinity of our own facets and expressions of ourselves, which deals with our body/physical, our mind/mental (which pulls us into the Universal energies of sharing while we are here on Earth), and helps us tap in to the expression of our soul/spiritual, to complete our "trip" in this lifetime? You have to ask yourself for those answers!

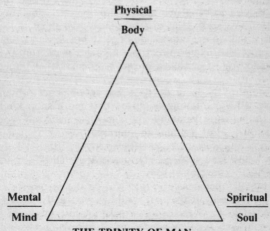

THE TRINITY OF MAN

ARE YOU A PSYCHIC COLLECTOR?
LIKE TO SHOP AROUND
FOR A QUICK FIX?

How do you find a "good psychic"? Just because a friend told you of a psychic whose predictions all came true is not the only determining factor. Most people want to deal with their truth, not *the* truth, so if you want an "instant fix," you'll most likely find one that serves you well. Some people will recommend going for professional therapy and choose a psychotherapist for this kind of help and guidance. They may say that a psychic is nothing more than a fortune-teller and that the experience can sour them for the remainder of their lives. In some deeply troubled cases I find that both kinds of professionals can and do work very well together. They come from two different states or levels of understanding.

With all the fraudulent people and charlatans working in the field, be aware that not all of these so-called psychics work for God and care how or whether you live or die. These frauds concentrate on the "unwashed public," or those who want to learn to do black magic on someone to achieve an end to their goals against another's will. If you find this sort of person, *walk out* the door. The "psychic showboat" is not exactly what you need either. This type may try to impress you with how many celebrities he's seen. If he claims to be a consultant to the stars, remember that most "stars" don't talk, but these psychics do. This type is also likely to hint that his rates vary from person to person–and you're getting a break. A good rule of thumb: find out the fee in advance.

Be careful of the handout flyers you get on street corners. You may find a fortune-telling booth by day and a soup kitchen by night. Or perhaps some of these people may tell you their problems instead of listening to your questions. Any person who judges you and makes you feel unworthy or "lays a holy trip" on you should send you heading for the door. These are not signs of a spiritually developed self.

The best "roller coaster" ride will be the fortune-teller who promises to break all the evil spells on you and charges you a small fee to do so. Some of these make interesting stories. I have seen people who say they were cured by climbing naked into the bathtub with twenty-five lit candles around them, where they are made to utter unintelligible sounds that sound like glub, glub. Some have gone a step further by adding some perfectly good brandy together with $3,000 in dollar bills to the tub. Of course, the psychic gets to keep the wet money. Another interesting act: stuffing dollar bills into a cantaloupe until it disintegrates (again, the fortune-teller keeps the cash). What lengths some people will go to! All these stories are actual cases. Enough examples. You need to learn how to sweeten your physical environment, to learn that no worthy counselor tells you what to do or takes any responsibility to do it for you. They can encourage and help you over the hurdles. They simply and instantly "know" you and what your needs are.

You may have to wait for a while to find one who is truly on the right path, who is working not solely for your benefit but for God, and needs you for his own spiritual evolution. These people know that when they guide others effectively, they guide themselves.

Psychic therapy should not be confused with psychology. Psychics simply are unblocked and detached enough from this earthly confusion to pick up precognitive information working with your own energy sources, and can *see* a clear path into your future. They work with the goodness of the positive truths of the Universe and can usually find your guides and personal panel of spirit judges who can and do help you. You are never alone. Each relationship with each client will be totally different, as each person's needs are different. The true spiritual practitioner will never make you feel dependent on him or her alone. Enslaving a client and projecting guilt onto him would take away time that is needed for others who are truly in need of help and ready to do their own work. Some practitioners will not immediately accept you as a student until you "get your act together."

When you awaken to your own deceits and expose your own motives to yourself, you may not feel exactly ready to grow and learn. Good psychic readers will sense this beforehand. (Please read the following pages on getting the most beneficial experience out of a session of guidance.) Before going to anyone, however, put the thought out there and state what your needs are. Chances are, you'll get it!

WHEN GOING FOR A READING FROM A CLAIRVOYANT: TIPS AND ADVICE ON HOW TO CONDUCT YOURSELF FOR A BENEFICIAL HAPPENING

1. Understand that in most cases psychic attunement is not fortune-telling, unless one happens to go to a fortune-teller.

Most Clairvoyants have first to attune themselves to your level of understanding—whether you are into basic Earth or material world structure or higher, spiritual realms. The understanding of your soul and soul's growth will be revealed (perhaps understood as a past life reading or regression).

2. *Expect truthful advice* for correct living patterns based according to the highest philosophy. See if personal development is separated from personal desires and prejudices.

3. Try to come into the reading that day in an even-tempered mood. Do this by abandoning your problems for a moment to see if a detached party will see a way out for you (there always is). Intense human emotions make it difficult. Of course, this is not always practical or possible, but do try.

4. Good teachers or Clairvoyants do not want excessive advance information, as this could confuse them. Just let them know, from time to time, if they are on the right path according to your own timing schedule and inner biological time clock. Impressions come through them from many different energy sources; thus, they may need some clarification to separate the information so you are both in sync. Be fair. You can tell them if they are misoriented or on the right track so you don't waste any of your time or theirs.

5. Don't be skeptical if they seem to be tuning in to the far-off future. By the time you find out they are wrong or right, you will either need another reading by them, or you will decide to find someone else. It always works out. Time is one of the hardest elements to predict accurately! Psychic information does not come through the linear time frame. Information comes in terms of words, pictures, concepts, and/or feelings. Some get it through audio or visual impressions. Discrepancies arise only when they don't know whether a picture is symbolic or literal. They do determine this, however, while working with you. *Expect good results.* If you do not, this is not a beneficial reading. Remember, is it your truth or the real truth you are dealing with? Be honest with yourself!

6. Don't be quick to say "no." The information may clarify itself later and you will have already changed the energy coming through.

7. Have patience. The psychic may have to proceed at his or her own pace. Your major problems may not be answered

right away, as they have to feel out the energies first to see what you can or cannot handle. If the major problem does not come through (as they may not see your immediate problem as a problem at all), any good reader will ask you at the end if there are any more questions. You can then bring it up and the reader can provide you with the proper insight.

8. Many things are destined and you may merely have to go through with a problem for your destiny to be revealed. Many traumas are caused merely by a free-will problem. Ask the reader to guide you through these to see if it is inherent or a karmic pattern you have set. A good adviser can answer that question and you will feel the truth by his or her words. (In your heart center, not your head!)

9. Some Clairvoyants see a spirit manifestation; some hear. Some see symbols or screen projections. It would help you to ask them how they receive this information so you can understand their work in relation to your knowledge and input.

10. Do not interrupt in the middle of a sentence. Wait until they have finished. It could interrupt their communication with their spirit guides.

11. Determine *how* they guide you. With love? By telling you about their own problems? Find out how they feel about themselves and how they handle their lives' stressful situations. *Guidance is a keynote.* Ask if your free will might change your own life situations.

12. Do not make unfair comparisons before they finish. If you go to consultants in good faith, you will definitely determine their worth. *But,* please evaluate them at the end of the session. It is possible that someone cannot tune in to you. You will know this at the very beginning, perhaps the first ten minutes. Sometimes you can be your own protection. Then thank them and leave. It is also possible you have just gone there to find out whether you *know* your truth. That negative experience could turn out positive. Nip it in the bud if it feels completely negative.

13. *There can be errors in some readings.* Try just to consider each reading as a new piece of information or helpful guideline by which you live your life. Feel it and compare it to your own inner voice. *You* might be right.

14. If you try to prolong a reading, the energies involved could dissipate for you and your reader. Your Clairvoyant is not your wet-nurse or therapist, as a different energy is involved. Energies can become lost. Abide by the rules established beforehand.

15. The truth is not always measured by love and kindness. Always, truth must be determined, not what you would like to hear, but always delivered in a positive manner by a good Clairvoyant. Perhaps they can show you how to turn your grief around. It may be that you are not prepared to work at your own problems and want the psychic to do it all. Be fair!

16. Let the Light of Truth guide you, and above all pray in advance that you will be sent to the right person for you. I can assure you, you get what you ask for. In time, you always get what your needs are.

Remember to bring your circle of protection, your white light. Then put it on!

PART TWO

—

GETTING
STARTED

5

Psychic Energy and How It Works for You

MOTION:
THE LAW OF THE COSMOS

A great philosopher, Hermes Trismegistus said, "Nothing rests, everything moves, everything vibrates." We all are a part of the vast sea of interpenetrating vibrations. Nothing exists that does not move or vibrate! This encompasses *everything in existence*. We are all energy receivers, whether we be man, plant, or pebble, moved either by the air, earth, water, or fire. We exist on Earth with all four elements.

ABOUT YOUR ENERGIES

What is consciousness in human beings? The philosopher Descartes said, "I think, therefore I am."

We go along in this world seeing with our eyes, hearing with our ears, smelling with our noses. Through our five physical senses and by their perceptions we become aware of consciousness. Can you exist only on that level of consciousness? When you think in one place you might be miles away and think of another. For example: while reading in a chair in your home, you see or read something that reminds you of a physical place. You can, therefore, return to a nonphysical state. Reading about the Civil War—an event that is not in your physically conscious world—you can feel the excitement and fear that era represents.

Perhaps you can tune in to a time you lived before your current lifetime. Or you can read a science fiction book set in the year 2500 A.D. Are you not focusing your consciousness on a time after your probable death? Such is the power of the imagination.

It all can feel very real to you, almost to the extent of your actually being there. You can, therefore, see or realize different time frames, in which a truly altered state of consciousness exists, compared to what we now know. It is another reality, one which we can perceive without our physical senses.

So if we choose to focus our consciousness beyond the physical body, do we possess, by a process of focus, the ability to visit, to go to another realm and have a coexisting life in another place?

PERCEPTIONS

You're thinking of a friend, perhaps one you haven't seen for years. Suddenly the telephone rings, and the person you were thinking of is on the line. Is it plain old coincidence? Can you define it as a life event that defies logic? Can you keep writing off such occurrences as pure chance?

Carl Jung coined the word *synchronicity*. He gave it a name and awareness, describing that which we sometimes overlook until it suddenly becomes concrete evidence. We then have to sit up and take notice!

Let's begin with the five physical senses: sight, touch (feeling), hearing, taste, and smell. Now, try to understand the senses beyond those. Go beyond, to the *Astral* senses, which can open the door for you to experience all there is. One meaning of the word *occult* is that existence beyond the one on which you can focus (beyond the physical senses).

Clairaudience, for example, is Astral hearing on the Astral Plane, different from what you can hear on the Physical Plane. Psychic powers lie dormant in everyone. The possibility of their awakening is always present. Different degrees of development depend on degrees of spiritual unfoldment. When you reach the point of *near opening*, you can deal with feelings that you get and then see coming true. The element of faith plays an important part. Disbelief tends to keep psychic abilities dormant, as does fear.

In the New Age the Astral senses of human beings are unfolding and becoming commonplace. Many think it only the *imagination* or foolishness. Some first use this power in their dream state. We use our Astral senses when we perceive occurrences and sense what is happening at a distance, perhaps quite far away. The Astral ether (merely a space pocket of air energy) allows us to see the future as it is thrown ahead of time. Time consists merely of mental impressions or images that we experience whether going backward or forward toward the future. The Astral body is an exact counterpart of the physical body of a person. It is composed of fine ethereal matter and is usually encased in the physical body of a person. In dreams it can become detached and sent on long journeys, over long distances. Sometimes distress can cause this. The Astral body may even be able to travel at a speed greater than light. The Astral body continues to exist after the death of the physical body but it disintegrates eventually.

You must understand all this before going on. Astral impressions are always received in the ethers. For example, if a few inventors scattered in different parts of the world are working on the same idea or project, they are all in tune with the ethers on the same plane to pull in from, and pick up from, the same information source.

The need to finish and patent it quickly is required to make the idea yours, or else someone else will be deemed the inventor. The attributes of the spirit, which we term *soul*, bears a correspondence to the physical senses of the body. The *soul* bears exactly the same relation to the spirit as the physical senses bear to the human brain. The intelligence, the mind behind the senses, utilizes and tabulates the impressions it receives from the outer worlds or planes. Mind is something above and beyond the senses, even though it is absolutely dependent on them so it can break down the impressions to this world's mind and the Universal mind. It is the same with the soul and spirit. All knowledge of eternal life from without or within the Universe is received by means of the soul. The mind utilizes all the knowledge and experience that the soul in its various cycles is continually receiving and sending to it.

In the mind we find the doorway to the fourth energy level, the fourth dimension. All that can be imagined by man is how we use this energy level. What is reality is in fact imagination brought forth into the physical level. Remember, everyone's views are different, so their conception of reality is different. Once you unblock the awareness and can be open to it all, you'll find that all thought is electromagnetic—energy of a high vibration—and that the brain is a powerful generator of energy. The process of thinking produces an emission of these electromagnetic brain waves. So Descartes was right: whatever a man thinks is what he is!

THE COSMIC LAWS OF ENERGY

Source: The Encyclopedia of Ancient and Forbidden Knowledge by Zolar

1. ORDERLY TREND: Under this law we have order in the cosmos, from the sun to the atoms and the Law of Cause and Effect. Thus, there is no "chance" or "accident" in the nature of things.
2. THE LAW OF ANALOGY: Under this law, we have correspondence and agreement regarding the various forms of manifestations and when we know one, we know, "As above, so below." "All is mind, the Universe is mental."
3. THE LAW OF OPPOSITES: A thing is and is not. A thing is subject to change, therefore it is and it is not at the same time. Also, if we carry opposite things to the extremes, they are alike, as in extreme light, we cannot see, or in the darkness we do not see.
4. THE LAW OF SEQUENCE: Under this law, we learn that everything proceeds from something and is succeeded by something.
5. THE LAW OF BALANCE: We find that everything has its opposites; love, hate, pleasure, pain. And we can see, we require the opposite to give us balance.
6. THE LAW OF CYCLICITY: Everything seems to move in circles, but by wisdom and strength of mind we are able to work the circles into spirals for the purpose of progress and attainment.

USING ELECTROMAGNETIC FIELDS TO CHANNEL PSYCHIC ENERGIES

We all swim in a sea of energies. *All* is energy—and that includes everything in our living existence. There is nothing magical or mystical about energy, nor about the limits to the usage of these energies. The only limits that exist are the ones we set. Negative energy is always close by and positive energy is farther away. Therefore, it takes us longer to achieve the positive energy. Do not let prejudgment ruin your creative thoughts of what you can allow to materialize. (Just be careful not to set up barriers.) Project those thoughts of what you want, when you want it. Specify "in your minds' eye." Use the end point: think only of the end result of what you want; do not worry how you get there. We have the ability to alter time if you believe it to be so. Our life on this plane is but an illusion. As we begin to experience a thought we can manifest it into our current material reality. By thinking you will create "cause and effect," and if you change your images or any preconceived ideas you will be able to think your wishes true. The power within depends on how centered you are in the here and now. The more you keep yourself here now, the easier it will be to make your dreams come true.

HOW TO USE AND CHANNEL
THESE ENERGIES

The Making of Energy Balls for
Healing and Stimulating Body Energy

- Rub your hands together briskly for about two minutes.
- While rubbing, picture the colors red and orange coming from your hands creating an imaginary rubber ball or beach ball.
- Utilize this energy for pulling out headaches by touching affected places on the head or any other area of the body that needs a self-healing or the immediate movement of blocked energy (perhaps in the knee, foot areas, or limbs).

Air Baths: Feel the Flow of the Wind,
How to Deal with Energies and Their Currents

- Utilize these energies to *avoid* blocked energy and to speed your evolution.

EMULATE THE WIND

- The sea of energy you should bathe in is the wind. Be it and become it. Since the entire cosmos is energy and we are the infinitesimal parts of this energy, we should wash ourselves in its currents.
- Do so when you are tired. "Hang out" in the pulsating, living part of the Universe. Any action you take should move you with the flow. The *movement* of the physical body, like the wind, is upward. If you have been bucking against the natural flow, reverse yourself; move with it in its natural groove. Walk with it, run in it, or sit by the seashore and feel the Universe's flow pounding against your face and body. If you step out of it, you will notice how you are floundering. You might feel disturbed, distressed, restless, or unhappy. Feel and know this within yourself. Move your body rationally in rhythm with the movement of the Universe. If you don't feel right, you are stepping out of the flow. As you place yourself in this flow, you can ride the currents of energy and reach your goals more quickly, safely, and easily. However, you must sense it! The Divine flow will bring the world and you into perfect ecological balance.

Dissolve a Cloud

- Select a small one and give it your undivided attention for a few minutes. Mentally tell it to dissolve and picture energies flowing through you and up to the cloud to increase its temperature. Keep watching and it will disappear and dissolve.
- Use your imagination, the power of thought energy. You can form images or shape the clouds into artistic designs.

Need a Parking Spot?

Visualize it, send the energy to it, and you will get it. Simply do the following:

- Visualize what you need
- Visualize and see where you want it to be
- Do all this while driving in that direction or place

Energize an Animal or Inanimate Object

- Rub your hands together as described in "The Making of Energy Balls," p. 51).

- While rubbing your hands, ask for God's energy to be sent down into your palms and feel it come through you. The intense heat will show you that this request has been answered. Make sure that there is a lot of green color in your palms, as green is the healing color.
- Your thoughts can affect people, pets, clouds, and inanimate objects. As you walk through your home, touch all your plants and pets with love and your hands will heal.

Group Healing with Prayer, Energy, and Vibrations

- A prayer should be made by the whole group (see Chapter 8). Have everyone in the group ask mentally to be bathed in white light.
- Have a period of silence for five to ten minutes in which everyone feels love.
- Place the group in a circle, with everyone holding hands. Place an empty chair in the center of the circle. Each individual will have a chance to sit in it. While arranging the circle, make sure someone is facing east, someone facing west, north, and south.
- Have everyone *mentally* direct energy and love and healing energies to the person sitting in the center of the closed circle. (The person in the center should feel healed of anxiety, homeliness, apathy, or rejection, or you can heal a particular part of his body.)
- The minds of all of you become the channels, and the receiver in the center has an experience. This is accomplished through electrical charge from the group to the receiver. This energy is your "life batteries," and the voltage is psychic power.

Remember, always start with a healing prayer and use the *white light* around yourself, around the person in the center, and around the whole circle.

THE ASTRAL SENSES

We are all born with the same *five physical senses*:

- Sight
- Touch

- Hearing
- Taste
- Smell

There are *five Astral senses* that correspond but differ from the physical. Collectively, these are called the *sixth sense*, the doorway to our intuition.

FIVE SENSES (Physical)	SIXTH SENSE (Astral)
1. Sight	A clairvoyant ability
2. Touch (feeling)	To read into an object's energy field (can be called *psychometry*)
3. Hearing	The ability to hear vibrations on planes of consciousness above that of Earth
4. Taste	The power to absorb life's energy waves through the body
5. Smell	Sensitivity to aromas other than those of the Earth Plane

OTHER SENSES	SOUL ASTRAL SENSES
6. Intuition (to use this, a person may perceive occurrences and scenes at an incredibly far distance)	The capacity to receive true inspirations
7. Thought transference	The power to receive, at will, information from the ethers with other spiritual beings in other dimensions

These energy powers may be dormant in many people. The degrees of "opening" depend on the person's unfoldment and evolution.

Let's divide the mind into these categories:

1. CONSCIOUS MIND. This is the receiving station of the five physical senses. It is your assimilating mind, your reasoning mind, your logical mind, the mind of language and ordinary perception.

2. SUBCONSCIOUS MIND. This is your storage house, the origi-
   nator of fantasy and dreams and creative imagination. Your
   subconscious is where you remember everything that has ever
   happened to you as though it were on a tape recorder and
   ready to be played at your command.
3. SUPERCONSCIOUS. This is where your subconscious blends
   into other minds and is connected to events that have not yet
   taken place. This is where you go backward or forward in
   time. This is the part of your mind that can travel about
   unlimited by your present position in space. It is through this
   activity of your mind that you get your truest extrasensory
   impressions.
4. DIVINE MIND. Divine Mind is that spark of *divinity* called
   your soul, which is in you and in every living thing. It is part
   of the Greater Divinity that we call the God-Power of the
   Universe or the Infinite Intelligence. It is the causative force
   behind all people, things, and events.

Note: When you listen to the voices of intuition, you should
automatically open your entire being. Judge each experience
individually. Judge reality as it exists, rather than view it in
preconceived categories.

A SOUL'S UNFOLDMENT
(OR EVOLUTION)

Fundamental laws and requirements:

1. Physical harmony in one's own surroundings (this helps you
   to be unblocked and therefore open to all new thoughts).
2. To be aware of impure thoughts. Isolation at times helps to
   clear our feelings.
3. Taking care of your inner growth, thus allowing a purity
   within; clearing takes place and the higher exterior states will
   then take care of themselves.

The "near opening" sometimes referred to by Clairvoyants
refers to those times when feelings come true. The element of
faith plays an important part. Disbelief tends to keep it dormant.
Awareness is where it's at. If you can unblock yourself at will,
you may and can tune in to these precognitive feelings. Imagination and creativity are the bases of all and any reality. No one's

views are the same, so there are no rights or wrongs. Only the truths of your convictions are your strengths. Learning to allow precognitive feelings to come in is essential.

Now we get to the good stuff. The *first step* in consciousness raising is to *know* there is a spirit force beyond everything. Don't view it as an intellectual truth. This world is the one place where the intellect by itself is powerless to penetrate. Remember: *The mind is above and beyond the senses, even though it is absolutely dependent on them.*

It is the same with the soul and the spirit. All knowledge from without or within the Universe is continually received by the soul in its various cycles. The mind then utilizes all this knowledge. The attributes of the spirit that we term *soul* bear a correspondence but are separate from the physical senses of the body.

All these Astral senses will unfold and soon become commonplace for all humans. Many may now think of it as imagination or foolishness. Some will experience this power in dreams. But someday we will all experience these highly developed senses.

So, do not view all this as an intellectual truth, since in this area the intellect is a "fraud." It deals with three-dimensional things, while we have become four-dimensional.

We must have the strength to find the truth. Truth must be put into action, by being lived. What you learn from it has to be absorbed within so that you can become a part of it, in the following ways:

1. BY REPETITION—it works its way into the soul. How you progress is up to the character of your soul and its development. Keep practicing! Say mantras (see chapter 8).
2. EFFORT must be extended. You have to sincerely want harmony with the spiritual energy. It has to hook up to the rest of your soul. Work hard.
3. MANIFESTATION is the real key. You must put forth the effort. The idea is not to grasp but to absorb until it becomes a part of you. This is along the lines of "seeing is believing." *Manifestation* means these advanced truths must move into physical action. In order to advance, the fulfillment of what you have already done or accomplished must be witnessed and understood by you. If you do not understand this, instead of going forward, you go backward.

4. SPIRITUAL GROWTH is the capacity to complete and manifest our spiritual truths. It incorporates our *character*, the one quality that we have to develop for ourselves, as it cannot be given to us. It advances when one dedicates himself to the soul's need without seeking rewards. A *need* is what the soul must have to mature. The *personality* is the unique one, as no two people are the same. We use our personalities as they are the means by which we choose to express our characters.

Truth above all, to thyself; all other truths will then follow.

RELAXATION IN THREE STEPS

- Learn to listen.
- Learn what to listen to.
- Unblock yourself so that you can tune in to the frequency you need; spiritual purity and complete isolation from impure thoughts.

FOR A HAPPY, HEALTHY STATE OF MIND: EXERCISE GUIDE TO THE ALPHA STATE

DEFINITION: IMAGINATION! Learn that there is no difference between imagination and human realities. Reality means that there are no rights or wrongs, only what you believe. Accomplishing peace of mind is the major factor. It is only the awareness of opening you to yourself that makes it right. This is a learning essential, as our life is all a dream in conscious reality.

AWARENESS: PROJECTING those thoughts of what you want and need when you want it—*specify!* No two people are the same; therefore, states of awareness differ. Use the end point of what you want, to be aware of where you want to be at the end of your extending opening of awareness. Don't wonder how you will get there. Change your negative images.

PROGRAMMING YOURSELF: DO IT NOW! Count down or create an image or picture of yourself in your conscious mind. Your conscious self will feed the data to the unconscious, where these messages will be stored in tiny little time capsules. You are never given anything you can't handle.

TECHNIQUES FOR INCREASING
PSYCHIC ENERGY

- By means of mind-directed breathing
- By mind alone (clear away those gray masses around the brain by visualizing it becoming a healthier color)

PSYCHIC ENERGY AIDS INSPIRATION

To apply it is to reach a higher conscious high-grade energy for greater awareness to do what you wish to accomplish. If you are a writer or a painter, seek this inspiration.

- Breathe in quickly and deeply to the count of five.
- Hold your breath to the count of ten. As you hold your breath, visualize a brilliant cloud of shimmering, pulsating silver-white radiance two or three feet over your head. See it being small and round, about two feet in diameter.
- Then breathe out to the count of seven. As you do, raise your consciousness up into the center of the cloud so that it pulls in and contains your head and shoulders. Do this with a rhythm. Proceed to write or paint. When you get tired, *rest*.

USE SCENT TO RAISE PSYCHIC ENERGY

- Use Tonquin Musk or V.S.P. Musk.
  (Do not take internally!)
- Place a few droplets on red or orange suede.
  (This will increase your sensitivity and help you make sound decisions). Keep the suede on your person or close to you.
- This method works especially well if you are run down or have depleted energy and need a quick pick-me-up.

HOW TO OBTAIN PSYCHIC ENERGY
FROM A TREE

- Be very conscious of what you are doing—*concentrate!*
- Touch your fingertips to the sharp ends of the needles of a living cedar tree or branch. (Cedar is good for unblocking the senses.)

- Lightly press the balls of the first two fingers and thumb of either hand against the tips of the needles. Retain this hold for a few minutes as you feel the energy of the tree flow into you.
- Do this every day for a week to become aware of the increased vitality you can feel.

BASIC TECHNIQUES
FOR DEVELOPING CONCENTRATION

Keep a diary of your experiences. It will help you improve results.

EXERCISE 1

- Relax, breathe deeply. Make your mind a blank.
- Decide where you would like to visit—a place, city, house. Have a destination in mind.
- Create a pinpoint of light about nine inches above your forehead (above your third eye). Move toward that light.
- Go into that pinpoint of light.
- Move the light gradually upward, out, beyond time and space.
- Then move the light into the sky and from there to the point you have chosen to be your destination. While you are moving, see the terrain below as you would see it in flight. (Stay in that light.) Picture the cities, rivers, mountains, towns, and buildings you are moving toward.
- Let the light descend at its destination, allow yourself to look around, picking up thoughts, feelings, visions, and voices.
- Return using the same process. When you have come back to the starting point, make notes on what you sensed.

EXERCISE 2

- Relax, breathe deeply. Make your mind a blank, create an empty screen.
- Let your awareness float where it will.
- Make notes on what you sense . . . what you hear, smell, taste, and so on.

EXERCISES TO REACH
THE ALPHA STATE

EXERCISE 1: RAINBOWS

1. Settle yourself comfortably in a chair in an upright position.
2. Take a long, deep breath—inhale to a count of 5—*hold* for a count of 5. Exhale to the count of 5.
3. Allow the mind to drift leisurely and relax the shoulders and neck. Hopefully the rest of your body will take a hint. Your conscious mind may be restless at first.
4. Begin your countdown. Begin with 21. Start by seeing the figure 21, then say 21, see the figure 20 and say it, and so on down to 1.

   You can count silently or aloud as you drift deeper and deeper with each number into the very core of your being. Let the numbers come to you at your own pace. There is nothing else to do . . . nowhere else to go. It might help for the countdown to be said in intervals of three, so that you can monitor your body's rhythms. In this way, you might be able also to be aware of your bones, nerves, and muscles and scan them all at the same time. Mentally program the descent into the cave of your soul's being. When you reach the count of 1, drift along and see nothing but space and sky, an open arena of air floating by. Continue to relax. Never worry that you have done it wrong; your subconscious will take over.
5. At this more inward level, visually pick out a passive scene from nature that is meaningful to you, one that creates your own inner sanctum of peace and serenity. Keep your eyes closed at all times and your conscious, imaginative mind will roam into a different state of reality.

   At this point, *think only once*, "Who cares what is reality or my own world of fantasy or imagination. There is nobody in here but me, so no one else can see or occupy my space."
6. Again, take a deep breath and, still with your eyes closed, tune in to the colors of the rainbow. See the spectrum of colors in front of you. Take each color separately at first and fit it into a color association of what that color represents. Try: *yellow*, bask in the reflection of the sun. *Red*: see a shiny red apple. *Green*: perhaps the forest. *Blue*: the azure sky. *Purple*: maybe a plum or a violet, or the haze of a misty sea.

A QUICK EXERCISE TO
REACH THE ALPHA STATE

First, do the relaxation and countdown exercise from 21 to 1. Some find, then, that the circle technique works. Form a circle with the thumb and index finger. You can automatically slip into the problem-solving stage of Alpha. It should be practiced daily, or the facilities can slack off and vanish.

Visualize yourself going into an elevator, feel it move down many floors; to the basement from the top of a hundred-story building, then to the sub-basement. Ask to have a shortwave radio put into your hand and listen to it for information on where to go or what to see when you get to the sub-basement. The radio is your director and will lead you in the direction you need.

You are now going into the inner levels of your mind. You are there to get direction to quiet your mind and to feel the safety of your inner sanctum. You are there to experience freedom from stress, anxiety, and pain, as this is where your personal workshop is to stimulate your creative faculties. You will feel perhaps an infinity of white light or a calm darkness of a loving, restorative quality. You may also feel a flow of energy as you are practically breathless with all fear and tensions gone.

The shortwave radio is the sound that will lead you to a center of awareness, an identifying strength that will intuitively keep you on the proper course. The answers always lie for us all within the deeper layers of the mind and our feelings about the Universal force about us.

Explanation:
1. You are going into a workshop, your personal one.
2. You might wish to furnish it with a desk or a chair. You can even imagine a telephone or several chairs there, your own private conference room.
3. Your shortwave radio is your only means of communication with the outside world, if you wish to speak with someone . . . spiritual or physical.

EXERCISE 2:
THE WORLD IN THE TREE

Find a tree; any one you wish to imagine would be okay, just make sure it is large enough to have a wide base. Look all around it for an opening or hole, perhaps one already dug out by a squirrel or woodpecker. Know that once you feel yourself diminishing in size you will climb into the tree. You will be going into the hidden cave of a world beyond the reality you have just left and begin on your journey.

Allow yourself to walk deep inside the tree. As you walk, know you are coming into the light of a strange new dimension. Perhaps you will see yourself there, in a strange new land. Notice the artifacts in that space. Let the images flow without fear, and view the whole of the entire scene; go slowly and let all these impressions come through. Set the conditions in your mind now, so that when you return you will remember every detail, every aspect of this journey.

When you are finished or do not feel anything further happening, set the condition in your mind that you need to go back where you started, outside the tree as you first viewed it, and either you will start to see yourself going back into the tunnel the way you entered or you will just be back outside the tree instantly. Ask then to be back in the room where you started . . . take a deep, long breath and open your eyes.

EXERCISE 3:
SCREEN PROJECTION

Get into the Alpha level again with your breathing and countdowns (see Exercise 1, p. 60). Close your eyes and keep your mind focused only on the darkness you see. Look for a pinprick of a white dot in the center of the darkness. Try to go into the light (it will get lighter) and ask to travel along in this "time tunnel." Ask to go into the "screen of the mind." (Remember in this and every other exercise to ensure your safety by protecting yourself with a white light before you start.)

See yourself now going into an amphitheater with a huge screen. Set the conditions: you will see only color images. Between each sequence of pictures, put a white light around the frame of what you see, the kind you see around bathroom vanity mirrors or a makeup mirror, to protect yourself in these images.

EXERCISE 4:
INSTANT REPLAY

Visualize a problem or perhaps a project you need to know about, surrounded by white light. On this screen, which should look like a huge color TV, visualize several images in a row. (Remember to protect yourself with white light.)

See what you may have done yesterday, *or* see what you perhaps felt about yourself or another, *or* play a scene of what you actually did in this earthly reality, only this time visualize it the way you wish you had.

Improve the scene to work out okay and forgive yourself for the mistakes you made. Changing the image to one you like will upgrade and improve your life, as it will erase all pent-up emotions and old "tapes" of thoughts and feelings.

The above techniques will help you relax, tune in, and center or calm yourself. They drop you into the *Alpha* level. People in this state most of the time are at their healthiest, as it is a relaxed, healthy state of mind.

A MORE ADVANCED TECHNIQUE FOR
DEVELOPING CONCENTRATION

The following *time and space exercise* is designed to make your past, present, and future all one, back and forth. Thus you will see the past, present, and future as one continuous line, unbroken.

1. Make your mind a blank while you are in a restful, quiet, relaxed, passive state.
2. Select a person or a place on which to concentrate.
3. Recreate that person or place in your mind's eye (either in the present, past, or future).
4. Create a setting. Allow the image to come through. Write it in your diary.
5. Recreate the original person, place, or thing. Then, move it backward or forward in time.
6. Describe the backward setting and make a note of it in your diary.
7. Describe the forward-in-time setting and make a note of it.

Explanation: You can either see it and remember it, or see it in your mind's eye and physically write it down on paper.

BE YOUR OWN THERAPIST:
PSYCHIC TUNING IN

Do this exchange with another person.

Preparation:

1. Have both people face each other. Clear your head of emotions and thoughts.
2. Breathe deeply several times to draw in energy, stabilizing your emotions.
3. Draw in your psychic energies also through your breathing.

Tuning in:

1. Focus your eyes and your total attention on the subject.
2. Probe into the subject's eyes with your eyes.
3. Let yourself be a receiver of sights, sounds, and impressions.
4. Begin to talk when you feel an impression.
5. As you talk, you are tracking in on the subject.
6. Try to probe into the center of the subject on a deep level.
7. Think of yourself as radar, scanning the wave lengths of the subject's subconscious mind and soul level.
8. Ask yourself questions regarding the subject to direct the pattern of your probe.
9. If it is easier for you to tune in to the person's voice, have him or her talk to you, answering your questions.
10. Try to find the karmic meaning of the person and be a therapeutic psychic. (See Chapter 17.)

Analysis:

1. Have experimenters face each other and call upon them to analyze their fellow student (five minutes).
2. A teacher should guide analysis and add amplification to analysis technique.
3. Do not look for negative information except to correct it or to offer solutions to problems.

A TRAINING DISCIPLINE TO
TEACH THE MIND TO BRING IN
THE THINGS IT WANTS

HOW COLOR APPLICATION HELPS

Prepare swatches of colors.

Close your eyes and feel what each color does to you while touching the swatches. When you hold each one up separately to your third eye, you will get a message.

Open your eyes and write it down. Look over your writings a week later; it will be helpful.

QUESTIONS AND ANSWERS COME THROUGH
WHEN YOUR MIND FOCUSES

Take a piece of paper and write a question on it. Put several of these pieces of paper in a pile and mix them up. Without knowing which question you have, hold the paper up to the third eye, writing-side up. You will get a message. An answer always comes for the question. Don't think about it, be spontaneous.

Save all these papers for a week without analyzing them. Then, at another time, when you look back, your mind will be as clear as your answers to yourself.

ADVANCED THERAPY

Listen to the energy of music that you ordinarily would not play or understand. The more foreign to your taste, the better.

Close your eyes. Decide how the music makes you feel. Happy or sad? If it makes you feel happy, meditate on giving energy to complete a project or end a problem you've been having. Work it out through the sound waves. It will give you reinforcement to decide which action to take and suggest solutions in your profession, home, love life, or in the more personal aims of your existence. It will give you a positive thrust!

If the sound of the music makes you sad, try to get the negative energy out from the sound of sadness and turn it around to a more positive outcome. Hold on to your needs and feel joy in that. Perhaps you really don't need your sad problem. The music will slow down your thinking and make you recollect the past, see where you may have fouled things up. Change the thought. Begin to feel forgiveness for yourself or another.

What this meditation asks is that when you listen to music you cannot feel, don't take to heart or interpret your own life in it. This will cause distraction and irritation for you. The music is simply to help you focus on your priorities. It merely aids you through the use of sound. The music's energy will help you steer your course by directly confronting issues and help to stimulate your mind to arrive at a decision with your problems. It serves as a background to help you focus more quickly and not hold on to old beliefs or situations.

USING YOUR SPIRIT GUIDE
AS A CO-THERAPIST

1. A spirit guide is a distinct personality with humor, perspective, insight, knowledge, and wisdom.

2. **The spirit guide is there to help you** to grow spiritually. Unless you invite him or her in, your guide cannot help you to grow. The guide cannot grow either if he or she isn't invited from the other realm to help you, since spirit guides often have learned your lessons during their Earth time. They need to work with you to get into the higher realms of learning.

   Many people are under the illusion that they should not ask a spirit for help, or that they must get all the answers on their own. The spirit guide acts as a go-between between you and the higher powers. It is a fallacy to think you can get all the answers you need on your power alone. Spirits can be awarded to you or can choose you. They could be with you some sixty to eighty-five years of your life, or much less. When the lesson is learned and you can go higher into the understanding of the Universe, a more informed spirit guide appears. There are no set rules regarding how long this takes. It is all up to you.

3. You invoke spirit guides through the power of prayer. State your needs to the guides. Call them in.

4. *Make them team members.* Some guides can go only a little distance with you, perhaps a short while if you have grown past them.

   Most guides will present themselves in whatever form you can accept. It might be an image, even an odor you're not familiar with, or they might appear as a bird or just a glowing light of energy. No matter what shape they appear in, welcome and accept them and your communication with them will remain constant.

5. *Acceptance* will help facilitate their helping you. Your guide will know what threatens you the least and will feel gratified when he can help you understand the spiritual realms. His presence there provides him with information and wisdom. He has to go out of his way to seek what you need on these planes. Since your mind can focus only on Earth's reality, you need a guide to function as a co-therapist. Learn to work with your guide in unison, as a team, as it will help you to cut through human emotions and biases that block your growth. Consulting with your guide can reinforce your good feelings about yourself.

6. Once you make contact, it is best to connect with the guide the same time each day. Try meditating to make contact each day. Consult with yourself as to what feels best. How do you do this? There are no set rules, but here are three methods I like:

   • Set the conditions—that is, you need a certain amount of time to speak or consult with your guide. You will automatically have it.
   • Wrap yourself in a cocoon of white light.
   • Say a soul mantra (this will clear out any negative energy). Examples: AUM   GOD   OM
     (Pick one of the above and exaggerate the sound until you cannot hold the note anymore. Do this three times.)

   or

   • Close your eyes.
   • Visualize a quiet place, maybe one of nature, that represents security, tranquility, peace, and safety. Always visualize the same place, as this is the meeting place for you and your helper to discuss your life's problems.

7. The most effective questions to ask when working with spirit guides are:

- What caused this to happen?
- What am I to learn from this experience?
- Have I learned all I can at this time from this experience?
- What have I not learned?
- Have I learned to release myself from the effects of this experience?
- Do I care?
- What caused me (or the others) to behave as I did?
- How can I handle the jam I'm in?

Now listen . . . Prayer means to ask, meditation is to listen within.

8. It might take three consecutive days of meeting with your spirit co-therapist to feel comfortable and gain answers. *Now, on day three*, go a little further and try feeling your guide's presence. Sense what qualities he has.

In step 1, I told you he has a distinct personality all his own. If you do not feel him, look for him. Perhaps there is a glimmer of a light, a heaviness nearby, a dark, shadowy figure. Maybe you see a cloak; perhaps you can see an eye looking at you. Anything that looks or feels the same on each succeeding day *is* the guide. Don't second guess yourself or you will be playing mind games. Maybe even a cluster of energies will appear, so accept it as being your spirit guide and test it for its validity each day. Spirit guides test you and even have fun with your awakening (they have a sense of humor!). You can test them as well: ask either out loud or within (they hear you either way). Imagine yourself holding out your hand and saying: *"Please take my hand and let me feel your energy."*

If you *feel*, you will be able to sense the quality of the energy. Determine if it feels like good energy. Or is it negative? Your guide will reveal himself at that point and you will be able to assess his quality and/or validity.

- As you get more familiar, ask your guide, *"What name may I call you?"* Most often a name will be given (listen within for it), but sometimes it is not. It is not important, but it does make it easier to work with.

- If you find after trying for a week or so in the beginning of your venture you feel uneasy by *not* hearing a name, demand within, *"In the name of God, speak out, or leave so I may have a higher energy force of light surround me!"* By Universal Law guides must answer. At least, you have released a prankster or other guide that is not evolved. This false guide will then be eliminated.

  Note: If you should see someone whom you know to be presently alive, then you have too much of a dependency on Earth. This is *not* a spirit guide, as "spirit" means just that.

  As you begin to feel more and more that your guide is a friend, a key person or energy in your life, ask this serious question:

  - What lesson do I have to work on in the here-and-now in my life?

  The answer to this may be anger, humility, prejudice, forgiveness, etc. You can ask then to be taken to an event so that you can experience this lesson.

  After you have experienced your lesson, you won't want to become bogged down in it. When you feel you have accomplished this, ask for a "cosmic perspective," so that you can release your emotional attachments to the problem. Then surround the whole situation in your creative visualization in white light, as if you put a white light picture frame around it. You can then perhaps move to another lesson-experience by asking the question again.

9. Always thank your spirit guide for helping you and send him or her some loving energy in a thought form. You can give thanks inside yourself or out loud. Express the joy of making each contact more meaningful.

6

White Light—Shazam:
The Uses of the Healing
White Light

I stand tall in your light, dear Lord, as I gather
strength, wisdom and knowledge to all thy ways . . . all ways.

He who has been given the power of the light shall be
sustained on either shore of enlightenment.

My realities are open to God's truth as I ask ascendancy to the
yet higher planes. Protect my pathway and repel any approaching
negativities that may touch me where I am. Lift me up to your
doorway of higher learning and truth.

THE WHITE LIGHT
AND THE MAGNETIC CORE

The white light is an iridescent light that you place around
yourself from head to toe. You can do this for yourself, your
loved ones, your friends, or any other person with whom you
come in contact. This will open up all the good energy and block
off all negative energy, whether that energy is real or imagined.
Negative energy cannot pass through white light.

If you feel times of trouble, whether for yourself or your loved ones, not only should you place this white light from head to toe around you or your loved one, but you should also visualize a wheel of white light lying horizontally around you. You are the center of the wheel. You will have this wheel of white light revolving around you as well as the white light from head to toe. This is the most intense use of white light as protection and is to be used only if you really feel it is necessary, because usually the white light from head to toe will be quite sufficient. You can put white light around anything, any animate or inanimate object or person. It works! If you wish to raise your consciousness or those of the people around you, put a vivid pink light around you or anyone you choose. Pink is the color of Universal love. This is a very high-vibration color, so be careful how you use it.

None of the other colors of the rainbow is useful for protection (see Chapter 7). You can visualize yellow to increase your intellectual ability or blue to increase your receptivity, but only white or vivid pink can be used as a *protective shield*.

When you feel drained, you can energize yourself with white light. You can energize yourself also through the pink light of Universal love. It can spread your aura out very far.

THE MAGNETIC CORE

Stand with your feet comfortably apart, back erect, and you will feel the magnetic pull of the Earth. Keep your hands at your sides in a relaxed fashion, eyes closed. Just think of the polar core at the center of the Earth that you are going to tap in to, and, believe it or not, you will feel energy entering through your feet or the tips of your fingers. You're going to feel tingling and you will feel this energy permeating your whole body. I suggest you start off outdoors, with bare feet touching Mother Earth. As you get accustomed to the feeling, you will be able at any time—even with shoes on—to tap in to this energy. You could be in a skyscraper thirty floors up and still be able to tap in to that magnetic core of the Earth and instantly re-energize yourself.

This is also a good means of protection. If there is a negative feeling within you, whether it is caused by disruption or anger or just someone who has bad vibes and you want to change that atmosphere, go to the center of the Earth, to the core, and take in the opposite energy. If you have a negative energy around you, pull up a positive energy. If you have an overabundance of positive energy that is making you nervous, go into the core and pull up some negative energy to counterbalance that positive energy. It's important to be centered, so use your core as your energizer, and use your white light and your pink light as energizers and protection.

To make this a bit clearer: you will use your white light and your pink light for the more emotional states, whereas the magnetic core of the Earth should be used for re-energizing or balancing out your physical state. If you feel fear, use your white or pink light. If your energy is dissipated, go to the core.

Try to use all three methods for their distinct purposes rather than just saying, "Well, I'll just use the white light because that seems to be the cure-all." If it's just a physical thing, use the core; if you feel mental or emotional disruption, use the white light; and only in intense circumstances use the vivid pink; as I mentioned before, it is an extremely high vibration. If at times your energy flow is a little bit off balance, using the pink light might make you even more off balance. As you start to work with the white light and the pink light and the core, you will understand better the distinctions I am trying to make here.

The magnetic core is one of the prime bits of knowledge for Yoga students. It is pure concentration; it is the energizing that people practicing martial arts use, which is why there is that intense quiet before they strike. They are using all of the Earth's energy, which is how they can almost defy gravity. There is a tremendous amount of power that will come to you mostly in the form of physical energy. As this physical energy is flowing through your body, you can transmute it into a concentrated mental energy. This is the mental energy called upon by the people who break boards with their hands. This is why there is that quiet stillness just before they strike the board.

ENERGY

As long as we are on the subject, let's talk about concentrated energy: *mind control*. This is what is done in witchcraft, in voodoo. I call it *posi-think*. Energy is there, and whether you want to use it for destructive or constructive reasons is up to you. Energy makes no distinction between good or bad. It is only there, just as the soil is there. Whether you plant a beautiful flower or a tomato plant or a weed, energy doesn't care—all it does is provide the nourishment.

If you wish to concentrate on an object or on a person, all you need to do is energize yourself from the magnetic core so that you supplement your own natural, normal, everyday physical energy. Once you've done this, take this energy to the center of your mind and think about the person, place, or thing that you are working on.

Throw all this magnetic energy out to that situation and you can at any given moment change a course of events, using Earth's energy to move people. Let the core's energy revolve around while you're thinking about a person, and then in a flash you will automatically release that energy to that person and they will get a big booster shot of this energy that you have just sent in their direction. In other words, you could think about someone and say, "I want so-and-so to get up off the couch and get me a cup of coffee." So, you pull up on that magnetic core energy, pull it straight up to the center of your head, then throw out that energy with the thought direction of what you want the person to do. Release it, and suddenly you will see the person get up off the couch and make you a cup of coffee, and the poor soul won't know what happened except that he really had to make you a cup of coffee. As you see, this energy can involve a certain manipulation of will. In its lesser intensity it is called *positive thinking*. This is the same concentrated energy that is used in black magic and voodoo. So, you can see all the ramifications of this use of energy.

I warn you that if you use this energy for your own willful, egotistical purposes, it is assured that within three weeks' time you will get some sort of a pay-back. So remember always that there is a check-and-balance system within yourself. While at first you might be guilty of innocent misuse, if you were to continue this way you would be in a bad pattern. Within three weeks, for just an innocent misuse of energy, you will get some sort of bad feeling, or the same situation will somehow return to you. It's a "boomerang" effect, so be careful not to use this energy unwisely.

THE USES OF WHITE LIGHT ENERGY

• *To heal.* The only way I know to heal people is to begin by putting a white light around them. You place the white light around the person and then ask him or her to visualize it. This way you are eradicating all negative forces so that the person who is to be healed will be more receptive to the healing energy.

• *To counsel a friend in emotional turmoil.* If you are acting as a psychic or adviser to a friend, first engage the conscious mind. The conscious mind can never be idle. It must be used. Ask your friend to think one distinct pleasant thought—such as about one particular element of nature. Do not let her think of a whole scene because it will take up too much thinking energy.

Once the mind is engaged, throw your white light around her.

While she is still thinking the pleasant thought, ask her to throw up her own white light—make sure she is still thinking the pleasant thought, since it will make her more receptive.

When you are ready to go to work, throw a vivid pink light around her—the light of Universal love.

Stand and pull up the energy from the Earth's core. Let the energy permeate your body, then bring it to your mind's eye and let it intensify there.

Direct this energy and shoot it out like a beautiful straight arrow into the other person's soul. The energy will take over and you will see immediate results.

Share this only with people you believe are on a spiritual path. Remember, do not misdirect this energy or it will come back to you in a negative way. Before you heal another person, make sure she wants to be healed. Leave her alone if she doesn't.

As you start to use your white light, pink light, and the magnetic core, you will become more adept at the direction of these things. You will notice that the more you exercise these powers, the higher your consciousness will be raised.

USING THE LIGHT TO
ADD TO THE HARMONY OF YOUR SPACE . . .
AT ANY PLACE

Here are some ways to use white light to improve the harmony of your space:

First, do some deep breathing until you are in a still, calm state. Project a beam of white light toward the object on which you are working.

- Use it to protect you and your car when you drive. Bathe the car in a shell of white light, almost like wrapping it in a cocoon. This will also help you avoid getting speeding tickets.
- The light will also protect you from many bugs hitting your windshield and from bumps at high speed while on a long trip.
- Use it to find a parking spot at your desired destination. The car is bathed in energy and you will find a spot more quickly.
- Project the light down the road when you are traveling. Traffic will move more smoothly and you will be safer; so will the other cars within your light's range.
- Place the light around long lines in stores or banks, to speed up service.
- You might even try it if you are caught in a bank robbery, though I'm not sure—I haven't.
- Protect yourself from mosquitoes and other annoying bugs in the summer by projecting an aura of love around you or by willing your white light to repel them.
- Use white light to repel attackers or muggers around your home.
- Use the light to protect your home when a storm or hurricane is approaching.
- Project the light around those whom you contact daily and *will* happiness, perfection, and love onto and into them.

The more you practice with the white light, the more automatic it becomes. Sprinkle, sprinkle, sprinkle it around all the things you think need protection.

LEARN TO CENTER YOURSELF
WITH A BAND OF WHITE LIGHT

It is a common occurrence for people to feel "zapped," or tired, as we unconsciously project cords of energy into other people's

force fields or energy systems. We live in a world of interaction
with one another. This sharing of energies is a natural part of life
and rapport between people. We do tug and pull on another
person's energies and feed them into our own energy fields.
After a period of time, and many problems, our myriad stresses
of daily living, and interactions with others, we can feel drained
and off center. You may feel a headache coming on, or a
stomachache. If you feel this happening, put a band of white
light or a ring of light around the area that you feel another has
just tapped in to. Certainly it can be a subconscious activity or
unconscious action you are reacting to. Nevertheless, manipula-
tions of this kind intrude on your energy system and cut off your
air supply. Sometimes the energy itself around another can be
disruptive to us as well.

You can help yourself by using the band of light to keep your
own energy systems intact and healthy.

WHITE LIGHT
AND ALL THAT RAZZLE-DAZZLE

- White light is the highest energy form. White is a name for
  light and represents a purifying, uplifting, and sterilizing
  vibration.
- Considered a symbol of the wisdom and protection of Divine
  Power, white is the most healing vibration there is.
- White light is a concentrated energy form. Pink is the Universal love color. Be careful, however, as pink is better for the
  emotional state.
- White light is a concentrated energy form, and the conscious
  mind should never go idle. It must be used for good thoughts,
  and the white light helps it along. Do not misuse the magnetic
  core's energy.
- Through the use of the light you will become attuned to your
  own healing and the healing of the Earth. Knowledge of the
  white light will raise your conscious thinking. We live in an
  energy world and the Universe's laws and knowledge provide
  our protection.
- You can go into a still state (deep breathing) and project a
  beam of white light to another person to heal them, physically
  or mentally. See it hitting them and dissolving all negative

fixations. Make sure they want to be healed. If they don't, don't. Use it only for people who ask for help.
- Don't think of healing and protecting yourself just in a physical sense. Power is in the mental and emotional understanding.
- Sprinkle, sprinkle, sprinkle the white light around all the things you think need protection.

7

Auras and Color Energy: Using Color to Enhance Your Life

**There is color in all of the world around us.
It reaches its highest state of vibrancy
when there is love.**

"COLOR YOUR WORLD"

AURAS AND ENERGY FIELDS

Those who are fortunate enough to see auras know that every living thing has an aura: people, animals, rocks, trees, flowers, and so on. An aura is made up of various colors; it hugs the body or object and radiates outward from it. The aura can reflect a living organism's health and emotion.

The more spiritual a person is, the more stable his or her aura color. These people radiate with a glow. If someone is fearful or depressed, the color can be muddy; if vitality is low, color can be diluted in strength, and if it is high, someone can seem to look brilliantly aglow. Some say that the aura around us is usually our favorite color.

If you are lucky enough to see them, you should look for a

break in the aura. It may tell you if there is an energy leak from the body at the point of the break. Many physicians are experimenting with these magical frequencies now to diagnose physical conditions before they manifest themselves.

Kirlian photography was originally developed in Russia, and now it is accepted internationally as a method of photographing glowing color. This technique reveals sparks and flashes coming from the hands as well as other parts of the body, and from plants and other objects. Such information provides photographic proof that living matter does radiate its own form of electromagnetic energy.

Darkness surrounding an energy field is usually the sign of poor health or, at its most serious, terminal illness. If you know a person who is suffering from emotional problems that are causing an ailment, *visualize pink or rosy pink* surrounding him. Accompany this with a feeling of love. However, if the condition seems to be due to a rundown physical state, *visualize bright orange surrounding them*.

Notes: With Kirlian equipment you can detect the body's systems in color and study this. You can also use a simple Polaroid camera. You might be surprised at what auras turn up around Polaroid photos of yourself and friends. If you photograph your pets, you may see little spirit friends attached to them. There seems to be a chemical in this kind of camera that makes the spirit clearer and plainer to see.

AURA COLORS

WHITE

A white aura is considered the highest of all. All colors are blended into white. White represents purifying, uplifting, and sterilizing vibration. It is also considered a symbol of the wisdom of Divine Power and thus the most healing of all color vibrations. The more dazzling the white, the higher the vibration.

There are many shades of white, although I will list only three:

Pearl white — Represents kindness, gentleness, and forgiveness.
Oyster white — Indicates that the soul is trying hard to
  unfold in spite of tests and lessons being experienced.
Crystal white — Indicates that the soul has acquired complete self-mastery. This is extremely rare.

RED

Although the shade determines its true meaning, red stands for
energy, strength, courage, and vitality. It is the badge of deter-
mination and perseverance. It is also the color of sacrifice—the
giving of oneself—and is thus combined with green as Christmas
colors.

People with a great deal of red in their auras have strong
physical propensities, strong minds and wills, and usually a
materialistic outlook on life. They often manifest a very warm
and affectionate nature. However, red can also denote the deepest of human passions, whether passionate love, courage, hatred,
or revenge.

Dark red — Means physical vitality only; not mental or
  spiritual strength.
Rose red — Indicates love of family and country.
Bright clear red — Symbolizes faith, hope, and courage.
Dark, muddy, or cloudy red — Person is mixed with negative
  conditions, such as nervousness, temper, even domi-
  neering qualities and possibly strife.
Scarlet — May indicate egotism.
Medium orange-red — A healing, vitalizing color, often
  seen emanating from the hands and fingers of many
  healers, including especially conscientious medical doctors.

PINK

Pink, especially salmon pink, is the color of Universal love.
Depending on the shade of pink, it can supply or encourage joy

and comfort as well as companionship. People are drawn warmly to those who wear pink.

Pink is also the color of human love. Used for others, it can be uplifting, joyful, and a key to abundance. In the aura, coral pink can mean a feeling of unsureness about decisions and/or happiness in one's surroundings.

A pink aura denotes a quiet, refined, modest character, one who likes a quiet life, beauty, and artistic surroundings. People of the pink-aura type exhibit great and lasting devotion and are rarely pessimistic, dogmatic, or aggressive.

ORANGE

Orange varies with the shade. Usually orange represents thoughtfulness and consideration. Yogis call orange the "soul of energy." Those with orange in their auras are leaders who tactfully manage others and are excellent mixers. They are the "live wire" type, yet well balanced.

Golden orange — Represents wisdom and energy and can increase mental and spiritual ability. It is considered a high, spiritual vibration and denotes self-control.

Brownish orange — May mean a lack of ambition, laziness, or repression.

Those with orange in their auras should watch out for kidney trouble.

YELLOW

Yellow represents health of body and mind; the more golden yellow, the better. Yellow is the easiest auric color to see; it is close to the hairline.

Yellow, except for muddy shades, is a good aspect in the aura. The golden shades symbolize not only thought, intellect, and mental concentration, but things of the spirit represented in religious ceremonies, such as golden crosses, vessels, and altar fittings.

Yellow is beneficial in dispelling fear, worry, or nervousness and is stimulating to health and mind. Yellow appears in the auras of bright and optimistic people.

Yellow mixed with red indicates timidity. If redheads have yellow in their auras, they may have inferiority complexes, be indecisive, or be followers instead of leaders.

> **Lemon yellow** — Indicates mental strength, or artistic, creative ability leaning toward scientific ideas and inventions.
> **Very pale lemon yellow** — May indicate sickness in the body.

BLUE

There are many shades of blue, all of them good, but the different shades have different qualities. Blue is the color of healing love, which is soothing. Blue is the color of calmness, of feeling at one with nature.

Blue represents inspiration; it is the spiritual color. The presence of much blue in the aura signifies an artistic, harmonious nature with spiritual understanding. The darker shades of blue, especially, show a high degree of spirituality, integrity, deep sincerity, wisdom, and saintliness.

> **Pale blue** — Represents less maturity but a strong desire to acquire it.
> **Madonna blue** — The color of obedience and fulfillment of duties, as in the obedience to the will of God.
> **Deep, rich royal blue** — More powerful than the lighter shades. It indicates honesty, loyalty, and, if it contains a tinge of purple, good judgment and an ability to handle material affairs efficiently. Those who have deep blue in their auras are highly involved in their chosen work, or are unselfishly dedicated to social causes, science, or art. Such people are also spiritually inclined.

When black or brown is mixed with blue, it causes heavy-heartedness. The vibrations are lowered and can lead someone to remark, "I feel blue."

GREEN

Just as green shoots indicate new growth and hope, green symbolizes newness, continuity of life, peace, abundance, and healing. Doctors and nurses often have green in their auras, and it is a strong, friendly, helpful color, indicating loving service, cooperation, goodness, mercy, hope, faith, and peace. It is calming, restful to the nerves, and good for overcoming fear.

High strung people should realize the beneficial effects of green on the mind and nerves. They should surround themselves with this soothing color, as its vibrations are extremely refreshing.

Greenish yellow, called "gaslight green," is a clue to untruth, evasion, and other forms of deceit. As green tends more toward blue, it becomes more trustworthy and helpful.

AQUA

Pure emerald green with a tinge of blue is a healing color. True aqua, which blends blue and green in equal parts, is high in vibration. It combines peace and healing love, fills one with high ideals, and is quieting to the nervous system.

VIOLET, PURPLE, AND INDIGO

Lavender (pale purple) — A color of humility and worship.

Orchid (slightly more pink) — The person is holy and spiritual.

Purple — Indicates an ability to deal with practical and worldly matters.

Indigo and violet — The person is searching for a cause or religious experience, though those with purple in their auras are often overbearing.

Blue-purple — Represents accomplishments through God's power.

Red-purple — Indicates power of body, human will, and individual effort, a lower vibration than the blue-purple.

Those who have indigo, violet, and purple in their auras tend to have heart and stomach troubles. Purple and indigo can also mean spiritual seeking or indicate that spiritual power is on the increase.

Violet is seldom seen in the average aura, since it is a highly spiritual color. Its presence means true greatness and unselfish efforts.

GRAY

Those with gray auras are persistent plodders who leave no task undone. They may also be the "lone wolf" type who like to live their lives in their own way.

Gray is the color of illness. When it is mixed with black it becomes heavier, vibrationally, and dull. Gray has also long been known to indicate grief, sorrow, and loss. However, it can be transmuted by adding red, pink, or blue to raise its vibration and become more peaceful, more harmonious. Silver is better than gray, since it contains a sparkle, which gray lacks.

BROWN

Brown is symbolic of the Earth and there are many shades that are beautified by the addition of other colors, such as red, yellow, or gold. Rich brown is symbolic of growth, effort, and the wish to accomplish.

Brown stands for industry, organization, and orderly management. It is the businessman's color, the ruling color of convention. Do not expect strong emotional feelings or tendencies in people with brown-tinged auras, but rather painstaking perseverance.

BLACK

It is true that there are various shades of black, depending on what colors have been added to it (blue, purple, silver, gold, and so on). However, black has the lowest vibration of all colors and should be shunned because of its heavy, dark influence.

Beware of black that seems to glow with crimson red shot through it. It is the most vicious combination of evil known. However; it does carry a neutral quality and holds sophistication. It should be offset with another color.

We show more white (opposite of black) in our auras as we grow toward perfection. This should be our goal.

An aura is an effect, not a cause. Thus, at any time, in any world, a soul will give off, through the vibrations, the story of itself and the conditions in which it now exists.

Those who can see auras can read these messages. Those who cannot, will not see the messages, but the vibrations and colors are there nevertheless. Kirlian photography has proved this to be true.

AURAS AND COLOR HEALING

There has been much written—even from ancient texts—on the effects of color and its applications and treatments.

The Sun is the source of all life, our source of light and heat, but the air we breathe is as important to our lives as well. Scientists tell us we receive all knowledge of the Universe through electromagnetic radiation. What we see with the eyes alone—visible light—comprises only a narrow band of that electromagnetic spectrum: a spectrum sequence ranging from short to long wave lengths of violet, indigo, blue, green, yellow, orange, and red.

This field of energy is all around us. What we perceive as a result of this energy is illusion; only is the energy itself real. Color is merely a sensation to our consciousness. When we analyze a beam of sunlight by means of a triangular piece of glass (a prism), we find that the beam consists of many colors. Black is the absence of color, while it is also a combination of all colors, and sunlight is a combination of all colors of the spectrum, visible and invisible. You already know what happens to plants kept out of light, as well as to people. We are all surrounded by color and have a love for it. We express our emotions through color and consider the effect of color itself on our bodies by either concentration or meditation. Color is a vibration. Vibration is a movement. Movement is activity of a positive and a negative force. Although we live in a three-dimensional world, we can now pull in the vibrational patterns of other worlds and dimensions of light to aid us in healings, the creative vibrations that are God.

Color therapy is centuries old. Ancient Roman, Egyptian, Greek, Oriental, and Atlantian cultures employed this therapy as a powerful treatment of ailments. In this chapter I will attempt to explain on a spiritual metaphysical level what the effects of light and color are on the body for health and healing of our energies at this time. This is a new age of enlightenment; old methods are coming to the fore once again for a new society of beings.

Every color is a power of energy vibrations, each color having a different vibration with a power all its own that can be used therapeutically to heal the minds and emotions of the ill. Depending on what color is used, it can help raise a person's magnetic frequencies in the spectrum of his life energy. Our future lies in working with this electrical body. For example, a holy man or guru has a vibrant light aura; he is in touch with the higher worlds. And when a woman is menstruating, her color (aura) changes. Her red spectrum changes, so she can benefit by wearing red.

In Atlantis, there was a Temple of Purification, and in this temple there was a color wheel. The Atlantians used colors and light to heal people. As was done then, some healers now stand in front of the person to be healed and run their hands up and down that person's body. The healer can comb the colors of the mental, physical, and emotional bodies of a person, using different colors to bring about mental, emotional, and physical changes.

COLOR BREATHING
TO CLEANSE THE CHAKRAS AND FOR
GENERAL REJUVENATION

We can do it sitting down, standing up, driving the car, taking a walk, or just being out in the air itself. Breathing and absorbing the colors in the air into our lungs will promote the necessary healing our bodies need each day.

By creating images—visualization—we can attract into us this general tonic, elixir of youth, rejuvenator, or whatever you choose to call it. Whatever color you choose or are working with, breathe in deeply and "absorb" the color into your body. Feel it permeating your entire body, reinforcing the action of the color. Breathe very consciously, very deliberately.

For a general tonic and pick-me-up, it is a good idea to use color breathing at least once a week. Use the seven main colors in turn to cleanse the Chakra centers. All color activity affects not only the nostrils but goes into the head and eye regions first before going into the body to restore it (see illustration on p. 90).

Here is one technique, to help you get wrinkle-free:

Take a few deep breaths of *pink* air (visualizing shades of lavender). Then choose an area of your body you wish to work on. If you see a wrinkle, breathe in pink air. Spread the area smooth with your fingers so you can see how the area would look if the wrinkle were gone. While you hold your breath, visualize the skin area, smooth the wrinkle, and exhale slowly. Repeat this breathing plus visualization technique two more times, taking three total breaths in all.

CAN COLOR SPEED UP THE
HEALING PROCESS AND SLOW DOWN AGING?
YES . . . THINK PINK!

* Breathe *pink* through both nostrils each day.
* Breathe pink every morning before rising and every night before bedtime.
* Breathe pink air directing the energy to your reproductive organs as both you and your mate sit in a cloud of *rose*. Wrap yourself in it, alternating with a shade of pink, to restore your sexual vitality. Your skin will rejuvenate as well and help to remake the body system for youth and vitality.
* Pink calms schizophrenic patients.

OTHER COLORS FOR HEALING HELP
TO RESTORE DIFFERENT PARTS OF THE BODY:
FOCUS COLOR ON ANY AFFLICTED AREA

* ROSE PINK makes you robust, virile, and sexual.
* PINK-RED is for sexuality, as sex is always associated with red. It inflames the emotions, but there is another side of sex, the spiritual, *rose* being gentler, more spiritual than red. Breathe in a deep shade of rose, at the same time mentally sending the air and the color to the area needing help. Visualize yourself being young and virile and then release the air slowly up the spinal cord, leaving the color down there.

- SCARLET is a variation of red. It acts as a stimulant; it can also reduce inflammation and can be a general healer and energizer and strengthener for the body.
- Use and surround yourself either with pink or red to attract others, lovely and interesting people.
  Now, while they are walking toward you, picture a nice bright *green* on them and visualize them swathed in it. Use your imagination. Therefore, both your energies and theirs will be in sync.
- "RED BLANKET" TREATMENT. This works well for the treatment of hives as well as to speed up post-operative healing. *Treatment*: Wrap yourself in a red blanket from head to toe.
- ASTHMA ATTACK TREATMENT. Put a *red* silk ribbon around your left wrist and inhale the color *blue*. This is **after** you have taken your medication and is for your stabilization.
- YELLOW relieves constipation and restores your nerves. It can be used in an arthritis sunlight treatment by placing a light behind a piece of cellophane and beaming it on the body.
  Yellow is also a muscle stimulant for nervous conditions, as well as an aid to digestion.
- GREEN is used to treat broken legs and running or jumping problems. Soothes bones, and promotes general healing.
- BLUE acts to calm and soothe. It encourages relaxation, reduces fever, and fights infection and migraines.
  Breathe blue air deeply and direct it through your body to your left hand. If you have trouble with this, imagine yourself in a *blue ball of light* so everything around you will be blue, so you can't help but breathe in the blue air. Visualize the *end* product—see the affected area cured.
- COBALT BLUE is excellent for laryngitis from shouting or singing.
- INDIGO relieves swelling and pain, is a good sedative, and produces muscular generation and strength.
- TURQUOISE helps decrease weight gain; it also aids in ridding the body of heaviness in certain areas—legs, hips, and fat spots.
- BREATHE IN COLORS OF THE WATERS for leg fractures or other broken bones. Take the nerve color *green* and add some *blue* (the life force color)—swathe the leg in the color of mist.
- VIOLET promotes sleep; a particular shade of violet can reduce tension.

- BONE COLOR/WHITISH GRAY is used for bones that have not knit or mended properly. Visualize this color being sent to that particular area.
- MIX COLORS ON YOUR MENTAL PALATE. Combine dark *blue*, a faint tinge of *green*, and an overlay of *white* mist. Put entire leg or both feet and ankles under this healing sphere of color for injuries to this area.

If you lose your voice, radiate and flood your body with *yellow/orange*. Focus it both on the liver area and the vocal cords.

COLOR PROJECTION
TO CLEANSE CHAKRAS AND BODY'S BALANCE
(FOR INFORMATION ON CHAKRAS,
SEE CHAPTER 15.)

You can also do this as a part of your regular meditation periods. Imagine the color against a black base. Direct the color through a cone or spiral effect, as illustrated on the following page.

See a blackboard of the mind. First, breathe in each color you feel you may need, for each center of energy or all seven centers.

Swirl the color energy in a clockwise direction for a full minute at each part that needs help. If you need more than one color, drop the first after a minute and move on to the next. Swirl each spiral of color for a full minute and rest.

The colors work as follows:

Red — Stimulates
Orange — Revitalizes
Yellow — Re-energizes
Green — Healing
Blue — Centeredness and calming
Indigo — Relieves congestion
Violet — Meditation—purity of thinking

WAYS TO EXTEND YOUR AURA

1. Envision your aura (field of light outside the body) expanding. See it going out at least twelve inches beyond your physical body, larger than you imagine it to be.

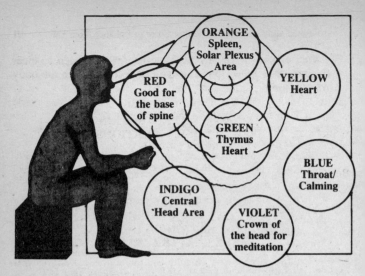

VORTEX OF LIGHT EMANATION (AS A CONE)

2. Visualize putting your whole body into a large open flower. Watch yourself walk into it until you are surrounded by the pollen. Feel the essence of this beautiful scented flower (sense the smell of the flower of your choice), and feel it opening and closing while you are inside of it.

   Do this as it opens and closes three times. On the third time, feel the energies of the flower energize you to that frequency and pick up the color of the flower chosen to be a part of your own aura. Feel the energizing pull of it fill you up.

   As you see yourself walk away, pull the energies around you as if you were putting on a cloak and see it extend past your physical body.

3. Imagine the golden Sun as you project this image into your solar plexus area. Feel the warmth of the rays of light and brilliance of the Sun.

   Watch it grow larger until it engulfs your whole physical body, until you begin to see yourself as a small speck in the Universe inside the Sun. It has now extended way beyond your magnetic field. Hold and focus on that feeling for two to five minutes. You can do all of these exercises while driving a car, in the shower, or in the middle of your day when fatigue sets in.

This can burn out any negative energy you need to clear out immediately, so that it doesn't collect or stay in the body system.

RAINBOW OF PROTECTION
TO SEAL IN YOUR VIBRATIONS OF
INNER COMPANY

Before leaving home in the morning, wrap yourself mentally (by visualization) with a spiral rainbow from head to toe.

EXPLANATION:
The rainbow does radiate and attract others to you. People notice you when you do this. It will give you a special glow and make you radiate alive with energy. Try putting it on in the morning before leaving your house to start the day outside. Maybe you need to use this energy when you first get out of bed and face your grumpy family, husband, or children.

Adopt this rainbow habit even before you leave home to go on a shopping spree or tour. Otherwise you might be drained of energy as you mingle with people. Protected by the rainbow of colors, you may not become depleted. You may even start being aware of seeing the auras of others.

SPECTRO-CHROME THERAPY

Color therapy is invaluable for the relief of pain. Color vibrates with a sound and vibration that your body can hear and respond to. It can break up the congestion of energy in your body and help it to heal.

METHODS OF PAIN CONTROL

Get colored panes of glass and place them in front of home windows. Put them in direct contact with the Sun or perhaps a bright light bulb. The colored light should come in direct contact with the area you are treating in the body.

If all colors are not available to you in glass or plastic, you can substitute colored gelatin sheets, such as those used to cover floodlights in theaters.

Colored light breaks up the congestion in the area, so it can be carried away by the body's elimination system. There could be a slight discomfort. If it becomes too intense, terminate treatment and use a complementary color to restore balance.

Beaming the color onto bare skin feeds the body's energy as the color makes it heal.

Some healers believe that underweight or overweight may be due to an imbalance between red and blue in the body. Underweight is said to be the result of too much red; overweight, of too much blue.

To correct imbalance: if you are underweight, increase intake of blue foods—actually the range of foods includes green, brown, and black—and sip solarized "blue water" daily. If you're overweight, the correction is the opposite. Eat more red foods—the spectrum that includes white, yellow, gold, and orange—and sip red solarized water daily.

SOLARIZED WATER

Put a jar of water on the ledge of a wooden cabinet. Put a red or blue glass on top of the jar. Place a 100-watt bulb overhead and leave on for twelve hours. Place the appropriate color cellophane over the lightbulb. Lie on your back or in bed.

Project the light at the afflicted area. There may be some discomfort. If discomfort is intense, terminate treatment and beam a complementary color to restore balance.

Rheumatism can be healed with color. It is an accumulation of wastes including uric acid. Flooding the body with red light dissolves these crystals in the joints and the body's elimination system carries them out.

FOR LIGHT TREATMENT

Use a red light bulb or red gel over the bulb. Lie on the bed. Red light is projected first upon the soles, then ankles, calves, knees, and thighs (five minutes on each location). It is best to have someone working with you to watch the timing.

COLOR THERAPY:
A MAGICAL ENERGY TO HEAL THE BODY, MIND, AND SPIRIT

Color is the second highest vibration, sound being the highest form. Color can affect and effect attitudes, moods, feelings, and thoughts. Color is truly in the eyes of the beholder. If you create a color to heal you, to protect you, to pick your spirits up, that color is yours.

We cannot live without color. It symbolizes the power of the life force itself. It can stimulate our minds, cool or heat our bodies, lift our spirits, enhance our homes, enliven our lives, and give us mental stimulation or concentration or create a calm atmosphere in which to work. It serves as a vibrator for our souls and a frequency to stimulate our minds.

Color therapy can be used to influence human health, either physical, mental, or spiritual. The healing comes from the effects of mental light waves, which are like rays of the Universe. The healing power of color rays created in you proves the statement "it's all in the mind." It's true! Your mind helps you tune in to the Universe for healing, helping energy. You have *needs*, not moods, to wear a certain color or colors. A message forms inside you if your aura is not right, if it is disturbed and requires a change to a certain color. Don't fight it, feel the need!

In lighting up our world, the beauty of living is all linked and wrapped up in this one word.

C *osmic Process of Energy*
O *the omnipresence of God's code in us*
L *ight is the God code beneficial to our being and existence*
O *de of alchemical harmony*
R *ays of the Universe*
S *even Rays of expression*

THE POWER OF THE RAYS

Color has power. In hospitals or institutions, patients feel more cheerful when rooms are bright yellow or orange. Their emotional recovery speeds up their convalescence. The right color in schools can boost students' grades. The right color clothing has impact on how you feel from day to day. Red toothbrushes, for example, should be avoided because they suggest bleeding. Yes—color has power and you can make it work for you.

People who have a need to feel insecure choose neutral colors such as gray and beige to surround themselves with. These people use few warm colors. People more confident prefer brighter colors and very light or very dark shades. I suggest that you choose your daily costume color according to the way you feel or what you feel you need when you wake up. These needs change daily.

Color in nutrition, meaning the color of food, is also an important factor to consider. One's diet should consist in part of foods grown below the ground and an equal balance of foods grown above, since these foods carry imprisoned sunlight. Consider the use of color intuition when you plan a meal. Your body tells you what color food you need that day.

Regarding your physical health and color: certain specific colors influence specific glands. Concentrating on a specific color will stimulate secretions from the gland corresponding to the color.

These secretions will aid parts of the body which need assistance.

STIMULANT WAVE	GLAND
Red	Liver
Orange	Thyroid/mammary
Yellow	Choroid/pancreas
Lemon	Pancreas/thymus
Green	Pituitary
Blue	Pineal
Indigo	Parathyroid
Violet	Spleen
Magenta	Suprarenals/prostate
Scarlet	Testicle/ovary

THE MEANING OF COLORS

These color rays can be brought to use through burning of candles of the right color, wearing clothing and accessories, or imagining the color you need.

RED
(Restores physical balance and spirit of activity)

• Passion
• Fast action
• Stimulation

Red is for firing up your emotions to prepare you for constructive action. Be careful: spiritualists use this negatively at times and they tend to bring in negative spirits and energies—either in the Astral Plane or in the negative side of the planet Mars, which has two sides, two different races of people.

Red is like a transfusion of energy and iron. Wear red when you are tired or are menstruating. Your chemistry is deficient then. You need to absorb the color red to bring about balance. If you need to wear red, it can be clothes, lipstick, or even jewelry. High-keyed people should not wear much red.

BODY BENEFITS:
Blood, heart rate speeds up, exaggerates respiration.

Red is the longest wave length in the visible spectrum.

Red draws out anger and hate; would be a useful color in a mental hospital or institution.

PINK
(Universal color for love and harmony)

Some say pink is helpful for getting a lost lover to come back or replacing him with a new one.

Don't believe it. Although it *can* work, do you really want to manipulate another's energies in this way? And suppose they aren't right for you? That is wasted effort, especially since you want the best that is truly all yours. Use pink positively. It is a Universal love ray. It mixes with youth and vitality and can increase the blood count and stabilize the body to keep back the aging process.

Wear pink, and use pink rays, when you meditate.

ORANGE
(Represents energy and control)

• Happiness
• Attraction
• Vitality

Use orange to inspire, to stimulate new plans and ideas. This color retards growth of unhealthy lesions in the body and dispels them. Orange works like a shock treatment on poisons or poisonous thoughts. A tremendous stimulation, orange brings a passion for doing, learning. It will counteract low-level energy and enhance sexuality. A person drawn to orange is an extrovert. This person has a need to touch and feel. This is a great color to use in a mental hospital to bring people out.

BODY BENEFITS:
Spleen, digestion, kidneys, thyroid, breasts.

GREEN
(Beneficial for harmonic balance and healing)

• Prosperity
• Success
• Health

Green is for good health and growth, for ridding the self and home of bad vibes, for bringing in much-needed cash, and for encouraging education and aiding plant growth.

Its physical healing gives growth and energy. It is the healer's color; a green light around someone is antiseptic. Green light bulbs act as tranquilizers.

BODY BENEFITS:
Nerve calming, lowers blood pressure.

BLUE
(The color of the spirit. Blue emanates a level of spirituality toward which we should strive. It also aids the mind and mental powers.)

• Peace
• Protection
• Friendship

Blue is for doing the right thing at the right time and making sure that an important business deal succeeds.

Use this color for meditation, mental work, thinking and concentration, and introspection. If you have a need to do very intense thinking, wear blue. It gives you focusing power and a clear mind. If you have to write, wear blue or go into a blue room.

BODY BENEFITS:
Throat, antiseptic, calming, reduces fever.

VIOLET
**(The color of the pituitary gland.
Good for protection and high spiritual attunement.)**

When the pituitary gland is opened through proper attunement to its creative source it can emanate a violet color. It is streaked with the color of the new man, the symbol of the Father or of heaven. People who are searching for a cause or a religious experience use the concentration of this color for work and the will. It can help you develop psychic talents along with a belief in God and independence. You can use this color to locate lost objects and for generally clearing up confusion.

PURPLE

This color has a very high spiritual frequency and vibration. People who stand above the crowd wear purple. People who are searching for a cause or religious experience need purple.

BODY BENEFITS:
All-around healing and peace.

INDIGO
(Intuitive color)

Indigo is the color of the perfect or ideal gland, which is the computer storage library of all that the soul has ever done. If you can open up your past lives memory banks, much will be recalled using this color.

BODY BENEFITS:
Eyes, ears, nose.

WHITE
(Completion)

White has no color. White helps you master a high state of learning, such as when you are seeing visions. A white room is good for a person of many moods. He or she creates his or her own mood levels by hanging various pictures (different colors) on the walls. White, as well as beige, is a neutral color. Its use benefits someone who wants to create.

BLACK
(Represents potential, future, the unknown, neutral.)

Black absorbs all. It represents the absence of color.

If you are required to wear black in connection with your work, or decide because of your state of mind to wear it, then brighten it up with a scarf or tie of some bright color. I predict that black will eventually be completely replaced with brighter, lighter colors of all hues and shades, in a future generation. It does nothing for our vitality and can pull us down.

BLACK AND WHITE TOGETHER

This combination works on getting rid of bad vibes and allowing the flow of good energy and thoughts.

THE SEVEN COSMIC COLOR RAYS

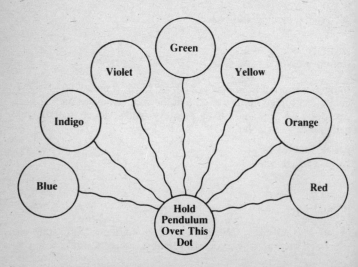

RAINBOW

The rainbow contains all the color components and if visualized around your own body or that of another, it will help to draw the correct color from the rainbow which is needed at the moment.

Keep asking each of these questions each day and watch the pendulum come to a halt with the best color for your needs of the day. Visualize the color shade you lack and breathe it in through your nostrils while you concentrate on taking it into you.

If you visualize all Seven Color Rays each day you will experience freedom from thoughts weighing you down. Feel the colors permeate and flow through your body and bloodstream. Use this ray healing every day to revitalize your energy and it will keep you in balanced health.

8

The Uses of
Breathing, Meditation,
and Mantras

One breath keeps life sustained.

THE BREATH, MIND, AND ENERGY
(HOW TO USE THE TOOL OF BREATH)

Correct breathing brings the mind under control. Correct breaths are deep, slow deliberate breaths. Hold out your hands before you, palms up. This lets the Universe breathe through you. (There are minor Chakras in the palms of hands.)

As you know, when you are angry, your breathing becomes hard, uncontrolled, irregular, and labored. If you are scared, your breath becomes shallow. You might find your attention drawn to your heartbeat, perhaps even hold your breath. In any condition, your breath reflects the inner condition of your mind.

Yoga calls breathing "Prana," the life force within our bodies. It can also be called the intelligent energy that lives through all forms of life or creation. If you learn how to control it, you can help aid or control others. It is what I call positive control or good ego.

We reap many rewards from good breathing: calmness on a deep satisfactory health-related level, earthly stability, physical stability, and vigor. The physical process of breathing involves using the life force of the energies of the cosmos.

When we practice Yoga the movements we make keep our physical body as well as our mind in tune with the energy of the cosmos. We learn how to move and control the air all around us to be beneficial to our energies, growth, and health. Yogis call this "energy control" or "pranic energy." It means the ability to control the flow of Prana in your body and to be able to draw energy into the body at will.

Respiration and circulation are controlled by the medulla oblongata, an organ located in the brain stem. The medulla is the negative pole at the center of energy and consciousness. It has its positive pole at the point between the eyebrows, the third eye. By focusing attention and tuning in to the third eye (spiritual eye or forehead), through certain focusing techniques and meditations, we can shift control of the breath from the autonomous medulla to the frontal lobes of the brain, which are the centers of conscious awareness. The spiritual eye is the doorway to cosmic awareness. Some literature about Yogananda says that when the human heart stops beating, upon death, you go through a dark tunnel toward a brilliant white light. This "tunnel" is in fact the inner spine, which can be entered in deep meditation. The light seen at death is the spiritual eye. The first part of the body to be formed in the womb is the medulla oblongata. Thus, it seems somehow appropriate for life to leave the body by the same doorway.

If we open ourselves to deep breathing, we can learn to internalize our own awarenesses. We can learn to stay calm amid many trials and tribulations, to feel peace, and to concentrate much better on our tasks and our work. Deep, open breathing accompanies an open, accepting attitude toward life. Inhalation is associated with an upward stimulating movement of energy in the spine regions. If you inhale good thoughts you also take in the good understanding of the Earth.

When you exhale you rid yourself of negative thought. Never force exhalation, as, done correctly, it rids the mind of toxic waste, bad thought forms, and negative energy. The movements and breaths we take, in and out, guide our subconscious while opening up our channels, expanding our energies to feel good. When you stimulate this flow with your breath, you will find your thoughts all changing automatically. Your subconscious takes over completely.

In severe cases of trauma, sometimes we need to learn to double-breathe. This consists of a short inhalation through the nose, followed by a long one, then a short and a long exhalation through the mouth and nose. This fills the lungs more deeply than plain deep breathing does. Slowed-down breathing makes less work for the heart, so of course it slows its beat. The heart Chakra is the "main switch" that controls the flow of energy from the spine out into the extremities. When the heart slows, Prana is automatically withdrawn into the deep spine. There it activates the Chakras, the spinal energy centers that control both bodily functions and fundamental states of consciousness. The body enters a state of suspended animation in which oxygen is no longer needed by the cells, and breathing stops. I quote Yogananda when he said that "cosmic consciousness is experienced when one has learned to pass through the Five Pointed Star seen at the spiritual eye center in deep meditation." Look at it this way: we can all learn to die daily and still keep ourselves at a peaceful level through breathing in the excitement of new life coming into us.

Breath is the vital secret of life, the highest and most subtle manifestation of physical man. To have thought and to think it through is the Great Manifestation of Intelligence in Man, making him one with the Universe.

CORRECT BREATHING EXERCISES
TO PREPARE FOR MEDITATION TO BE
ONE WITH THE UNIVERSE

Breathing position—Head, neck, and chest straight to avoid pressure on the nerves of the spinal column. Posture should be natural since new sorts of vibrations will occur in the body as a result of these exercises. Count to 10—out to 10 (to establish rhythm that generates "nerve energy"—flows over the nerves and feeds the nervous system).

Exercise—Close right nostril by pressing forefinger against it. Feed and fill the lungs with air through left nostril. Remove finger immediately and close left nostril with finger (to your capacity), then exhale through right nostril. Keeping left nostril closed, inhale through right to *full capacity*, remove finger from left nostril and exhale through it.

Repeat the alternative-nostril breathing three times at each sitting. Practice three times a day. Do not repeat before eight-hour intervals.

PRACTICE!

Purpose—To bring about an internal purification especially to nerves. Proportions of oxygen, hydrogen, and nitrogen in the body of an individual at any time are not only an indication of his bodily condition but also indicate his spiritual condition. For character and development of self also will blend proportions of oxygen and nitrogen and balance good and evil in man's nature. Every evil thought increases nitrogen, having an adverse affect on body and soul.

TO PREPARE FOR MEDITATION

When going into any meditation or any creative visualizations, always light a white candle in your mind. Wrap yourself in a cocoon of white light before you start. Ask your higher sources of God-Power or higher spirit sources of the light to be with you.

Then . . . set the conditions. Always set the conditions for your needs, whether it is to remember all that you have seen or done, or where you want to go. Perhaps to a past life or to settle a future or current problem. This way, you will be ensured a safe and happy voyage or experience.

HOW TO BUILD UP THE
VIBRATIONS IN A ROOM BEFORE
YOU MEDITATE AND HOW TO DILUTE
NEGATIVE ENERGY

1. Music lifts the spirits.
2. Light many candles. They should be white.
3. Have lots of glasses, vases, or urns of water around.
4. *Incense*: A way to clear the channels to the spirit world (sandalwood).

5. Laughter and humor.
6. Flowers.
7. Programmed crystals can be an aid (see Chapter 12).

MEDITATE TO FIRE ENERGY

**Note: Learn to focus with the sixth sense
before beginning elemental meditation.*

1. Room is darkened and white candle lit and placed in the center of the room where everybody in attendance can see the candle. Put it in front of yourself when you are alone.
2. Stare at the flame of the candle and feel the rhythm of the fire for about fifteen minutes.
3. You will begin to stare with narrowed eyes to view the world inside the fire or flame of the candle.
4. Go into the fire visually. Put yourself in and focus and tune in.
5. Remember what you felt, saw or heard. Record it in a journal or diary.

MEDITATING INTO THE
ENERGY OF SMELL

Room should be darkened once again. All those in attendance experiencing this should be instructed to open up their sense of smell by commanding it to open mentally! Go *into* the odor that is being introduced into the room—such as sandalwood incense. Meditate on that odor (ten minutes). Write down what you felt.

MEDITATING ON ENERGY
OF WATER

Room is darkened except for small lamp shining on a clear glass of water in full view of the experimenters.

Everyone should be instructed to stare into the glass of water and mentally go into the water to pass their tensions and tiredness into the water.

*Time: fifteen minutes

Each person should then relate what was seen, heard, and felt.

MEDITATION EXERCISE
WITH THE ENERGIES OF SOUND ONLY

CHANT on INHALE—AUM
CHANT on EXHALE—OM

You can do this yourself or with a group.
Begin with:

1. *Chant* to the sound of AUM (six times).
   This will clear out all negativity.
2. All are to take three deep breaths *inhaling* and *exhaling* slowly through mouth and relax.
3. Close eyes and let it all go.
   Go into the *silence*.

1. Have the room you are in darkened and all close their eyes. You have already done your AUM chanting. Relax and concentrate on your breathing. Make sure it is slow and in tune with the rest of your bodily rhythms.

2. Have someone sound a bell, or both a bell and tuning fork.
3. Go into these sounds (bell, tuning fork, or both).
   *Time: fifteen minutes

Do all of the above: chant, deep breaths, relaxation, closing of eyes.

1. Listen for ticktock sound of clock and to hear time and space between the ticks and tocks.
   *Time: fifteen minutes

FOR THE MEMORY OF SOUND

Have the room dark. *Chant* in deep voice (six times to AUM sound).
   Keep your eyes closed and meditate on memory of the residual vibrations of the sound you have heard.
   *Time: ten minutes
   Relate what you saw and heard.

GROUP MEDITATION ON
EACH OTHER'S AURAS AND ENERGIES

• All of these meditations are important to groups who have come together to fundamentally understand meditations and psychic energy.

1. The room is darkened and the group is instructed to look at each other's faces in the dark. Have a white candle burning somewhere nearby.
2. Each person stares at each of the others in order to see their auras and electrical energies in darkness of room. This should be done for ten to fifteen minutes. Look at auras around head outlines and see electrical energy and electrical plasma in the room.
3. Each person should relate what is seen and heard.

WHAT IS MEDITATION?

Meditation is a form of mental exercise to take you into other dimensions. It is an effective rest period to help with relaxation and to incorporate the use of this rest to help you with stress management.

What do you actually do when you practice meditation? You actually achieve a state of "perfect rest" and experience sensations that benefit you, which permeate every minute of your daily life. It allows you to feel the positive effects of correct breathing and its techniques while recharging your body with energy and vitality.

I will not go into the how-to's of meditation or TM they appear in many other books. I *will* touch on the therapeutic effects I've learned from working as a channel. This can help you use Prana, or breath control, for vital health and toward the restoration and strengthening of the energy flow of your body. This natural healing, of restoring the power to your own body, can strengthen and affect your own immune system, to help your work performance and speed your clarity of thought.

Meditation affects the memory centers of your brain and helps with the decision-making process. It may also relieve any unpleasant mental state your mind or body is in. When you meditate, your breathing is no longer labored. Your heartbeat slows down and establishes a good rhythm as your circulatory system evens itself out and you rid yourself of hypertension. The aging process is also affected, as your body revises and revitalizes itself. You can *get addicted to mental rest*. The therapeutic value of meditation is that it can reduce the pain of acute trauma, headache, upsets in the quality of your nightly sleep, toothaches, and so on. The concentration of a deep level of Alpha can be achieved through the process of learning to let yourself go into thin air or space.

If you like, you can experiment with psychic communication when your mind is up there in the clouds, pointed in this direction of *release*. An expanded awareness and being in touch with yourself are the first steps.

These experiences come to us in two ways. First, there are karmic lessons that we are put here to learn. Also, we attract certain experiences by our positive or negative outlook in life. Remember, if we project negative energy, then we receive negative energy in return (boomerang effect). If we put out positive signals, we are more apt to get positive feedback. These are simple procedures and principles that anyone can use, whether or not they already believe in anything psychic.

Another important tenet in this system of beliefs is that there is a body of knowledge outside of ourselves that we can tap in to through the use of our subconscious minds. Religious leaders call it "God." Emerson called it the "oversoul." Carl Jung called it the "collective unconscious." Whatever it is, the wisdom and knowledge it contains can be made available to us through prayer and meditation.

But Karma and our own thinking can get us into trouble. We can make negative things happen (Law of Attraction) by putting out a thought about someone that is not very nice. Be sure that we'll get it back somewhere along the line.

Nature must be balanced and should not be manipulated for entertainment. When there is a legitimate need or something in us causing havoc, recognize that something must have gotten out of balance. An enlightened person may need meditation to help restore that balance. If we meditate we may become aware of total subjectivity and total objectivity as a single phenomenon, witnessing a duality that exists between subject and object. Awareness, simply put, is nondoing. Witnessing implies a doer. It is a technique toward awareness. We cannot say that the mind is aware, only conscious, which is a *quality* of the mind. Awareness is a transcendence going beyond the mind.

Man is chaotic and neurotic, molding himself into a particular pattern of life. The pattern creates the neurosis. Things within us are contained and never allowed to take shape or form. Everything within us is divided into abstract thought patterns and we call our neurosis *havoc*.

All meditation is a kind of passivity, because it is a doorway to consciousness, freeing the mind of all that is superfluous. When these extraneous fragments of the mind are thrown out, you become open and allow yourself to take in what you need. Enlightenment comes where there is no desire but just *to be*.

BEFORE GOING INTO A MEDITATION

Your circle of protection is your white light. It will protect you from anything unknown while in meditation and serves as a protection from evil or negativity.

By leaving yourself open by exposing your own energy systems, anything negative can come in. A broken line in your aura is an easy way for anything seen or unseen (spirit as well as people) to break through your force field. Your own health is, therefore, at stake! A crack in your auric field affects your immune system and you can be open to illness and psychic attack.

Reinforce your aura by demanding (mentally) a cocoon of white light to be put over you. Then *ask* your higher self, God-self, and higher power to seal and close off your aura with a band of *golden light*.

Now meditate!

HOW TO RESTORE YOUR INNER BALANCE

MEDITATION

I am still.
I am relaxed.
I am one with the Universal mind.
I project love and harmony to all life.
I am Love.
I love the higher way of living.
I love the higher way of thinking.
I am surrounded with a sphere of white light that purifies
     and protects me constantly.
I radiate goodness and love, day and night.
So Be It!

Repeat each line slowly, absorbing each aspect of the words before you get to the next line.

When you are finished saying: "So Be It," draw a deep breath, exhaling any unnecessary residue of frustration you may have left inside of you. Mentally surround your aura and bathe it with a pink glow.

HAVE TROUBLE WITH MEDITATION?
DOES YOUR MIND DRIFT
FROM ONE THING TO ANOTHER?

This will help get you in the mood:

1. Buy purple eyeshadow or lipstick or a little swatch of purple cloth or paper.

2. Paste or draw this color on your third-eye area.
3. Stare at yourself in the bathroom mirror and concentrate on the color purple.
4. This will put you in an altered state.

EXPLANATION:
I hear you snickering at me on this one, as you have taped a piece of paper on your forehead or have put makeup on your third eye. You will not chuckle long if you continue to stare and concentrate on that area for a full five minutes. You will begin to switch into an altered reality that will steer you into a new dimensional state. You will drift into another level of being and be ready to drift into nothingness and rest.

HOW TO MEDITATE
CONSCIOUSLY AND SUBCONSCIOUSLY
WHILE DRIVING YOUR CAR

A lot of answers to questions or problems come through while you are *releasing*. You may think your mind is on first gear, but as soon as you have your travel instructions down pat, know where your destination is, what parkway or street to drive on, what direction to take to get there, your mind goes into "automatic pilot." You switch gears to second, even to third. You become your own judge and jury. You speak to yourself and see yourself as a different person outside of you and go over what you didn't do, or should have done, or will do. Ever notice how so many ideas come to you in a car? The motion is helpful; in a car you feel disconnected from any pressure or from anything that has pressured you.

Why not do all your deep thinking in a vehicle of this kind? Remember, this is a place where your mind talks back and gets results.

In the silence you become your own inner parent and approve or disapprove of yourself. You let your inner voice tell you which way to go. Why not take a small tape-recorder in the car with you? Speak your thoughts into it. Then, play it back at the end of the week. You will be surprised what you figured out and what conclusions you came to (if only after the fact).

AT-THE-KITCHEN-SINK MEDITATION*

Ever notice how fluid and loose-tongued you feel at the sink? How messages and ideas come to you in rapid succession? Perhaps you can contemplate new ideas, new concepts can come to fruition and reach a stage of maturity in your mind. You are merely *meditating consciously*. You have allowed your mind to drift from one sequence of thought to another. You are as a spectator, detached, viewing your life from another level. You can roam in and out of one frame of existence or thought to pick up all those loose, fragmented pieces of incomplete understanding and put them where they belong.

THE SUN MEDITATION

Reason: To increase your energy, push your aura outward, and keep your force field strong.

How to: Imagine the Sun in the sky. Take the glowing rays of warm light and project the image into your solar plexus region. With your eyes open or closed you will feel the warm, revitalizing energies of our solar system as you feel the Sun grow larger and larger, enveloping your entire physical body's outline. While extending its rays outward, past your auric field, you will indeed look smaller inside our Sun. Hold the image for between two and five minutes each day, for a period of ninety days (three months). This time will suffice and give you added strength and power.

---

*One need not go and sit down to reach a deep level of mind concentration through use of meditation techniques. This is a conscious meditation to show you that you can *consciously* be in two realities at once. Release the blocked energy—it helps with the flow of feelings and emotions. If you don't act on it physically, if you put it back inside your mind, it will cause you stress. If you manifest the knowing and reach the understanding in your conscious reality, if you keep it on the outside, you will be able to help yourself, to transcend any difficulties you may be having, and to settle many problems efficiently and with relief within. The bathroom, the shower, or anyplace where there is running water will do.

MEDITATION (STAND-UP)

(You can do this meditation to cleanse and purify your aura and magnetic field by using a golden light.)

1. Stand up straight, hands at your sides.
2. Enter the silence or still state.
3. Say, "I am still." . . . Relax.
4. Visualize yourself surrounded with golden light (*will* all negativity to be dissolved in this light).
5. Picture yourself as a bar of pure golden white light. (See the negativity coming off you like little gray globs, all dissolving in the golden white light.) *Hold* this vision for about fifteen seconds or until you feel the light is pure and no negative cells are coming off.
6. Dismiss it and return to *full* normal awareness by counting from 1 to 5—1 . . . 2 . . . 3 . . . 4 . . . 5 . . . *Aware and alert*.

If you become aware that a person you are speaking with is responding negatively, use this. If you are listening to a bad speaker or lecturer and you do not want to receive these vibrations, this is what you do:

Mentally create a wall between you and the speaker. The wall should be of a white light. Make it as thick as you can. *Will* this white light to dissolve any negativity coming toward you. It will be absorbed by this wall before it ever reaches you. When you leave the lecture group, do a white light cleansing and cut the cord to any and all people who are at that meeting.

GROUP MEDITATION
DEVELOPMENT METHODS

The principle to follow is: spontaneous experience.

1. The subconscious mind can receive and send extrasensory impressions. Impressions are like hunches, flashes, or daydreams. They can be seen, heard, or felt. They can be literal or symbolic.
2. Impressions come in from various sources. Sometimes they come from within, or from other living people, from discarnate spirits, or from God.

3. Impressions are meaningful because they give us some insight into our present feelings and conditions, explain the past, or indicate the future. They are used as guides to explain decision making.
4. You can send impressions to other people. Thoughts can become experiences for those to whom you are sending them.

MYSTERIES OF THE CHANT AND MANTRA

These are charged words of power for energy-center balance and activation.

The mystery of the chant lies in the power of the "word." Some words are so powerful you can use them only on special occasions. The necessary ingredients are belief and desire or the right words (The Lord's Prayer can be used to accomplish and aid the desire to chant if said over and over again.)

The hold rhythm and rhyme is repetitive with a heavy, sonorous beat. This contributes to the gradual raising of vibrations, just like successful rock song artists do. According to the First Book of Moses (Genesis), God created the world with words: "And God said, 'Let there be light' . . . and there was light. And God said, 'Let there be a firmament in the midst of the waters.' . . . And God said, 'Let the waters under the heaven be gathered together into one place, and let the dry land appear.' . . . And God said, 'Let the earth bring forth grass.' " Here is the perfect example of the *constructive* power of words. This power, which God used in creating the world—the Power of the Word—was believed to be a power that could also be acquired by man. Chants and incantations are the earliest forms of magic known and can be found recorded on tablets dating back five thousand years.

Sumerian and Babylonian people generally believed that sickness was caused by evil spirits entering the body. They believed a magician could draw out these spirits by the use of magical chants. I believe they can. Burning incense, the smoke of incense, carried the words up to the Gods. You can possess the *Power of the Mantra* by using the sacred and powerful words from the story of Ali Baba. The all-powerful, mystical "abracadabra" is still used today. Hindus and Buddhists use mantras.

The mantra might be a single word or whole phrase. *Repetition* of this word or phrase produces the necessary vibration to cover what is desired. The magical chanting by the Egyptian magicians was what enabled them to lift the great blocks with which they built the pyramids. It's *your* magic, enabling you to do and have what you desire. Take it, and use it well.

MEDITATION MANTRA (OIIM)

When you prepare to use a mantra, let it be understood that sound opens the doorway from this dimension to another.

The mystic chant of the OHM said before meditation will assist you in increasing your sense of mental and emotional stability and also raise the frequency of your meditation.

OHM is pronounced exactly the way it is spelled. OHM-PIE-CHEE-SOO-OHM. The OHM is from the Tibetan Sanskrit and is used in that country for meditation purposes.

Begin by repeating this mantra, OHM-PIE-CHEE-SOO-OHM (five times) before getting into your meditations.

OTHER MYSTIC MANTRAS

I am God
OM
AUM
OM-MANI-PADME-HUM

CHANTING MANTRAS

1. Touch thumb and forefinger of each hand together while chanting a mantra.
2. Visualize white light flowing through your bloodstream to center and balance you.
3. Draw in white light from the source above you; with sound vibrating through your body, align your energies.

(Energy does circulate through your body in a circle. Be aware of this as you nourish each cell through this sound and source.)

To *call in* the energies into your system to raise your vibrational frequency, *chant*:

AUM—TAT—SOM—AUM

To *activate* these energies rising from the Kundalini, *chant*:

I—AM—THAT—I—AM

OVERCOMING NEGATIVE LIFE KARMA BY MEDITATION

If you've already been told you are on a karmic trip, this will help you to release it all!

The ancient Egyptian and Tibetan chants can help you to release and lessen any negative Karma.

It is suggested you understand first the spiritual laws that rule the Universe. They include:

1. The Ten Commandments
2. The Sermon on the Mount
3. The Golden Rule
4. The Law of Love and Forgiveness

Sit in meditation each day and repeat your meditation mantra (at least five times), OHM-PIE-CHEE-SOO-OHM. Say it more often if you need to quiet yourself down.

Say:

I am now in control of my mind and my emotions.

I rise above it all to control the negative force field that surrounds my life.

I control my thoughts and feelings to feel peaceful, harmonious, loving, and kind.

The winds of misfortune that blow me off course I push from my doors.

I accept my spiritual self and am prepared to meet the challenge of life head-on without fear or worry.

I am prepared to meet with the spiritual challenges that come my way as I have been purged by the spiritual flame that burns through me.

Say:

I feel the Divine presence of God and it makes me poised, peaceful, powerful, and loving.

I accept only this as I will not allow the petty misfortunes of life to touch me where I am.

I ask for the pure golden ray of spirit to come through to help control my higher mind.

I seek only those experiences to come into my life that will shape my destiny in the direction of infinite peace, infinite good, infinite love, fulfillment, infinite creative wholeness, and I am in the light, free from the darkness of despair, to meet my higher truths!

CHANT TO OVERCOME LIFE'S PROBLEMS

Say or chant:

I call in my outer armor of my earthly presence the physical shell. I enter into the innermost plane of my soul where I go into the light and understanding of God's ways and protection.

I know it will dissolve all fear of my problems, give me inner joy, peace, love, and fulfillment. I realize now that although I occupy a physical body entrapped by physical existence, I am also on a mystical journey through time and space in many dimensions and dimensionless worlds. My soul needs to grow and evolve with the karmic pattern I have chosen for me. It is reserved for me, although I wish the stress problems and obstacles that stand in my path to dissolve. I defy the negative Karma that has built a wall in my path and I ask to overcome my negative misfortune. Show me the way so I can no longer be tied to these burdens and worries. Give me the strength and courage to endure and place me on the path of my truth to uplift me.

I now invoke the power of cosmic magnetism to attract only good into my sphere of influence and life experience— all that you wish for me. I use the art of cosmic alchemy to turn hate into love, poverty into riches, misery into joy, failure into success, and evil into good.

God is Good and God is Love.

Shower me with Your light of my Divine heritage.

CHANT AND MEDITATION FOR
ROMANTIC HAPPINESS

I now attune my higher mind and the energies of the higher forces of God to come through me to show me the way to perfect my life, my inner expression, my outer—the personality.

My needs are to perfect all the lovingness I hold within me, my soul. I ask my beloved to recognize my mind, my good qualities that are the God within my nature, and to respond accordingly to me.

I ask to overcome my supersensitivity so I am not open to unkind remarks or any negative actions my loved one has directed to me. I need to control my emotions so I don't feel I am a target for attack. My expression is to remain loving, cheerful, positive, and optimistic always, even in times of strife.

My moods should reflect my aura of beauty, magnetism, and charm so he or she can see my deep need for spiritual guidance.

I ask to overcome all holds of jealousy and possessiveness and am under the understanding that we are two individual souls who need each other's space.

I bless this union and know that I will bring joy and contentment to my beloved.

CHANTS FOR YOUR RELEASE OF
CREATIVE POWER

To program your higher brain centers with genius and inspiration, say your mantra five times.

Say:

I am a channel for the preservation of life and the beauty of the Universe.

I channel all this creativeness within—to light a spark to the celestial music and sound of the spheres of higher life. The motion of the creative images of the arts, the sciences [or *whatever your needs are*—state them], is part of me.

As I attune my brain cells to these higher wave lengths of

color, sound, and motion in my world, my environment, my creative lovingness to everything I touch . . . I ask this Universal mind to release these creative patterns of thought into me, to crystalize my own images to this beauty. Send the rhythm down to me as I wish to inspire humanity with my great dreams of creative imagery.

I vibrate to the golden Sun, the silvery Moon
In the purple veil of night.

I send these images in power into me to reflect in my personality, giving me dynamic power and inspiration
So, I may give to the world. . . .

CHANT AND MEDITATION
FOR BUILDING MONEY, POWER,
AND SUCCESS

To bring to the front power and success, say mantra five times, OHM-PIE-CHEE-SOO-OHM.

Say:

My concentration is now to reach awareness and achievement, follow my high ideals to my chosen path or profession.

My needs are a source of your supply—money so I can help myself—family—others to achieve a higher standard of living.

State now what you need: (*example*: house, car, better clothes, jewels, or other).

I know *it is* possible for me to upgrade my existence and I ask Divine guidance for these things and the things money can buy.

I will use it wisely as I dedicate myself to be a channel and receptor of God's Divine inspiration so I can give freely to an evolved community of higher understanding.

I will avoid greed, miserliness, and avarice, so that I can help those less fortunate than myself.

I am a dedicated chalice for these Divine gifts and now accept the responsibility placed upon me for these to be bestowed from the Universe without waste and with appreciation of this beautiful Universe to fulfill my life's road and my tasks.

Thank you, as I am your Divine creation.

Amen

LAUGHING MEDITATION

This meditation serves as a release from tension and suffering. We laugh only with a cause. There is fun laughter or pain laughter but one rarely laughs for no reason at all.

Laughing is a beautiful way to deep-cleanse the spirit and deeply purify it.

METHOD:

When you awaken each morning, before opening your eyes, stretch in a catlike movement. Enjoy the feeling of your body and body parts coming awake. After a few seconds you will obviously see humor in your knees creaking, perhaps, or your stomach sticking out.

Start laughing. After a few minutes you may feel yourself an idiot, but soon you will genuinely laugh. At first you may have difficulty if you are not accustomed to laughing and have forgotten how. Soon it will become spontaneous. Enjoy!

Do this also during your rest periods midday.

9

Prayers and How to Use Them When the Unusual Happens

Guide me while I am here
Entering the unknown
I feel lost, confused and angered by the changes
    surging through me
I say now I am in touch with my emotional state
    which I can now release and turn over to you—
    my guardian and keeper at my door—
Behold and see the images of light and changes working
    through and over me taking place
I alone know the torture and turning to find
    my place, my home, my truth

PRAYERS AND THE BUILDING OF FAITH WITHIN

*Lord . . . grant us the right
to go beyond the realms of eternity.
So Be It!
Amen*

Prayers are important as you walk down this special path. The power of prayer helps you open up to your higher self. Let the word and sound of prayer, said daily, fill you up with faith, hope, and peace, through which you will find happiness and communication with your source of higher power and enlightenment.

It is through prayer that we reach for faith. Not only can we uplift ourselves to higher levels of learning with faith, but we can release ourselves from the lower levels of consciousness. We cannot hold on to both higher and lower levels of knowing, and faith helps us be sure that the higher level is always there to grasp. Faith is manifested in the act of surrender, which is prayer. Hope activates faith, for true hope is the conviction that you are capable of the necessary actions to get to the higher plane of understanding. We also pray to open the doorway to love—love of others as well as of ourselves. Love is the motivating force that propels us to achieve more than we think we can. Every action that is prayed for *is* charged with love.

I offer this humble explanation to open you up to the reason behind the praying you have always done, whether consciously or unconsciously. Our needs and wants must be explored on a higher plane or level of thought, and prayer is the vehicle that drives us there. A prayer is an honest, earnest entreaty, petition, or request. The energy of asking through prayer is sent out to communicate with God. The words explain what we are asking for.

I offer you the following prayers. Some worthy ones I have here collected have helped many preparing for the New Age, while others have been channeled by me and have been most effective.

The following prayer is the invoking of the aid of the Forces of Light and is sent out daily by disciples everywhere. It has been translated into twenty-six languages. It can bring the light and love needed to save our planet from destruction. The Forces of Light have to be invited to come in and help. They will not interfere with man's free will. The first verse invokes the Buddha, the Lord of Light. The second verse invokes the Christ, Lord of Love. The third verse invokes the planetary hierarchy whose center is on the Etheric level over Jerusalem (the New Jerusalem that will not pass away). The fourth verse deals with mankind and brings the power of love and light to Earth.

If enough people all over the planet will use this prayer, the planet will be lifted into the heaven it was meant to be.

NEW AGE PRAYER:
THE GREAT INVOCATION

From the point of Light within the Mind of GOD
Let Light stream forth into the minds of men.
Let Light descend on earth.

From the point of Love within the Heart of GOD
Let Love stream forth into the hearts of men.
May Christ return to earth.

From the center where the Will of God is known
Let purpose guide the little wills of men
The purpose which the Masters know and serve.

From the center which we call the race of men
Let the Plan of Love and Light work out
And may it seal the door where evil dwells.

Let LIGHT and LOVE and POWER restore the Plan on Earth.
—ALICE A. BAILEY

INVOCATION

The Sons of men are one and we are one with them.
We seek to Love, not hate
We seek to serve and not exact due service.
We seek to heal, not hurt.
Let pain bring due reward of Light and Love
Let the Soul control the outer form and life and all events,
And bring to light the Love that underlies the happening of the
    time.
Let vision come, and insight,
Let inner vision come, and insight.
Let the future stand revealed.
Let inner union demonstrate and outer cleavages be gone.
Let LOVE prevail
Let all men LOVE.

MEDITATION FROM THE
ASHTAR COMMAND

This is a special meditation for peace, harmony, love, and
prosperity in the New Age—beamed to Earth by the Ashtar
Command.

One must meditate on the goodness of creation.
Meditate on the Light in front of us.
Meditate on the glory of living.
Meditate on the fruitfulness of life.
Create a glow of unity with the Space Brothers in your third
    eye and make that glow expand. Let that glow consume
    you.
Let that glow consume everything around you.
Meditate on the wholeness. Meditate on that which is
    beneficial.
Meditate on kindness, say to yourself:

> I AM THE LIGHT OF THE UNIVERSE
> I AM POWERFUL
> I AM GLORIOUS
> I AM A LIVING BEING

Send out positive thoughts, send out harmony, send out LOVE.
Meditate on the wholeness of the solar system.

THE AFFIRMATION OF
THE DISCIPLE

I am a point of light within a greater light
I am a strand of loving energy within the stream of Love divine
I am a spark of sacrificial Fire, focused within the fiery
    Will of God
And thus I stand
I am a way by which men may achieve
I am a source of strength, enabling them to stand
I am a beam of light, shining upon their way
And thus I stand
And standing thus revolve
And tread this way the ways of men,
And know the ways of God
And thus I stand

—ALICE BAILEY

PRAYERS AND MANTRAS
THAT HAVE HELPED
by Isabel Hickey

I CLOTHE MYSELF WITH A ROBE OF LIGHT COMPOSED
OF THE LOVE, POWER AND WISDOM OF GOD. NOT
ONLY FOR MY OWN PROTECTION BUT SO THAT ALL
WHO SEE IT OR COME IN CONTACT WITH IT WILL BE
DRAWN TO GOD AND HEALED.*

O LORD OF LIFE AND LOVE, REVEAL THYSELF TO
ME. OPEN MY MIND. O LORD OF LIFE TO TRUTH
THAT IS FOR ME. THY SERVANT, LORD, AM I. GRANT
ME THY HEALING GRACE, I PRAY, AND AS I GO
ABOUT MY WORK THIS DAY GIVE ME THE POWER
TO KNOW AND DO THY WILL, AND THROUGH THY
PRESENCE AT MY SIDE, HEAL AND COMFORT THOSE
I CONTACT AND THOSE FOR WHOM I PRAY.

I have always loved this prayer and use it constantly.

IN THE CENTER OF ALL LIGHT I STAND. NOTHING
CAN TOUCH ME THERE.

See yourself in a pyramid of light. Light is substance.

THERE IS ONLY GOD AND THERE IS ONLY GOOD.

When we cling to this truth and affirm it with all our being, there
is no dark force that can stand against it. This conviction will
root out any negative power and it will have to leave. The forces
of darkness do flee!

HOW TO SET IN MOTION
YOUR OWN MIRACLE POWER

Affirmations are declarations of your intent. Say whichever ones
you need.

---

*Many of us use this prayer every day, putting on our robe of light before we travel the
highways or walk the streets of the city. We also circle our cars with light. It works. Try
it. You can prove the power of light for yourself.

AFFIRMATION 1

My higher self, the God within me, gives me the power to forgive all those who have brought me pain and suffering past and present.

AFFIRMATION 2

In perfect order is my all-powerful higher self bringing me all the blessings more wonderful than can be imagined, including perfect health, love and happiness, and abundant wealth.

AFFIRMATION 3

I humbly request the all-wise Spirit of God to reveal the answers of this problem at exactly the right time for my greatest good.

OUR FATHER

Our Father who art in heaven
Hallowed be thy Name
Thy kingdom come
Thy will be done
On earth, as it is in heaven
Give us this day
Our daily bread
And forgive us our trespasses
As we forgive those who trespass against us
Lead us not into temptation
But deliver us from evil
For thine is the kingdom and the power and the glory
Forever and ever
Amen

The Our Father should be said three times in succession. It is especially good in a group meditation when wanting to clear out the debris of negative thought forms of energy.

The sound of these words goes from this world into the ethers of space as if by a pyramid of light. It sends out the loving vibrations to these higher worlds to balance us and carries us to our sources of spirit or enlightenment.

TO SAINT JUDE, PATRON SAINT
OF IMPOSSIBLE CAUSES*
(Say for nine days in a row)

O Holy Saint Jude, Apostle and martyr, great in virtue and rich in miracles, near kinsman of Jesus Christ, faithful intercessor of all who invoke your special patronage in time of need.

To you I have recourse from the depth of my heart and humbly beg to whom God has given such great power to come to my assistance.

Help me in my present and urgent petition—in return I promise to make your name known and cause to be invoked.

Saint Jude, pray for us all who invoke your aid. . . .
Amen

Say three Our Fathers.
Say three Hail Marys.
Say three Glory Bes.

PSALM 23

The Lord is my Shepherd: I shall not want
He maketh me to lie down in green pastures:
He leadeth me beside the still waters
He restoreth my soul; He leadeth me in the paths of righteousness for His name's sake
Yea, though I walk through the valley of the shadow of death,
I will fear no evil: for thou art with me; thy rod and thy staff comfort me
Thou preparest a table before me in the presence of mine enemies;
Thou anointest my head with oil;
My cup runneth over

---

*Perhaps known to those of Christian faith, although many others have used this and have had remarkable results. We are all children of God and only our known heritage accepts or rejects. Be open to all.

Surely goodness and mercy shall follow me all the days
    of my life: and I will dwell in the house of the Lord
    forever:

A PSALM OF DAVID

MEMORIZE PSALM 23

Recite this psalm when you are troubled by a big problem. You
will feel a sense of tranquility and inner calm. It will build up
your mental strength and you will feel calmness and peace so
you can overcome difficulties.

A CALL TO OUR FORCES
OF STRENGTH

Father, Mother, God, Good Spirit Guides, Archangels, Galac-
    tic and Intergalactic Generals, and Servants of God:

We beseech you to answer to us in the name of truth and love;
We thank you for this day of learning and in any days we may
    have ahead in our journey ever-upward to find God the
    source of all Light.
May he generate in us all the love, faith, and hope to further
    and help mankind to a most positive end as that is our
    goal.
Establish our trinity on Earth as a pyramid of light
Guide, protect and keep us through any approaching negativity
    and dissolve them instantaneously.
We wish wisdom and knowledge not for our own egos and
    goals but to receive a higher understanding of your work
    in all worlds, with Your love and your light.
We thank you, for all your caring, sharing, love, and concern
    that has brought us this far in our never-ending journey
    and search for knowledge.
Bring down your positive beacon of light [say three times].
May it descend on us all, bringing in rays of lights that go
    from this world to other worlds.
While taking our negativities and throwing them out, we ask
    them to be transmuted into love wherever it is needed.
    [Say the last sentence three times.]

Transmute them back into this world with love. [Say three times.]

We are love with all our Godly attributes, concerns, and sharing from this world to other worlds.

We thank you for the answers to our mind, our bodies, and our spirit!

Amen

PRAYER TO RAISE THE ENERGIES FOR A GROUP MEDITATION— A DECLARATION TO SPIRIT AND THE GOD FORCE

We have set the conditions in place, with this prayer, as we call out to our higher energies on higher levels of existence in physical as well as a general meeting with spirit beings to surround us with love and protection to help us here on the Earth Plane.

We have asked them to guide and assist us in helping to raise world consciousness among man.

At the end of your meditation, with a group or singly, envision the planet Earth as a ball of green light. This concentrated thought will help heal the earth.

Or—ask for any extra healing energy to be sent to the person or persons of your choice. The members of the group will decide whether they should pray mentally or announce verbally.

PRAYER BEFORE READING THE TAROT

Dearest Father-Mother God (or the Holy Trinity)*
Use me as Your vehicle, as Your worker and messenger on Earth
Put Your words on my lips as pearls of wisdom and knowledge
Let my words flow like wine and honey

*We have offered this prayer to the Holy Trinity. Or you could focus on the two inverted triangles that make up the trinities of the Star of David.

Pause, before starting prayer and feel the salutation's energy force before you begin the prayer.

Assist me to aid those who come to me for counseling and let
    them be surrounded by my love and my light
Allow me to destroy in them the negative crystalized energies,
    and let me penetrate into their being with my light and
    my love

Dearest Father-Mother God, help me to lift them into a new
    awareness
I have asked and it is given on this day
Thank You

I CAN DO ALL THINGS, FOR YOU ARE WITHIN ME
So Be It!

PRAYERS:
FOR AN UNINVITED SPIRIT THAT HAS
ATTACHED HIMSELF TO YOU

Somehow, when you encounter the presence of some truly negative individuals you may feel awful when they walk away and
leave your presence. That person could have "dropped" a spirit
or two around you after he has left you. They may decide to stay
with you as you feel better, and then zap your strength. If you
feel at a loss, blue, melancholy when these people leave, say the
prayer below so they do not stay hidden in your home or on you.
Prayer helps to relieve you of your anxieties or tensions. Also, as
you send these invisible beings into a white light you will
experience a lightness.

Spirit be gone [say three times]
That has come through with [*the name of the person who has
    just left you*]*
Go with her/him
Remain with her/him
Be with her/him
So Be It!

[*End it with:*]
I am in God's light and under God's protection
Nothing less than God's perfection
Can touch me where I am.

*Say the full name of the person from whom you feel you may have picked up the
negativity. You will send all his bodies packing and all burdens will be lifted.

A QUICK CLEARING PRAYER:
BEFORE SERIOUS MEDITATION TO GET
SOME ANSWERS TO OUR PROBLEMS

Bring down, dear Lord, your powerful white light [say three
times]
Fuse and bond your ray of light and love
with your Eternal Essence of love and protection
Bathe us in your glorious field of protection so we
may walk this Earth Plane unafraid of any negativity,
on all planes of existence, as we call out Your Name*

PRAYERS:
RIDDING OF RANCID ENERGIES

Dear Lord, please send down purifying energies to remove
(*State the problem*) and erase the vibrations of (*name*)
that affect me.
Send it to my conscious mind, subconscious mind, and
superconscious mind and from the cells of all of me, that
is pure that ever was, and ever will be.

After saying this prayer, transfuse an orange light into yourself
coming from the top of your head down into your body. Picture
it if it would be easier (orange clouds over your head that
disperse as a shower all over you, a cosmic shower for cleaning
out and through all the unneeded, unwanted negativity.)

PRAYERS FOR GENERAL USE

I call on the energies of God's power and love to raise my
vibrations to the attunement of God's perfection—to the
State of Supreme Protection. I direct this energy to my
higher self, lower self, and God-self by the Laws of the
Elohim.
I stand tall in your light, dear Lord, as I gather strength,
wisdom and knowledge to all thy ways . . . all ways.

*The name of any higher power will do (spirit guides as well). Say the name eight times
in succession, as if chanting.

I humbly ask by Divine right . . . for the power of your
strength to guide me through my stormy days and guide
me toward the light of eternal enlightenment, for I need
to be under the canopy of your guidance . . . *Amen.*

My realities are open to God's truth as I ask ascendancy to the
yet higher planes. Protect my pathway and repel any
approaching negativities that may touch me where I am.
Lift me up to your doorway of higher learning and truth.

I give myself up to my earthly demands of what I believe to
be right and ask for your direction as what I feel right
and just . . . just doesn't seem to be working for me.
Focus in on my truth, dear Lord, and if it is not as you
deem it to be . . . cast me into a different direction. I
pray for my salvation . . . *Amen.*

PRAYER TO GIVE IT AWAY
(CONFUSION AND PROBLEMS)

(This is a prayer of Abandonment, in which you ask God to help
you communicate with Him, and help your soul find the way out
of difficulty.)

When you know *not* what to do or know not how to resolve
your problem, you are putting yourself into God's hands to
abandon yourself to his wisdom fully and completely. You are
asking your higher power to take the problem from you.

Visualize an arc of white light coming down from the skies and
an arc of white light coming up from the center of the Earth and
stand in the rays of the arc, which resemble the form of a crescent
moon, and say this prayer while you visualize yourself being
lifted up on this beam of light, with your palms facing the sky:

Father of the Universe, I, [*say your name*], abandon myself
into your hands.
Do with me what you will, for I no longer know which way to
turn or what road of understanding to choose to help
myself.
Whatever you may do, I thank you, as I am ready for all your
assistance and humbly accept all you can give me to
terminate my problem [*State your problem*].

Into your hands I put my soul, for my soul IS your soul.
I offer this with all the love in my heart for I love [*your name*]
    and need to give myself and surrender myself into your
    hands.
This is without reservation and with boundless confidence as I
    am your child and I need you, in order to know myself.
I, the creator too, need to see and know you, [*your name*],
    your creation.
Amen.

HEALING PRAYER:
NEEDED TO RESTORE YOUR INNER BEING
AND PHYSICAL HEALTH

Say each line out loud by chanting in a vigorous rhythm with
absolute belief. Pause and visualize when reciting each line's
words and think the words through. A good way to build up your
energy systems. If there is a particular problem in one specific
spot on the physical body, concentrate heavily on that area with
healing white light (green and pink can also be used with white).

Loving Father,
I recognize, that my life is one and the same with your eternal
    and supreme power [visualize a ray of white light coming
    into the top of your head and merging into your body].
Your constructive mind is now within me building my mind
    and body into a fortress of strength and perfection.
I open, my mind to the influx of your mighty presence of
    health, tranquility and peace, which exists as a power
    fountain of vitality flowing into every faculty and organ
    of my being. [See this begin to happen.]
I am, the creator of my nature and my life and health have all
    the power to regenerate and heal my body.
I am, organizing my life and strength into a mind body of
    health and perfection.
Thy substance, is feeding and restoring every part of my body
    to positive health.
I call, on thy healing life force and intelligence of my brain to
    alert every organ of my being, every nerve cell and every
    atom of my flesh to regenerate. [Visualize a pinky flow
    coming into the cells.]

I ask for thy glorious wisdom which is illuminating my soul
    and purifying my mind of every limiting thought and
    limitation. [Pour more energy into yourself to illuminate
    you with power.]
I ask thy healing tender love which invigorates and upholds
    me to dissolve away all fear. [Take deep transformational
    breaths and exhale deeply.]
O Loving Father, my body is thy holy temple.
Make it a perfect dwelling place from which shall radiate thy
    healing light and love, as you give wisdom and health to
    all thy children.
Father, glorify me with thy healing power that I also may
    glorify thee . . .
So Be It!

HEALING FOR SELF:
ALL-PURPOSE

Prepare by saying:
    I honor my own divinity, the real myself which is in perfect order
    Harmonious and balanced
    My mind, body, emotions and spirit are together and centered

    God bless my mind, God heal my mind
    God bless my body, God heal my body
    God bless my emotions, God heal my emotions
    God bless my spirit, God manifest in my spirit

PRAYER MEDITATION FOR
PURIFICATION OF A SOUL WHO IS:

• Ill physically
• Mentally
• Emotionally (yourself included)

To Lift the Spirits Upward into the Hands of the Higher Energies for
Healing

This prayer is to be said daily for a period of three weeks.

1. Get to meditation level by deep, deep breathing. Inhale and
    exhale to the count of 5 (three times).

2. Light a white candle and a yellow and a blue candle for healing. Set white candle in front of you, other two in back forming an upside-down triangle. The white candle should be at the point. *Example*:

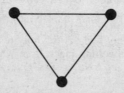

3. Say a prayer of protection for yourself even when you are in the process of healing others.

   Say a prayer of protection for the person you are healing. Put him or her in a white light first, then enclose the person with a blue light (your subconscious will see that this is done).
4. Call in the soul you are healing as you begin by envisioning the face or put a photograph in front of your vision.
5. Call on your highest power or guide to come through God's light to assist you. Yes, Angels are included also.
6. Ask them for help to bring down God's Golden Spiral Staircase and know there are seventeen steps for this soul to climb up to for a healing of this sort. (Count steps with your fingers.)
7. Have the soul face the staircase. Visualize the soul and his or her guide by leading the way mentally to the first step of the Golden Spiral Staircase.
8. *Say* on step 1

We three are in the hands of God and with the powers of the highest light. May this light shine upon our way to these higher energies of the light for a healing and purification to our physical, mental, and emotional states of being. So Be It!

Feel the presence of the Angels and the powers you have called forth and see the white light shine on you all to guide you up the staircase.

Say:

"I call [*person's name*] to step forth and ascend the Golden Staircase of God." See (visualize) them climbing up to the ninth step on staircase and *start your prayers.*

> Dear Lord, take [*person's name*] into the waters of purification to have them purified and cleansed, throw away all of their negativities and turn them back into the world with love. Fill their heart center with love, fill them up with love, as you take away all the negativity keep throwing away my/his or her pains, sickness and ills and the causes of them [say this three times]. Submerge [*person's name*] fully and completely, fully and completely into the Etheric waters to cleanse their physical, mental, and emotional bodies. Turn them back into this world with love. [Say this three times. Now name the situation causing their problems as best you can.]

I ask all of your love and healing, blessings, mercy, compassion, patience, understanding, love, and high-energy vibrations to come to them (say three times). Also, your love and spirituality, love and your godly attributes to heal and bless [*person's name*], dear Lord.

Have your Angels with [*person's name*] always, dear Lord, so that he/she is never afraid, frightened, and alone giving [*person's name*] guidance and direction.

Purify and cleanse his/her soul, his/her spirit, his/her Etheric and Astral body, mental and emotional bodies and his/her physical body filling [*person's name*] up with your love, healing and blessings.

Shine down your holy white light on [*person's name*], dear Lord, with your love and guidance, your health and your healing and may he/she always dwell within the sight of you, dear Lord, and drink from thy Divine chalice of love, protection with peace and abundant happiness.

I give this situation to you in Divine order. May your love and your glory shine upon [*person's name*] soul always.

I ask and it is given

Thank you, dear Lord, thank you

Amen

ANALOGY:

The above prayer is done for emergency situations to help uplift them when the difficulties of the being have made healing impossible. When you start, continue every day for a three-week period as it is most effective to help with the causes of illness. Repetition in certain places is essential to take the soul into other worlds for a healing also. Say these prayers exactly as they are.

PRAYER MEDITATION
FOR PURIFICATION OF SOULS
UPON PASSING INTO THE
NEXT REALM

REASONS:

1. To lift them to a higher plane when they have passed over (so they will not be earth grounded or bound).
2. To help these souls rid themselves of their earth emotions, anxieties or fears they have hung on to (impurities).
3. To take their spirits from earth and ascend them to a higher place for learning what this present life was all about; to prepare them to be in their rightful place and not be taken over by Astral "intruders" or negative spirit life.
4. To put them directly in the hands of God.

BEGINS:

1. Get to meditation level and breathe to the count of 5 (inhale). Exhale to the count of 5. Do this gradually, very slowly, very deeply. Do this three times.
2. Call in your spirit guides and ask for high protection. Ignite a white candle.
3. Say the Our Father three times *or* the Ancient Hebrew Prayer

   Kadosh, Kadosh, Kadosh
   Adonoy—Tsuaos—Milo—Chall
   Had—Avetz—Kivodo

MEANING:

   Blessed, blessed, blessed, Blessed is the Lord, the one Lord over Earth.

(This gives great positive protection.)

NEXT:
Visualize the soul that has just left Earth and passed over. Call out his or her name. If you do not know what they looked like, call out the name fully (Son of, friend of, mother of, whomever you know on Earth who is related to this being and can see their form. Mentally envision this.)

THEN:
Ask for his or her spirit guide to take the hand (see their forms in your mind's eye). Visualize a Golden Spiral Staircase coming down for them both from the ethers or space (if it's easier to picture the Golden Staircase coming down from the sky, that is all right, too).

ADDRESS:
The souls needing help with their guide or guides embracing them and holding their hands. Ask them all to feel or see them facing the winding Golden Spiral Staircase.

SAY:
"Dear Lord, send down your Golden Staircase [visualize it coming down]. [Say three times, addressing the soul]. Climb up the Golden Staircase, climb up the Golden Staircase and go through the white light into God's world of perfection and protection.
    "God loves you, God wants you, God forgives you [say twice]. [Name person and his guides, repeat name again. Take them through the white light into God's world two times]. See the white light pouring over that soul and the guide. [Name person], climb up the Golden Staircase and go through the white light into God's world [two times]."

SAY:
"God loves you, God wants you, God forgives you" [say twice]. Keep repeating this phrase until the soul has gone through white light.
    You yourself can be the guide, and astrally project yourself to the soul, and help guide the soul up the steps, to go through the white light. And call to the Angels, say, "God's Angels, God's Angels, God's Angels . . . please come out of the white light and take this soul from me. Thank you, Dear Lord, thank you, Amen." (Go by feeling throughout the prayer.)

NOTE:
If there is any reluctance by the soul to leave this Earth Plane

then, wait for a period of eight days and repeat the process. You can only be and feel energized and refreshed as well as having your energies perked up.

THE SUN-SETTING PRAYER:
A CANDLELIGHTING CEREMONY FOR PURITY
IN THE HOME—TO VIBRATE LOVE

Beauty in the candles we hold illuminating the night as the brilliance of the stars

Oh, how the fear never surfaces upon it

We are one with the Sun, and the stars show their luminate glow for joy and peace within thy soul

Shine into the night and bring forth a white light of peace

Shine, oh great one, so that I may step forward to take thy hand

Lead me not astray from all I seek

Help me to accept my destiny and my journey although hardship may arise

At a time beauty is needed, I shall know henceforth, it is for me to seek what is truth in the ways of the Lord

Seek and thee shall find one's own courage amongst the realms of dreams and hidden realities stored away from great wise men of lifetimes before

Those who saved time's elements for the future to be sought and found by all those who search

Allow me to search without fear, and if by fear, guide me with hope and love in the name of the Lord

As the peaceful vibrations of the night set in, be at one with the serenity of the passing day.

—LAUREN STABINER

PART THREE

THE TOOLS
OF THE TRADE

10

The Uses of Water: The All-Powerful Elixir of Vitality—The Exceptional Element

WATER HEALINGS AND THERAPY

These waters can be used for healing and to serve for ridding your own or other people's negativity.

• Sea water
• Fresh water (rivers, lakes, streams)
• Spring water
• Distilled water
• Holy water

WATER POWER

Water has been called our ages-old elixir of youth. It can also be our rejuvenating energy to restore our bodies back to health. Our bodies need water, and little can sustain life without it whether it be animal, vegetable, or mineral. Our Earth has life because it has water. Whenever there is life, water is found, but where the supply is limited, few people and little life exist. That is why so few people live in deserts or around polar ice caps.

Man needs only a small amount of water each day to live, but civilized man uses water for other purposes such as cooking, bathing, and washing our dishes and clothing. It irrigates our food crops and runs our factories by the use of its energy, it flushes away human waste, dirt, and grime. Its energies are not only a source of power to be harnessed (hydroelectric power) but in this era we find its healing uses as well.

Natural sources (spring) supply the cheapest water available. Underground wells exist everywhere beneath the surface of the ground, near the surface or very deep down. This water can be salty, fresh, soft, or hard. Underground water seldom contains bacteria because it has been filtered through the soil. Rain water helped most of civilization during its early growth periods. It is usually drained from a roof into a cistern and pumped. It is soft water and contains no dissolved mineral salts from the ground. It does have, however, dust from the air and from the very surfaces it touches. This can be removed by filtering the rain water through sand.

We do purify water for drinking through these processes: (1) coagulation and sedimentation; (2) filtration; (3) disinfection. Much research has been done to purify the salty water from the seas and oceans by removing the salt but it is quite expensive. Distilled water is free from minerals and impurities in general.

Water can also be a magical force, a vital resource that can restore health and healing to a body. From the old sitz bath to magical treatments, water can make you feel alive again.

WATER CLEANSINGS

FRESH WATER

(rivers, lakes, streams)

Fresh water can be used as well as *sea water* at times, as it does pass into the oceans. You must, in using it for cleaning, simply command (through the power of prayer) that the negative particles be removed and taken to the ocean. This type of water has its own unique function and does fit in to the Universal scheme as well.

Holy water that is consecrated by the Roman Catholic Church is tap water exorcised and blessed over or prayed on, with consecrated salt or alcohol added to it to remove impurities. It has the virtue of God placed within it and when sprinkled through a house will lighten and strengthen the vibrations in it for the believer.

On Rosh Hashanah, one of the Jewish High Holy Days, after certain prayers are done, the congregation gathers alongside a body of water to throw their sins away. So it is for more than drinking purposes alone that we need water to survive; perhaps water has other virtues or properties as it comes from the light, as it is sought by the light, to bring about our spiritual elevation.

THE SEA

Somehow I feel that because the Earth is made up primarily of the oceans and seas, *all* of us alive on Earth need the constant cleansing of the air and water elements. For the ancients, for Jew, Christian, and Moslem alike, sea water has always been the symbol of life. It has been known to cleanse us. Water can be charged to remove all the evils that cling to us and remove the negativities we hold on to. Even a bath of water and salt can remove negative influences. Water helps us remove spiritual blocks and some physical blocks that we would otherwise hold on to for a lifetime. Sea water can be bottled and it is very worthwhile to do so for healing minor ailments. Incoming tides are more pure than outgoing tides.

Did you ever feel, when tired, depressed, angry, or ill, that you are feeling a need to become one with the water? That's not only a need to return to the womb! Water also helps us to even out our physical and emotional balance and synchronize all our energies, to be in tune with it all. It clears our spiritual/emotional burdens as it removes all toxins. The ocean is one gigantic tumbler, a kind of psychic washing machine. The seas were created to absorb and hold every evil thing. They are powerful enough to absorb and remove negative influences.

MAKE YOUR OWN HOLY WATER

INGREDIENTS:

1. Double terminated crystal (points at both ends)
2. Clear glass vase of water (amount of water optional)—use spring water (I use an oversized brandy snifter or wide-mouth jar)

Cleanse crystal first (see Chapter 12)

MAKE SURE GLASS IS
Thoroughly clean. Then add a small amount of hot tap water to cleanse bottom. Pour out and add spring water and cleansed crystal.

MAKE A PRAYER AND SAY:

> God of my energy come forth
> Surround me in prayer
> Send forth your light to shine into my elixir of vitality,
>   my strengths
> Eliminate the gases and chemicals of negativity
> Add and use these sparkles of healing to be used in
>   my time of need
> Be it of mind, body, or spirit
> So Be It!

When done, pour in a drop of brandy to preserve this mixture. Ask to have your hands guided as you pour. Use a small drop for a small container, a little more for a larger container.

Now you may also use this "cleared and charged water" to cleanse the face and put it on any area of your body that might have bothered you or been giving you difficulty. Pour it into your hands, too, for a refreshing face wash. It's ready for use immediately!

THE ENERGY OF STORING SUNLIGHT
(SOLARIZATION)

Water can also be a means of storing sunlight. It also acts as a magnet for the Sun's energy. Place a closed, ordinary gallon jug filled with water in sunlight for twelve hours or more. It purifies the water and improves the taste by exposing the water to the sunlight.

For a smaller amount of water (pint or glass), let stand for five minutes in sunlight and say a prayer over it. Water can magnetize energy. Put water vessel in sunny window with a colored filter between the sunlight and the water *or* in a colored glass jar or bottle placed in sunlight. The Sun can transfer the colored wave lengths into the water to give your body what it needs before drinking it. It can be supercharged in one hour.

Use *red water* or *blue* to make beverages for morning coffee. Red water stimulates; blue water is a sedative. Try it at the end of the day.

Blue water is good for insect bites or skin irritations. (You can manufacture this by putting red glass panes or blue over a jar of water. Cover and install 100-watt lightbulb overhead (for twelve hours). (See p. 92.)

PRAYER

May the Sun, the source of all light
Increase our vitality, illuminate my path so I can grow and
    prosper
I am raised to the presence of your rays of energy for my
    needs and body's requirements

WATER/GLASS SOLUTION FINDER

As you go to bed, place a glass of water on the table next to your bed. State out loud, or write down in one or two clear sentences, one problem to which you wish an answer. *Example:* Why can't I get along with my sister (or mother)? What can I do better in to affect my business positively? Make up your own questions about anything that bothers you in your daily life.

After stating the question, drink one-half of the water in the glass. Go to sleep, and make up your mind to sleep soundly. When you wake up the next morning, drink the other half of the water in the glass. In seventy-two hours you should have the answer to your problem. It could hit you over the head. After you work out that problem, try another one. The water will help the sleeping but working mind to absorb a single problem and solve it. It will work as a computer to store energy and knowledge in your mind.

GO TO THE BEACH
TO BE HEALED

AT THE BEACH

First, go into the water. If there is no beach nearby, project yourself there mentally by sitting quietly and imagining a part of your body leaving you.

1. As you are bathing, or imagining yourself to be bathing, throw away all anxiety into that body of water. Unblock all of your inhibitions as the water churns around you and throw all

of your problems into it as if it were a giant melting pot. Salt water will sweeten and purify your body's balance. The feelings of failure, fear, and of being overburdened by crisis will disappear. The water serves as a gigantic tumbler. The Earth's gravity pulls out negative particles of energy from your aura and auric field and can serve as a body purifier and relaxer. Water pulls with the motion of the Earth and helps the body's elasticity. You, in that water, are pulled into that energy field. As you ease it all out by concentration or movement, keep throwing out into the water all negative emotions or feelings. Feel the water churning around you as it washes out the body's tensions. After getting out of nature's "washing machine," sit quietly on the shore.

2. As you sit on the shore facing the water, rest awhile and contemplate the sea gulls as you watch them. Sea gulls fly into the wind currents and they can stay still or fly as they do this with the magnetic pull of the wind. We can do the same as we watch them and feel at peace with these energies. Prepare for your "flight" home.

3. You are now ready to encase all that good energy for the trip home, now that all fatigue is leaving you. Imagine and create a scene of the mind of your being encased inside a crystal pyramid (all clear glass). Feel the crystal pyramid, with you inside it, lifting you up into the air far above the water. Ride with the air currents as a sea gull would do, as you tip your wings and glide over the water. This will seal in all your good energy. Sea gulls work with electromagnetic energy to move up and down; why not do the same as you ride out the wind and set yourself back on shore? As you walk out of the pyramid, bring that state of mind home with you.

TO RID YOURSELF
OF OTHER PEOPLE'S NEGATIVITY

1. Bathe in a hot bath to which you've added a lot of sea salt.
2. Add vinegar when you're tired, or achy, too.

THERAPY FOR THE MIND

Examine an acorn in a glass of water.

DRINKING A GLASS OF
THERAPEUTIC WATER

1. This water can rearrange your metabolic rate in less than one hour.
2. It will help your dieting process.
3. It will hasten your recovery from stress.

- Fill a glass with spring water.
- Say a prayer for God to energize this water.
- Command your higher power for a *blue light* to come from within and project outward for your third eye or forehead.
- See the blue light or ray going into the water glass.

Let the glass distill for about five minutes, and while doing so imagine the bottom of the glass filled with "sparkly golden stones." Ask that it be energized by the love and healing rays of God, and while doing so put your right hand over the top of the glass in mid-air and make three complete clockwise circles over the glass top. Wait two minutes or so, then drink down all the glass's contents. Do this three times a day until you feel a change within.

WATER AND THE BED PAN

- Put a pan of water under the bed of an ill person.
- Three times a day command the negative energy in the room to go into the pan of water.
- Change the pan and add new water once a day.

The pan holds all of the negative energy, so the patient gets well faster.

WINDY AND RAINY DAYS ARE BEST
FOR AURA CLEANSING

Water or wind can cleanse your aura. You can stand in a breeze and *will* all of your Astral garbage off to be cleansed by the wind or rain. Do this riding in a car with the windows open, too, or in any situation in which the wind is rushing past you. A fan works, too, as does water or rain.

You can release the negativity in a drop of water or an ocean full, while you wash your hands or take a shower. Simply *will* all the garbage and dissension into the water, or swim and bind it there by commanding it so.

• When it *rains*, the atmosphere is charged with energy.

BATHROOM THERAPY: WATER, WATER, EVERYWHERE, BUT *PLEASE* DO NOT DRINK!

EUCALYPTUS FLOW

METHODS:
Total relaxation . . . sit on it!

1. Make a steam room with hot water as you draw a bath.
2. Put eucalyptus oil in the bath (do as the Egyptians). It will open your pores and allow the flow of energy to drain out negative energy from fatigue.

CRYSTAL BATH FOR THE HEAD

METHOD:

1. Put four quarts of quartz crystals around the tub, using all four corners.
2. Add sea salt in a glass and sniff the salt water. It will purify your nasal, throat, and sinus tracts. This is also good for colds.
   Salt is a basic purifier. Nature knows what it is doing.

WHIRLPOOL BATH WITH CELLS OF SOUND

METHOD:

1. Draw a bath and feel its hot goodness as you "melt" in the tub.
2. Ask your guides to help you start creating a circle or whirlpool of energies starting from the outer perimeter of the tub. Create in your mind the circles moving clockwise, outer circles larger than the small ones around your body.

3. Start to sing out loud while you feel this whirlpool motion and feel the sound of your voice circulating in that energy body of water.
4. Feel the energized water circulating, and hear the sound of each cell being nourished as the frequency of the sound waves works through your body.

KUNDALINI BATH
(For Base Chakra or spine)

INGREDIENTS:
3 beryl gemstones
Epsom salts

While bathing with beryl and Epsom salts, be conscious of inhaling the vapors. It should stimulate the Base Chakra (at the base of your spine) as a test point. On an anatomical level it is applicable to the intestinal tract and cardiovascular system, and can prevent hardening of arteries or hemorrhaging. Also, restoration of the skin's elasticity can be obtained.

CORAL BATH

With coral in the tub, this bath will help to alleviate arthritic pain.

TALC BATH

Bathe with talc chunks, sea salt, or Epsom salts added to the water.
   Float talc chunks on the water and imagine yourself to be in an isolated, abandoned pyramid.
   Your male and female qualities or androgynous state will be balanced.

COLD WATER TREADING IN TUB

PURPOSE:

• Headaches
• Insomnia
• Rundown feeling and nervous problems
• Poor circulation

PROCEDURE:
In the morning; walk back and forth in a cold-water tub, mid-calf high, for five minutes. Dry off and get on with your daily activity.

FULL-TUB TECHNIQUE

PURPOSE:

• Head cold
• Nervous conditions

PROCEDURE:
Sit in the tub with two inches of water (85 degrees). Lie down in it, turn on the cold water, and relax as the cold water fills the tub, coming up to your chin. Then, turn off the water and keep as still and relaxed as possible for twenty minutes.

Do this once in the morning and once at night and it will turn off your cold.

EPSOM SALTS BATH

PURPOSE:
This helps rid you of toxins and poisons in your body. Good for lumbago, sciatica, rheumatism, colds, and neuritis. Softens the skin.

Warning: Do not take Epsom salts bath if you have a heart problem of any kind.

PROCEDURE:

• Run a hot tub with about two inches of water.
• Add one pound of Epsom salts.
• Mix salts into the water, then sit in the tub.
• Add more water, and as you do, start rubbing yourself all over with a saltwater washcloth.
• Add more hot water and relax.
• If you begin to sweat, get out. The treatment is terminated. Stand up and take a quick cold shower and rub down your body with a dry coarse towel. Rub from head to toe.

BATH CURE FOR INDIGESTION

Relaxation Bath:

- Put hot water in the bathtub.
- Add pine oil for fragrance.
- Sit in this hot water for no more than thirty minutes.
- Your digestive mechanism will be organized.

"CLEAR MENUS" WATER BATHS

SPRING WATER AND PURE ESSENCE FLOWER BATH

By adding some bottled spring water to your bath, perhaps four to five gallons with a tub full of tap water, you can raise your spiritual vibrations and increase your sensitivity. You can also add pure flower essences—pure white—or place only white flowers and petals into your tub. It will heighten your sense of being. (Lilies, gardenias, white roses, and daisies are good for this.)

GEMSTONE BATH
(A toner to tune up Chakra system for balance)

Add at least the twelve stones of the zodiac to your bath water: garnet, amethyst, diamond (herkimer or crystal will do), emerald, ruby, topaz, tiger's eye, lapis, peridot, sapphire, rose quartz, and carnelian. All can be bought very inexpensively in a lapidary shop. *Say a prayer* while in your mind you wrap your bathtub up with white light.

> Condition me, oh Lord, with your vibrant
>   rays of life from the earth.
> Raise my energies and attune them to my
>   highest spiritual centers.

This heightens the sensitivity of the spiritual centers (Chakras). Color rays attract healing to the tissues and act as an aid for the magnetic healing from the poles to align with your own meridian points.

INITIATION BATH

Every choice that we make regarding spiritual law should always become a ritual. It is through ritual that our needs are met. At the same time each day, praying a certain way, for a certain purpose, calling in Divine help, all constitutes the word *ritual*. Rituals must incorporate our needs. Always say the same thing: "The Divine energies of God are put into the ingredients with the minerals in this tub. God is in the center of this experience."

This is for the advanced occultists who are in the process of having their energies upgraded and going through an intense initiation. You'll know who you are!

- Mineral water
- Cleansing herb (hyssop or rue)
- Ginseng tea (draws out poisons in body)
- 1 teaspoon herb in:
- 1 cup boiling water
- Strain
- ½ tub water

PSYCHIC TENSION BATH

For healing without soap:
   Soak for twenty minutes.
   This will release psychic tension and heal physically as well.

- 1 cup baking soda
- ½ cup Epsom salts
- 2 tbsp. sea salt (table salt will do, too)

FOR ALL THESE BATHS

Chant: "HA-JO-HA," to call in the energies of the Father.
   Chant the vibrations of these sounds twelve times when first entering the bath water.

POWER PERFUME BATH

Want your power back and all negativity that has clung to your body removed?

RECIPE:

Fill the tub to the brim with lots of water, any temperature you like.

Add 1 cap of Clorox bleach.

Sprinkle small handful of kosher or coarse salt into water.

Add a drop of your best perfume, or one drop of White Flower oil.

If you can manage to hold your nose and dip under the water until entirely immersed before you climb out of the tub, do so! Remember to keep your eyes closed.

11

Gem Therapy

**Look under each stone in your path right now,
as you will find others of the same
size, color, and dimension.**

**A stone that can soften remaining intact is
often a miracle you can trace back.**

GEMS: THE TREASURES OF
THE EARTH'S ENERGY STOREHOUSE

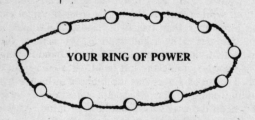

YOUR RING OF POWER

GEM THERAPY
Body • Baubles • Beads

The beauty of magic stones is that they benefit both body and
mind. They act as attitude- and health-balancing aids and for the
body's adornment.

154

Gems and stones raise the body's electrical frequency and amplify bodily energies for our benefit. Through history, many monarchs, religions, and empires have used gemstones. This has been principally for beauty, for adornment, but also for the active use the gem had on its wearer. There have been many superstitions regarding the use of gemstones. In some cultures, some gems were considered worthless, while another culture thought them priceless and used them for ritualistic purposes. Some had great legendary power and were used as energy generators. Gems were used as healing devices as well as energy magnifiers and, certainly, as protective amulets.

Every object, animate or inanimate, is surrounded by its own energy field, but a *stone* or *gem* usually has an energy range of effectiveness at about three feet. Whether you wear it or keep the stone in a range of three feet around you, it has an influence on your person.

Wearing a stone serves a double purpose. The head has a different energy, and the neck and each finger also act as individual energy conductors. As a rule, what I have discovered is that the thumb should never have a jewel on it since the thumb relates to your free will and shouldn't be hampered. Gems worn on the neck have a total effect on your energy field and should be given great care when chosen. They have an effect on your desires as well. Jeweled belts and buckles can affect your vitality forces. A stone such as a turquoise can relax and calm your midsection, while others will increase your physical endurance.

Also, remember that the two hands, right and left, have different energies. The right hand is for action, the left for receiving sensitivity or response. The right hand is outgoing (the sender of energy), while the left hand takes energy in and is the receiver. The index finger has the highest influence in receiving and sending energy. The wrists are a matter of choice. Don't wear stones on the wrists to stimulate your mind. As you will see in this chapter, some gems have tranquil effects, some protective, and some do trigger off energy to different parts of the body depending on the metal used in the gem's setting. Gems worn on the ears can influence perception and discernment. Remember, any stones carried in your handbag, attaché case, or personal pouch will have an influence only if they are kept within three feet of you.

Each stone has healing powers that can pertain to certain body organs and emotions. Holding or wearing the right stone at the right time can provide a shield against bad influences. What do you buy? What will work for you? First, rely on your instincts, what appeals to your eye, but do not rely on looks alone. Pick up the stone and feel it in your hands. Do you like the weight and shape of it? Sense anything special about it? Go to a good mineral store to buy, or perhaps to the gift department of a natural history museum.

UNDERSTANDING GEMSTONES

For healing and esoteric usage in coordination with the body, mental, physical, emotional, and spiritual applications:

- Gemstones have psychic vibrations and shield against negative energy.
- Gemstones have a great value to work to benefit either with energy or therapeutically.
- If you are attracted to it, *wear it*.
- If you like it, *get it!*

Our bodies, like the Universe, are atomic in nature. Outside stimuli such as rocks, gems, and metals create an electromagnetic influence that affects our bodies. These are aids to the soul's growth as they strengthen and guide the will of an individual. They add energy, healing agents, vitality, and luster to our upliftment and existence.

PSYCHIC AND SPIRITUAL VALUE
OF GEMSTONES FOR HEALING

Minerals were the first life form on this planet, long before the plant kingdom. The latter is more integrated and better self-adjusted on this plane. Gemstones were put here from the beginning of time itself for future use in healing and conscious growth. They contain properties that can have a direct correlation within an individual's vibration and that are based on our sympathetic molecular structure. Gemstones can stimulate the healing within a physical body based on the principles of resonancy or harmony and vibration. These harmonics in "empty space" or the air generate fields of an electromagnetic and electrical nature, so that a being's force field is activated. It works as an energy transfer if utilized as such.

Some stones work within a person's specific points of anatomy to which their healing properties are attributed. Certain minerals work on specific organs.

I wish to impress on you that fact of how gems work through thought amplification. As the thought form passes from our minds into our crystalline structure it gains empathy with it. The thought form is then received deeper into the body physical, thus completing the connection between the vibration of the gemstone and the biomolecular level of the individual. This amplified form of resonancy occurs when the mind creates or shapes into a living form a structure through the process of meditation. It can stimulate a person's vibration when thought through, can influence specific Chakras or energy points on specific areas of the physical body. The gemstones can be used to get into the vibrational frequencies through the meridian points and amplify the healing faster. Tremendous activity occurs as the gem acts as a kind of laser beam. The Atlantean and Lemurian cultures capitalized on using gems in this fashion for all healing purposes and the raising of consciousness to understand higher concepts of the Universe, including achievement of extraordinary extrasensory perception.

Gemstones do draw the physical body up to higher spiritual levels by working with the body's own natural evolution toward the crystalline dynamics. It integrates with the body's own cell salts and the parts of the physical that contain crystalline and quartzlike properties, especially the Chakra associated with the pineal gland, which activates higher consciousness. Diseases in ancient times were eradicated with the proper use of crystals and gemstones, and often removed a person's imbalances.

Understand: history always repeats itself. There is nothing new in our vast Universe, only that which has to be reopened and tapped in to again. We are now, at this point in our evolution, ready to receive all of its blessings. Our ancient recorded cultures—from Egypt, Babylon, China, to Persia and the Aztecs and Toltecs—were inspired by the records from Lemuria and Atlantis but developed their own specialized forms. Gems were used in healing, as well as to increase the capacity for levitation and to develop technologies that produced sources of electrical power. These things contributed to a more highly advanced society, and paved the way for the development of good for man to advance our planet.

GEMSTONE: AGATE

Color and Description

Variegated chalcedony, showing colored bands, spots, and markings. They appear in many colors.

Use and Benefits for Healing and Therapeutic Use

For health, wealth, and longevity, as an attitude-balancing aid for the physical and emotional changes.

- Guards the wearer against danger.
- Drives away bad dreams.
- Banishes fear; makes wearer more agreeable and persuasive.
- Cures insomnia.
- Helps with vision and the hardening of the gums.

VARIETIES OF AGATE

Banded—Attracts strength and courage especially when energy is drained.

Blue lace—Emotional, as it works with the body fluids.

Carnelian—Provides protein and endurance. Helps with anorexia nervosa.

Dendrite—Traveler's stone for security. Good for safe car and air travel. Elevates blood sugar level.

Eye—Counteracts negative thinking. Protects from bodily harm.

India—Offsets physical and emotional weakness. Gives psychic strength.

Lace—Stimulates happiness. Relaxes muscular tensions and spasms.

Moss green—Balances discordant emotional energies. Detoxifies the blood, lymphatic swelling, sinuses.

Moss red—Increases physical stamina. Purifies and influences the flow of blood.

Plume—Decreases fear in job hunting or direction finding. Strengthens the veins.

Tree—Helps relieve tensions. Reduces fevers and toxins.

GEMSTONE: AGATE (BOTSWANA)

Color and Description

Shades of pink and yellow to gray with unusual markings in the form of an eye. Only found in Botswana, Africa.

Use and Benefits for Healing and Therapeutic Use

- Used as a protection against strain and stress.
- Can go through the doors of extraterrestrial realms by looking into the higher frequencies, thereby putting yourself into a higher altered state.
- If you need added insight on a problem, it can unlock a pathway to psychic worlds by tuning in to the right-brain capacities. There is usually a keeper of the doorway or guide to help you do this. When you center yourself to get inside, this stone's effects can stretch the mind and aid insight to higher worlds.
- Botswana agate aids in the complete reoxygenation of the physical—any area needing oxygen, such as glands, red corpuscles, and lungs. Helps with tissue regeneration or smoke damage and inhalation. Good for drowning victims; also used for overexposure to X rays.
- Put in bathtub for emotional body to be eased and balanced. A few work with it in tub for throat area to be balanced, too.

GEMSTONE: ADVENTURINE

Color and Description

A variety of translucent quartz; green, blue, red, or white spangled throughout with scales of yellow mica. Found in India and several South American countries.

Use and Benefits for Healing and Therapeutic Use

- Cleanses the Etheric, emotional, and mental bodies.
- Stimulates opportunity and motivation.
- Increases perception.
- Creates insight.
- Used to aid near-sightedness.

- Used for good luck and wealth.
- Adventurine specifically alleviates psychosomatic illnesses. Especially works on buried fears that originate in the first seven years of childhood (current life, not a past life).
- Good for psychotherapy in developing a more positive outlook on life and emotional tranquility. Creative visualization increases. Heart and throat Chakras open.
- Amplify the properties by placing beneath a conical structure and bathing it in a blue light for ten to fifteen minutes.
- This is an androgynous stone but feminine qualities are slightly accentuated.
- A child can meditate with it nicely.

GEMSTONE: ALEXANDRITE

Color and Description

Red, green, or orange-yellow.

Use and Benefits for Healing and Therapeutic Use

- Best for the nervous system (spleen, pancreas, testicles).
- Diseases of central nervous system such as lymph adenoma, spleen disorders, leukemia (can assimilate some forms of protein).
- Ability to appreciate joy can be induced while wearing alexandrite.
- The mental, emotional, and Etheric bodies are aligned to create a more relaxed emotional state.

GEMSTONE: AMBER

Color and Description

A yellow or brownish yellow translucent stone. Found in alluvial soils and on some seashores.

Use and Benefits for Healing and Therapeutic Use

- Soothes nervous system and relates to electromagnetism, Prana, and Etheric power.
- Lifts the spirits.
- Reduces fluid retention and helps to detoxify the urinary system.

- Good for throat problems, asthma, and aiding of kidneys and liver.
- A key to Earth's stability. A ground force and anchor. Possesses powerful magnetic electricity. Polarizes healing magnetism, that which contacts and contracts it.
- In ancient times, was ground into a powder and added to water to make a potion that would relieve stomach pains.
- Eastern people believe that amber is a filter against germs and infections and has the power to disinfect.
- Often worn around the neck to help fight respiratory diseases and infections.
- All-around healer, especially helpful in memory loss, inability to make decisions, and problems with thyroid and inner ear.

Miscellaneous

- Harmonizes, helps balance your Yin and Yang aspects.
- Activates altruistic and passive nature.
- Spiritualizes the intellect as it opens the brow and emotional Chakras. Aligns and stimulates the mental body to proceed toward elevating the spiritual body.

GEMSTONE: AMETHYST

Color and Description

Purple or violet variety of quartz (crytop-crystalline).

Use and Benefits for Healing and Therapeutic Use

- The Greeks believed amethyst to be the preventative of intoxication and was meant to be a protection from overindulgence as it resembled the color of the grape.
- It is known to have a calming and soothing effect when worn or applied to the physical body, as it controls the temperament and its depth of feeling is constancy. Improves the memory.
- Relieves nervous headaches, pain, and tension, as it has an effect on the brain to induce mental clarity and to aid in meditation to lift the spirit. We can say that it is a master key to transformation as used as a direct hook-up between the brain and nervous center that brings about adjustments in ourselves and is used in integration of these systems to bring on healing of the feeling centers and brain.
- Purifies blood.

Miscellaneous

- Ultraviolet. Can act as a purifying ray and as a disinfectant. Remove mental or emotional energy blocks.
- Stimulates intuitive awareness, and increases it as a thought amplifier.
- Good for expelling all types of poison and generally toning the body.
- Wear amethyst preferably touching your skin, as a necklace, ring, or bracelet. All stones must touch the skin for them to do any good.
- Augments the activity of the pancreas, pituitary, thymus, and thyroid glands.
- Metabolism is balanced while it stimulates the midbrain and right-brain activity.
- The pineal and pituitary glands are enhanced. Helps even a collapse of the immune system and those diseases influencing blood-sugar levels, such as hypoglycemia and diabetes.
- Offers protection against radiation.
- Spiritually, it is good for people with low self-esteem and a sense of feeling off center. It enhances meditation and an awareness of God.
- Benefits those who need to feel a visionary capacity, for or greater attunement of the God energy within, especially if one feels that he/she is battling with atheism.

GEMSTONE: AQUAMARINE

Color and Description

Pale, bluish green.

Use and Benefits for Healing and Therapeutic Use

- Cleanses liver, spleen, thyroid, and kidneys. White corpuscles are stimulated in association with the spleen.
- The gemstone of sailors, aquamarine is believed to possess the calming effects of the sea; soothing and cleansing. Take it with you when you travel on water.
- Aids eyesight and reduces fluid retention.
- Acts as a stabilizer and has calming vibrations for nerves and spirit and balances an individual's feelings.

- Good for the protection of newborn babies.
- Helps stabilize fluctuating or ambivalent personalities.
- Relieves ailments of:
  - stomach
  - jaws
  - liver
  - throat ⎫
  - spleen ⎭ Chakras can open
- Used to rid oneself of disorientation and disarray.

Miscellaneous

- Charge aquamarine in direct sunlight with copper around it for a period of eight to twenty-four hours. It will amplify the stone's activity and aid in the filtering process of the body for each individual.
- An inspirational stone especially for the expression of self, as it reduces fear and an inability to express oneself. It opens the doorway to mind, body, and spirit.
- Feminine qualities are enhanced with the use of this gem.

GEMSTONE: BERYL

Color and Description

Unusual shade of green, with a resinous luster. Can appear in shades of yellow, blue, and white, also.

Use and Benefits for Healing and Therapeutic Use

- Banishes fear.
- Enhances happiness and long-lasting youth.
- Good for liver complaints.
- Amulets worn of beryl can quicken the intellect and cure a person of laziness, hiccups, bowel cancer, eye diseases, and swollen glands.
- Pituitary gland is strengthened.
- Helps anxiety and overstimulation of the mind-set.
- Can act as a sedative in its ability to ease tensions of the physical body.
- Aids in the absorption of nutrients, silica, silicon, zinc, and vitamins A and E.

GEMSTONE: BLOODSTONE

Color and Description

Semiprecious dark green variety of quartz, spotted with red jasper. Becoming a major gemstone in our time.

Use and Benefits for Healing and Therapeutic Use:

- Gives wisdom and courage.
- Relieves urinary troubles.
- Protects against sunstroke and headaches.
- Stops hemorrhaging of a wound or injury. Perfect for nosebleeds when applied directly to nose.
- Clears bloodshot eyes.
- Use for removing *energy blocks* and circulates energy on all levels for an all-around flow to help healing begin. Removes *emotional blocks* and limitations too.
- Combats physical traumas.
- Stimulates blood circulation.

Miscellaneous

- Has a use similar to that of the ruby and can protect against spells and negative hypnosis attack.
- Legend explains that bloodstone was formed at the crucifixion of Christ. Blood from his wounds dripped to the ground and solidified in the green earth. Hence, the name for this green stone with spots of red jasper. Some say it has the power to bring the mental self into balance to give wisdom and courage and provides a righteous shield against the "evil eye."
- Bloodstone's effects are similar to those of niacin.
- Wear bloodstone close to ear lobes, as it generates and connects the conscious mind directly to the circulatory flows and increases the capacity to mentally send the blood to specific parts of the body.
- Can be good with biofeedback.
- Said to help ease acute stomach and bowel pain, and also leukemia if worked in conjunction with professional therapy.

GEMSTONE: CARNELIAN

Color and Description

Ranges from light to dark orange, or can be red, brownish red, or brownish orange.

Use and Benefits for Healing and Therapeutic Use

- Helps as blood purifier.
- Capillary and respiratory systems are strengthened. Tissue regeneration, elasticity of blood vessels, and other cellular tissue.
- For eye diseases, epilepsy, tender gums, boils, ulcers, indigestion. For all imbalances of kidneys, lungs, and spleen.
- Prevents misfortune.
- For good luck and general contentment—receptivity for self.
- Often called an endurance stone.
- Prevents against "evil eye" and helps maintain a good sense of humor.
- Activates the sense of touch.

Miscellaneous

- Properties similar to those of varieties of bloodstone and agate.

GEMSTONE: CORAL

Color and Description

Ranges from red to white, including all shades of pink and orange.

Use and Benefits for Healing and Therapeutic Use

- When worn around the neck can be a protection against upper respiratory infections.
- Known to turn pale in color when wearer becomes sick and regains color when wearer is healthy.
- Used for balancing physical endurance and physical energy as it relieves tensions.
- Effective as a blood cleanser that helps prevent stomach cramps and indigestion.

- Worn around the neck, helps relieve throat and voice ailments.
- Mystics believed that it averts the "evil eye" when worn around the necks of children.
- Good for healing scars and ulcers.
- It aids in evolution of the ego and humanizes you.
- Helps diseased gums, nightmares, bile problems, and mucous membrane secretions, and is astringent.
- Since coral is exposed to sea salt, an odic barrier is created around each coral. This odic force promotes free flow through its highly conductive properties and draws salt water through air, advanced conductor.
- Good for strenghtening the heart and circulatory system.
- Capillary action increases.
- Red coral differs from coral as it stimulates metabolism by activating the thyroid. Steps up expulsion of toxins. Emotions are better expressed, too.
- Pink coral increases one's sensitivity and is good for spine and the sympathetic nervous system.
- *Nutrient properties* influenced include silica, vitamin E, cholesterol, lecithin, and protein.
- Tape to the brow Chakra for a few hours to release these energies.

GEMSTONE: CRYSTAL

Color and Description

Crystal is the clearest form of quartz (see Chapter 12). All crystals emit color rays. The clear, pure crystal of quartz also has common varieties of color and transparencies. They are clear pink, red, purple, yellow, smoky, and black.

Use and Benefits for Healing and Therapeutic Use

- A personal healer for the mind and body associated with the spirit forces and an energy power.
- Crystal energy is good for healing in all aspects—spiritual, emotional, and physical. Pure crystal is essentially used for the absorption of energy to be utilized for power. As a power source, for electricity, a source for generators in the future.
- Amplifies and purifies surrounding energies in healing, meditation, and psychic work. Crystals have the ability to align one's

consciousness with the electromagnetic energies of the Universe. It not only stores energy but heals and is used for other spiritual matters as well.
• Some practical uses: enhances clarity of the mind, banishes insomnia, protects against infection, elevates thoughts, releases bad habits, combats negativity, relieves pain, reduces fevers, and breaks up detrimental habits of smoking and drinking.

Miscellaneous

• Held in high esteem for centuries, especially utilized on the continent of Atlantis for its elevating and healing properties.
• When worn or carried around the neck it is a high spiritual protector, as it has limitless energy. It purifies and amplifies from the source of all light, provides sonic protection against negativity.
• Clear quartz is identified with magic for crystal gazing, as many psychics can see images or pictures in it.

GEMSTONE: DENDRITE

Color and Description

Shades of blue/green.

Use and Benefits for Healing and Therapeutic Use

• Strengthens the security of one's physical body.
• Used as a traveler's stone that goes with you wherever you are. Good in a car or in any motorized vehicle, protects you from bodily harm.

GEMSTONE: DIAMOND

Color and Description

Diamonds are transparent crystals of pure carbon.

Use and Benefits for Healing and Therapeutic Use

• Known for its power of refracting light, has purity, and gives comfort.

- Diamonds have no color of their own, no psychic power, and no inherent healing properties.
- Reflects light and thought, both positive and negative. They are also known to absorb through vibrations. They may *not* be your best friend. It all depends upon whose thoughts the gem holds for the receiver. It may be cleansed of all negative vibrations by soaking overnight in an ionic solution of a teaspoon of salt and a teaspoon of baking soda in eight ounces of water, followed by a clear-water rinse. Used as a true love-bearing gift, engagement or wedding ring, as this ensures the wearer of security.
- If one can bear the responsibility from the radiations wearing a diamond can bring, the self can be drawn upon and magnified by the mind. Your feelings, thoughts, and energy patterns give you a magical sense of upliftment.
- Diamonds give a sense of desire for the finer things in life. If that is how you feel, then it can be a powerful amulet for you. Thoughts of negative power can have a reverse effect for the diamond wearer.

Miscellaneous

Usage for healing and spiritual growth:

- A diamond can be a master healer and the most neutral of all gemstones. The brilliance is in its light. It does not amplify or unify but is powerful for the removal of blockages and negativity in the Crown Chakra and in the personality.
- A diamond, being crystallized carbon, adjusts the cranial plates and is focused on the brain. Place by the medulla oblongata, temple, or at the top of the head. Then meditate. There should be an alteration in the muscle structure of the jaw and shoulder blades. Tensions should be released. It has a self-adjusting balance as it improves the circulation.
- On the cellular level, diamonds can have a slight impact on the RNA activity between individual neutrons and the cranial capacity. Diamonds radiate energy and assimulate energy. They broadcast thought forms and can draw toxins out of the body, but use them with other gemstones to increase vibrational properties in the cleansing process.
- A diamond can be powerful, so use with caution, as it can

radiate too much energy if used in conjunction with the throat
and heart Chakras.
* Amplifies all emotions—jealousy, anger, and feelings of security.
* In symbology, a diamond means you have evolved to the
  highest degree of learning. Diamonds contain curses more than
  any other stone. Wear them only with purity of heart, inno-
  cence, and mental clarity.

GEMSTONE: EMERALD

Color and Description

A precious stone of the beryl variety; rich bright green and
highly valued.

Use and Benefits for Healing and Therapeutic Use

* Stimulates truth and perception and promotes creativity.
* Enhances wisdom and strength.
* Aids neurological diseases.
* Used in the healing of the eyes.
* Used for antiseptic and cleansing purposes, as it is believed to
  contain chlorophyll.
* Strengthens adrenal glands.
* Helps to improve memory if meditated on and acts as a medita-
  tion balancer.
* Prevents diabetes, strengthens heart, kidneys, liver, and pancreas.
* For medicinal purposes it can be ground and crushed to a fine
  powder and dissolved in water for use as an antidote to poison,
  a salve for wounds and sores, or a lotion applied to eyelids.
* Balances the heart Chakra, which is the test point. The Etheric,
  Astral, and emotional bodies are aligned, giving insights into
  developing dreams. Increases psychic and clairvoyant faculties.
* People with paranoia, schizophrenia, and severe mental illness
  should be treated with emeralds.
* Heart and kidney meridians are strengthened.

Miscellaneous

* The emerald, like the diamond, harmonizes with all the rays of
  color energy in your body to cope with the physical, mental,
  and, especially, emotional equilibrium. It can help the wearer

ascend into higher levels of consciousness if you put yourself into an energy spiral. Inspires and balances, but doesn't purify energies.

- Tauruses and Libras especially benefit with this stone. The force field of the green spectrum uplifts them as it is especially therapeutic. Capricorns, be careful!
- Emeralds have long been considered the gem of great price. Additionally, they provide gifts of perception, insight, hindsight, and foresight.

GEMSTONE: FLUORITE

Color and Description

Delicate pink, blue, green, gray, and yellow.

Use and Benefits for Healing and Therapeutic Use

- Grounds excess energy and allows more efficiency. It is best used with copper and silver for healing the physical body as it is a strengthener.
- Acts as a catalyst, a transmuting agent.
- Wear close to tooth enamel or by the ear lobes.
- Expose to a blue light for a half-hour to amplify its properties.
- Strengthens bone tissue and stimulates the mucous membrane tissues and inside lung tissues, viral inflammation.
- A strengthener, too, for the ability to perceive a higher understanding of reality.

GEMSTONE: GARNET

Color and Description

Deep transparent red (wine).

Use and Benefits for Healing and Therapeutic Use

- Known to stimulate success in business endeavors, as it enhances self-esteem.
- Can influence the action of the pituitary gland, and affects balance and thyroid disorders. A preventative against arthritis. Good for the cells and treating precancerous conditions.

- *Body correspondence*: Aligns with the spinal column and blood-stream fluids. Helps the spine.
- A master regulator polarized to the Base Chakra, completing its own circuitry with the spinal column. Garnet becomes the middleman or transmitter between the self and gem energies entering the orbital field.
- *Keynote*: Garnet is important for integration and regeneration. It integrates the past and future for a high level of vitality to balance your energy field. Test point is the brow Chakra. On the physical level, it increases capillary action, especially with the lung tissue and flexibility in the skin tissue. Assimilates vitamins A and B complex.

Miscellaneous

- A general stimulant but has very little psychic vibration for contacting the cosmic consciousness. It would be best to use a ruby instead as a stimulant.
- Wear this stone by the heart or ear lobes.

GEMSTONE: HERKIMER DIAMOND

Color and Description

Colorless, crystalline in structure. The name comes from where the stone is found: Herkimer, New York. Looks like diamond or quartz.

Use and Benefits for Healing and Therapeutic Use

- Used in healing and conscious growth and releases stress and tension throughout the physical body, especially in muscle tissue.
- Herkimer broadcasts energy. Good to keep next to diamonds as energy is enhanced. It can gather the toxins in the body and allow them to be eliminated properly, balancing all.
- Spiritual effects are similar to those of quartz. It stimulates clairvoyance, healing ability, and balance within the individual. Also, draws forth memories of past lives.
- It is a double-terminated stone. Good for using as a pendulum to scan the body and draw out toxins. Auric cleansing takes place, too. When the pendulum turns counterclockwise, toxic-

ity is present; when the movement is clockwise, a healthy pattern of energy is present. The movement of the pendulum circles itself around the physical body and helps to balance the Chakra points.
- The Herkimer diamond can store information like quartz and because of its two pointed ends can release energy that is stagnant as good energy is felt in its vibrations.

GEMSTONE: IVORY

Color and Description

Creamy white, sometimes pinkish.

Use and Benefits for Healing and Therapeutic Use

- Promotes spiritual protection and protects physical body from injury. Stimulates bone tissue regeneration.
- Promotes an abundance of red corpuscles and also eliminates toxins.
- Certain races seem to benefit from it. Attracts physical things and is good for the animal magnetism in some people. For the sensitive being, it could be disastrous, and can cause conflict and emotional disturbance. Be careful with ivory: it can attract voodoo energies, as it comes from various parts of a lower negative place in the world.

Miscellaneous

- Not actually considered a gem but rather an extension of the animal that produced it.
- People who need to exert inner discipline should wear it.
- Can alleviate anger and frustration.

GEMSTONE: JADE (GREEN)

Color and Description

Various shades of green.

Use and Benefits for Healing and Therapeutic Use

- Inspires mind and good fortune.
- Stimulates widsom, practicality, and feelings.

- Takes a long time to work into body systems as it is a consciousness raiser.
- Promotes healing of vital organs; soothes eyes and nervous system.
- Helps strengthen muscles and articulate feelings.

Miscellaneous

- Good for water-sign people (Pisces, Cancer, Scorpio).
- Chinese associate green jade with occult wisdom. It is said to inspire the mind to make a precise decision.

GEMSTONE: JADE (RED)

Use and Benefits for Healing and Therapeutic Use:

- Used only as a healer.
- Combats female disorders, particularly the ovarian and uterine functions.

GEMSTONE: JADEITE (GREEN JADE)

Miscellaneous

- Sold in this country as jade and is a good stone to a certain degree. Used in Yoga or primary development, jade is good. However, it cannot stand up to high teachings.

GEMSTONE: JASPER

Color and Description

Opaque variety of quartz, green, red, yellow, or brown. When colors are in stripes or bands, it is called banded or striped jasper. When it has layers of chalcedony, it is called agate jasper.

Use and Benefits for Healing and Therapeutic Use

- Eases emotional stress and upsets. Works with the gastric system.
- Helps with pancreatic disorders, hormonal problems.

- Aids intestinal functions. Reduces constipation and intestinal spasms. Good for combating ulcer problems, too.
- Stimulates the use of smell.

GEMSTONE: JASPER (RED)

Color and Description

Orange-red. An agate that is porous. Good for stress, a balancing of the physical body.

Use and Benefits for Healing and Therapeutic Use:

- Balances gastric and pancreatic disorders
- Protects against external stresses to influence hormonal problems in the *physical body*.

GEMSTONE: JASPER (GREEN)

Color and Description

Green shade that carries an Earth feeling.

Use and Benefits for Healing and Therapeutic Use

- Promotes a positive *mental* attitude for understanding people's needs.
- Can help with intestinal functions and spasms, ulcers, and constipation.

GEMSTONE: JASPER (BROWN)

Use and Benefits for Healing and Therapeutic Use

- *Decrystalizes* conceptual illusions. Especially good for emotional security.
- Aids female hormonal functions as it works with internal organs (also skin, kidneys, thymus, neurological tissues).
- Lowers immune system problems and premature aging.
- Treats allergies and skin conditions.
- Sleep with it after meditating as it can be helpful to stimulate psychic faculties. Use it to connect with a past life recall to bring oneself to the present life.

- Wear often by the heart, throat, or on ear lobes, as it will stimulate the throat and pituitary Chakras to clear one's thinking and actions.
- Expose it together with quartz crystals as a family to heighten its energies.

GEMSTONE: JASPER (YELLOW)

Color and Description

The yellow is due to sulfuric oxide that on the Etheric and physical levels creates a force field that works as a disinfectant (bowels, colon, or intestinal tract), especially when used in conjunction with other gems of a physical nature.

Use and Benefits for Healing and Therapeutic Use

- On physical and cellular levels, it can stimulate general tissue regeneration.
- Good for burn victims.
- A high-quality gemstone that can provide help with the proper nutrients including a raise with the energies of vitamins A, B, and E, and aluminum, magnesium, and zinc. Test it on top of the head, under tongue, and ear lobe areas.

GEMSTONE: LAPIS LAZULI

Color and Description

Deep royal blue with traces of pyrite and white calcite.

Use and Benefits for Healing and Therapeutic Use

- Lapis has a psychic cleansing energy to open our channels otherwise blocked and not utilized, and also develops inner discipline.
- Very *powerful*—it energizes the throat Chakra area by the thyroid as it also aligns the Etheric, mental, and spiritual bodies.
- Helps those who are autistic deal with reality. Shy, retiring, laid-back individuals also benefit from the use of this stone. It can tap in to the higher self and release blocked emotions.

- Brings your thoughts together and helps in speaking out. Especially good as a meditation stone. Best in a cone or pyramid shape for this cleansing process.
- Activates pituitary and thymus glands. Use for diseases on this area.
- Good for general health of the body and stimulates creativity.
- Has very powerful stimulation for mental vibrations, as it is excellent during contemplation and meditation exercises as well as Universal insight.
- The ESP centers expand with lapis, and the physical and Etheric bodies respond to it for the opening of the spiritual centers of man. Lapis is the epitomizer of our awareness and lifts our efforts up the ladder of higher achievement. It is used as an integrator with the highest intuitions of the mind and intelligence centers. The lapis atoms contain a polarization factor and adhere to the neutron factor, the Law of Equilibrium. It gives us structure. It oscillates to our higher frequencies, resonates to the ductless fields, relays to our intuitive substance, and opens the doorway of instantaneous knowledge with no reason or logic thinking.

Miscellaneous

- Practically, the lapis will stimulate the sixth sense of creativity, giving the wearer an inner sense of truthfulness, wisdom, and Universal insight.
- It is suggested that lapis be worn on the hand or around the neck because it has very powerful stimulation to the mental vibrations. It would be best not worn on the ear or facial areas as it is very strong and should be used only for short periods of time.

GEMSTONE: MOONSTONE

Color and Description

Soft, fluidlike translucent substance of milky white, light gray, or rose. Pearly moonlike luster.

Use and Benefits for Healing and Therapeutic Use

- Opens the heart to humanitarian love and brings forth experiences while protecting sensitive natures.

- Moonstone can be placed on the vertebrae and will help the breathing process during childbirth.
- For tensions in the abdominal area to be released, wear over the solar plexus region. Especially effective during time of new or full moon.
- Worn on the ring finger, will help strengthen meridians in the body.
- A woman's stone, as it strengthens female emotional energy and power over intuition. Magical qualities associated with the moon and female energy. A water-retention stone that helps those with premenstrual problems to regulate pituitary gland and stimulate pineal gland function. It works with female imbalances to clear lymph glands when blocked, and in pelvic disorders helps rid body of toxins.
- *Body correspondence*: Digestion and assimilation.
- Pituitary gland secretion is enhanced.
- Used for trances, mediumship, and as an aid to letting go. Place it on your third eye to meditate for Astral projection.

Miscellaneous

- Moonstone acts as the "mother" of our subconscious mind, connecting the intuitive essence to a practical basis and interacting with self-confidence.
- Increases access to the subconscious mind.

GEMSTONE: OBSIDIAN

Color and Description

Shiny black and often translucent. A hard glassy volcanic rock from lava flow.

Use and Benefits for Healing and Therapeutic Use

- Some use obsidian as an amulet. A protection stone and an aid in balancing effects of the outside stress on the emotions. It provides protection for the supersensitive and boosts immunity only.
- Acts as a shield against fearful thoughts and deep depression.
- Meridians and nadis are strengthened and masculine qualities accentuated.

- Testing point is the heel of the foot.
- Balances the stomach, fights viral and bacteria inflammations as well.

GEMSTONE: ONYX AND SARDONYX

Color and Description

Veined, opaque quartz gemstone in shades of white or natural black.

Use and Benefits for Healing and Therapeutic Use

- Onyx is not a receiver of energy and can handle a lot of negativity and at the same time pick up a positive frequency.
- It stimulates self-control and acts as an asset to physical coordination. Its low-level frequency serves the human race as it stabilizes earth's atmosphere.
- Helpful for the person who needs greater balance and help in *letting go* of difficult relationships.
- Nails, hair, and eyes are strengthened.
- Stimulates hearing, objective thinking, and spiritual inspiration.
- Test point is the head.

GEMSTONE: OPAL

Color and Description

Colors range from milky white to blue to rose with opalescent fires within.

Common opal—Milky appearance
Black opal—Very dark green background
Fire opal—Flamelike color
Jelly opal—Like the common opal, but colorless or transparent

---

- Has rejuvenative qualities that affect the stomach area and spleen.
- Aids in cellular-level alignment.
- An aid in the absorption of all nutrients.

- Enhances meditative practices.
- Thought amplifier that accentuates third eye.
- Stabilizes the emotions.

LIGHT OPAL (white, yellow, or pink)

- Hemispheres of the brain are balanced.
  (Eases dyslexia, epilepsy, neurological discharge problems, visual, physical coordination, also pineal and pituitary glands.)
- Stimulates white blood corpuscles.
- Solar plexus and brow Chakras can open.
- Intuition increases.
- Wear by the throat Chakra.

BLACK OPAL

- Can help the sexual Chakra, testicles, ovaries, pancreas, and spleen.
- Helps with filtration of red corpuscles and influences generation of white.
- Individuals who are depressed may benefit from dark opal.
- Helps release sensitivity and individuals' creativity and intuition.
- Thought force is strong when meditated upon.

Use and Benefits for Healing and Therapeutic Use

- Carries and passes enormous amounts of energy, both good and bad. Held between the eyes, it gives proper direction to thoughts and enhances images.
- Promotes psychic stability and capacity to share.
- Somtimes used for mental illness and increases the assimilation of protein in the body.
- Some practitioners believe it can open the third eye. Good for expanding the aura. The aura will change colors to reflect the feelings of the body as it opens the emotions.

Miscellaneous

- Only those attracted to its beauty should use an opal. It is a fragile stone that shatters for those who have no compatibility with it. It absorbs human duplicity and dishonesty and therefore it works with the karmic Law of Returns and can work as a stigma to the unlucky wearer of the gem.
- Australian opal is the best.

GEMSTONE: PEARL

Color and Description

Organic gemstone that is smooth, often highly lustrous. The energy of the sea formed as a concretion by a mollusk. From the same material as a mollusk shell.

Use and Benefits for Healing and Therapeutic Use

• The pearl is worn to stimulate feminine and maternal qualities and is used to bring about the maternal instinct so that the wearer will feel happy experiences of love.
• Promotes antibodies and fights infection.
• Works with irritability. Peace of mind comes from pearls; so does wisdom. Some ancients have ground them up to a fine powder as a cure for irate feelings. They also aid in the wearing of other stones and sensitizing emotions.

Miscellaneous

• In all legends, all folklore and history, pearls seem always to have been associated with femininity. Legends claim the pearl's power to relax the mind and free the energy for physical balance, thereby bringing in engagements and love relationships.
• Used for developing the third Chakra to enhance sensitivity.

GEMSTONE: PERIDOT AND CHRYSOLITE

Color and Description

Green and olive green. A protective stone.

Use and Benefits for Healing and Therapeutic Use

• Peridot has a direct relationship to the Sun's energy and is used as a tool for expansion and enlightenment of physical burdens. Activates physical and spiritual sight.
• Peridot is sometimes referred to as chrysolite; is believed to have direct connection to the Sun and is used as a protective agent. It is a healing stone to remove fears, depression, sadness, and guilt. It balances physical energies to ward off emotion and stress.

- Aids adrenal functions and works to prevent fevers and nightmares.

Miscellaneous

- Peridot is a very underestimated gemstone, as it can be especially effective when utilized by a trained healer who appreciates its functions for the maladjusted or manic person. One who is possessed cannot hold this stone in his hands, as the energies from the light come through and make him drop the stone on contact.
- A trained healer can detect possessions as well.

GEMSTONE: PETRIFIED WOOD

Color and Description

Brown, yellow, red, white, and okra. Displays growth rings of trees that are millions of years old and hardened into many minerals.

Use and Benefits for Healing and Therapeutic Use

- Replaces cells of organic matter with silica or other mineral deposits and changes it into a stony substance.
- Gives emotional security and acts as a grounder. Restores physical energy to tune you into Earth.
- Helps hip and back problems. Protects against infection and can stabilize you. Vitality is induced and back and hip problems alleviated.

Miscellaneous

- Holding a lead pencil in your hand will give you mental clarity while speaking in front of the public, as it will focus your thoughts and also helps against nervousness.

GEMSTONE: RHODOCHROSITE

Color and Description

Ranges from pale pink to raspberry red with a lacy design.

Use and Benefits for Healing and Therapeutic Use

- Used as the *rescue stone* for trauma and stress.
- Balances the traumas and stimulates forgiveness. Hold rhodo-chrosite in your hand and rub between the thumb and index fingers. It will calm your inner body. Worn around the neck, also will keep the nervous system at an even pace.
- Treats psychic and nervous systems and helps to prevent nervous breakdowns by adding mental stability. A definite rescue stone to ward off mental stress and feelings of complete depression.
- This stone has a force that centralizes on the kidneys, spleen, and pancreas. Put on the vertebrae, it also stimulates healing. The subconscious mind gets cleansed and self-identity process begins to keep a better emotional state.

GEMSTONE: RUBY

Color and Description

Clear, deep red variety of corundum; a valuable precious stone that ranges from pink-red to deep wine. Called "the king of precious stones."

Use and Benefits for Healing and Therapeutic Use

- Fire-sign people can receive special benefits from the ruby as it broadens their fire energies into manifestation, through acting as an emotional stimulant. Fire signs are: Aries, Leo, and Sagittarius.
- Develops the heart filled with love and the will, as it works with the Earth's evolvement. As the consciousness of man rises, the ruby expands its energy field. The lightest and brightest shades of its user affect the higher bodies for instant energy. The darkest, the physical heart and the generative system relating to the pituitary gland and central point in the midbrain. Do not misuse a ruby, as it causes a break in the auric field opening, letting in undesirable energy.
- *Body correspondence*: Balancing the heart.
- *Keynote*: Emotional magnification. Transmits life and energy the "spark of life," as it cleanses the bloodstream, circulation and heart of transfiguring love into Divine will. The ruby

governs the field of all emotional magnification since it rules the emotions; it also handles all our psychic connections from the inner bodies (Chakras) to the physical body.

- Can be placed under the pillow to ward off bad dreams.
- When worn on the left hand, it relates to receiving of life forces by the human body and provides protection. When worn on the right hand, it transmits life and energy to others. It is truly a gem of courage and high spiritual devotion.
- Strengthens the ears, eyes, nose, pituitary, and spleen.
- When all vitality has been depleted, the ruby can act as a pick-me-up!
- Also good for preventing varicose veins, swollen arteries, and eye infections. It also wards off greed.
- Protects sensitive natures and prevents schizophrenic attitudes. The ruby is the best gem to ward off negative energy for psychic self-defense.

Miscellaneous

- The Burma ruby is the most psychic and has the highest vibrations. It should be set in a round setting of yellow 18-karat gold.
- Hold the ruby in your hand and to your lips to put an energy sound into it. Meditate into the stone, chanting AUM (three times). It opens the vitality field through our auric fields. Feel the loving energies evolving from old habits to new ways. We can go deep into the ruby light spectrum for enlightening reactions leading us to special insights and revelations.

GEMSTONE: SAPPHIRE

Color and Description

Faceted blue and green shimmering, ranging from deep azure blue to dark royal blue.

Use and Benefits for Healing and Therapeutic Use

- *Body Correspondence*: Brain.
- *Keynote*: Intuition, mental stimulation, constancy, truth, and virtue. Goal orientation.
- Will contribute to mental clarity since it aids in perception and discernment and is used for protection. Acts as an antidepressant.

- Has a good mental range, good for meditation, keeping a clear head, and has a soothing effect on the mind. Gives awareness of cosmic realms as it serves as a mind filter. Activity centers on the solar plexus and pituitary Chakras.
- Sapphires can sweep away all mental illusion from the intellect and bring reason to the inquiring soul for pure insight, intuition, and instant knowing. It helps put together all your abstract thoughts and cooperates with our "debts in life." Guardian of the superconscious mind and a strong polarized energy from Earth. Ends limited thinking.

GEMSTONE: SAPPHIRE (PALE BLUE STAR SAPPHIRE)

Use and Benefits for Healing and Therapeutic Use

- If you want to meditate and you need a psychic aid, use this ring.
- Good for people who become distracted. If they focus on the star it will help get their heads together. The three bars that cross to form six points represent faith, hope, and destiny. Spiritual awareness, special visions, and clairvoyant gifts increase if this stone is meditated upon.

GEMSTONE: SHELLS (FROM EARTH'S OCEANS)

Use and Benefits for Healing and Therapeutic Use

- Keep them around you for domestic organization and efficiency power.
- Increases the levels of potassium, magnesium, and calcium in the physical body.
- Gets the energy to start flowing and works with the Earth's energies for grounding a person. Grind them up . . . put ground shells in a small sack and sleep with it under your pillow to ground you when you are involved in an important project.

GEMSTONE: SODALITE

Color and Description

Blue with white and pink streaks. Resembles marble when polished.

Use and Benefits for Healing and Therapeutic Use

• This is a soothing stone that has been used to rid one of guilt and fears.
• Sodalite is an esthetic stone that has a tranquilizing effect when stroked. It combines thoughts with inner feelings.
• Used to dispel headaches as it promotes a balance in thyroid metabolism and for physical deficiencies within the glands. Controls insulin in the body, too.
• Strengthens lymphatic system, works against lymph cancer and excessive swelling.

GEMSTONE: TIGER'S EYE (CAT'S EYE; TOURMALINE)

Color and Description

Semiprecious yellow and black stone.

Use and Benefits for Healing and Therapeutic Use

• Warns the wearer of danger and troubles; is considered a gem of good luck to increase the wearer's perception as it stimulates clear thinking and discernment.
• Reduces headaches and helps the nervous system.
• Offers psychic protection as it brings greater power to the mind and thought process.
• Sixth Chakra is opened, producing activation of visions and awakening to concepts of God. Protects against Earth's radiation.

GEMSTONE: TOPAZ (SMOKY; THE BROWN COLOR GOOD FOR NERVOUS PEOPLE)

Color and Description

Occurring in white, yellow, pale blue, or pale green crystals. Yellow variety mainly used as a gem.

Use and Benefits for Healing and Therapeutic Use

• *Body correspondence*: Generative organs.
• *Keynote*: Manifestation.

- Usually hung around the neck to treat emotions. It has a soothing and calming effect and promotes general tissue regeneration.
- Worn on fingers, a protection against untimely dying including death from an assassination, drowning, or falling.
- Topaz heals, most of all by calming the emotional nature against external stresses.
- Strengthens the eyes, especially when used with emerald. Treats disorders of the lungs, such as asthma, and acts as an appetite stimulant. Good, too, for liver ailments, kidney and bladder ailments, and insomnia. Fights diseases including gout and blood disorders.
- Aids in newly stabilized emotions.

Miscellaneous

- Topaz is a creative form of energy that blends with the physical body and links to a correspondence with the generative organs for sexual expression.
- Both ends of this crystal give off positive and negative currents, hooked up to the psychic atmosphere through desire.
- Topaz triggers our wants and needs as it intensifies by automatically obeying the input it receives through magnetized currents of the individual's orbit of energies.
- To amplify, expose stone to blue illumination through the Sun for ten minutes and place it on a quartz base.
- *Blue Topaz*: Hold the stone over the solar plexus area for two minutes. Pause as you breathe deeply two times and repeat. Blue topaz contains a vibrating calm that is good for the nervous system. Wear as earrings as well.

GEMSTONE: TOURMALINE

Color and Description

Shades of red, black, green, and multicolor.

Use and Benefits for Healing and Therapeutic Use

- *Body correspondence*: Endocrine glands.
- *Keynote*: Fusion and regulation—cause and effect.
- Neutralizes discordant energies.

- Can work with all seven Chakras. Gives inspiration and dispels grief. Sleep becomes more tranquil.
- Blood poisoning, consumption, and anemia are eased.
- Rubellite tourmaline strengthens the heart and willpower and gives an individual greater wisdom.
- Has strong electrical and magnetic properties. Cancer is treatable with tourmaline. Hormones are regulated and genetic disorders helped.

GEMSTONE: ZIRCON

Color and Description

Transparent, colorless mineral.

Use and Benefits for Healing and Therapeutic Use

- Reduces emotional negativity and promotes positive attitudes. Like all crystals, can be an all-around healer. May be used as a focus for hypnosis or occult focusing. It fascinates and magnetizes. Looks like a diamond.
- Alleviates bowel disorders and helps rid one of temptations.
- Hold on forehead to clear the mind.
- Protects against insomnia and melancholy.

METALS

Metals are a good conductor of electricity and heat. They are used with gemstones to hold the gems in place with their powerful electric frequencies.

ALUMINUM

- A whitish, light, malleable metal, good when lightness and strength are desirable.
- If you get the right kind, the purest kind, it can help keep you buoyant because it has very little weight and will lift you with its lightness.

MAGNESIUM

- A silver-white metallic element, light and easily worked.
- Especially useful for psychics as it draws their energies and uplifts them.
- In medicine, used as an antacid and laxative. Prevents body odors and tooth decay. Protects against high blood pressure and strengthens the heart.
- *Key point*: With this elixir comes detoxification on the anatomical and cellular levels. Cleansing opens stomach Chakra. Test point is the abdomen.

PLATINUM

- A heavy, silver-white metallic element with a steel gray luster. Sometimes magnetic. Used in jewelry, platinum is good for space vibrations. It has no healing power.

COPPER

- A malleable, tough, reddish metal and one of the best conductors of heat and electricity.
- Worn next to the skin, copper can be either a good or a bad energy source for you. If you have trouble with your nervous system or your spine, copper is a good energy conductor of the highest level for you to release blocked energy. Helps with bone or arthritic ailments as well.
- For some who are sensitive (such as psychics), copper may not be a good energy source as it sends up heat. (It acts as a conductor of your energies and can overheat you.)
- It is too electrical and can cause imbalance as well as bring you down to a level of animal passion sexually.
- Copper can treat a wide variety of inflammatory disorders.
- In homeopathy, copper is used to treat cramps, convulsions, nervous disorders, sexual organ imbalances, and mental and physical exhaustion from overexertion of the mind or loss of sleep.
- Wearing a copper bracelet can ease arthritis and rheumatism and aids in copper assimilation.
- The person in need of copper could be restless, neurotic, excitable, or apathetic. It can help with self-acceptance.

- Hold copper with both hands to alleviate throat problems including hoarseness, difficulty in swallowing, and coughing. Said to release a fear of death and aid ability to retain things in memory banks.
- Eases anemia, aligns the bottom five main Chakras, and opens the heart Chakra. This increases total awareness of self and generates much activity for psychospiritual awareness. Be careful how you use copper. It can be used for total amplication of thought. Placed on the third eye, could possibly stimulate electromagnetic fields for a connection between pineal and pituitary glands. Unified, this creates third eye activity.

SILVER

- A soft, white metallic element that has a high polish.
- Has a passive stabilizing quality and helps improve self-image while healing oneself.
- Balances central network of nerve endings for transmission of energies.
- Silver can clash with the aura of the wearer. Therefore, some can and some cannot wear it.
- Primarily a purifier and has a passive vibration rate of energy against negative energies.
- Can protect you if you wear it next to your skin.
- Develops self-respect and does away with despair and feeling sorry for yourself.
- Conducts electricity and has a certain pull and magnetism for those drawn to it; restores emotional perspective to those in harmony with its use. The moon influences silver.
- Good for doing exorcism and for protection. Wear a silver cross, or hold a silver bullet or silver spike.
- For protection against hypnotism, wear a heavy silver chain plus a silver cross.
- In homeopathy, sometimes used for mental imbalances, headaches, chronic hoarseness, brain and spinal problems, loss of control and balance, congestion of the windpipe.
- Many psychotherapists use silver, as it frees the memories from the subconscious and fantasies can be stimulated.
- Acts as a healing metal as nervous system can be eased when wearing silver. Wear on either index finger.

GOLD

- A precious metallic element, yellow in color. An Earth element that traps the qualities of solar energy for a positive charge. Gold is the highest vibration of the color orange. A source of vitality as the positive side brings out the joy in you, but beware: negativity can attract greed and jealousy to the gold wearer. It promotes a feeling of self-acceptance and self-enhancement along with wisdom. It is a strengthening agent that carries high vibrations of the highest frequency as it quickens the body's electrical impulses. Eighteen-karat gold is too soft to be used as jewelry.
- When you wear gold you have the power to heal; it serves as a protective shield against anything negative coming at you.
- Gold is a most magnetic conductor as it tunes you up and turns a psychic on. It never unbalances you. The sound of gold in ancient Egypt raised the psychic frequencies.
- White gold combines the cosmic energies of the Sun and the moon. It has the power to act as an integrated whole for the conduction of subtle energies.
- Pure gold, molded into fine thin sheets and laid on the body can heal arthritis with its magnetic energy and help with heart and gallbladder conditions. All gold is part of the Sun and produces our warmth.
- Improves circulation and breathing, relieves chills, fever, night sweats.
- There may be a need for gold when there is ego conflict or when one is overburdened with responsibility. Good for depression.
- Gold has been used for dental work, skin cancer, and overexposure to radiation. Also good for various arthritic and syphilitic disorders, bone implants, surgical instruments, and acupuncture needles.
- *Healing and therapeutic*: Gold is the balancer for the heart Chakra. For best results use the purest metal and that is why it is the alchemical link with man.
- The heart is critical to the circulatory flows of the physical body and gold is a master healer. It interconnects with the thymus, which both balances the psychophysical structure of the first seven years of life and rejuvenates the entire endocrine system.

- Aids tissue regeneration.
- Stimulates devotion to the higher self and storage of thought forms.
- Can be worn anywhere on the body.

USES OF METAL COMBINATIONS

COILS OF COPPER AND GOLD

- Can set up a magnetic field between themselves to create heat and can heal with the warmth. It should be wound and twisted together, good for arthritis.

COPPER AND CRYSTAL

- Good for making a healing bed (see p. 222). It draws the energy to you as the copper wire conducts the energy from crystal to crystal, creating the desired force field for a healing.

NEVER MIX GOLD AND SILVER

- They are not to be mixed. Always try to get the purest of whichever you are working with. Pure metals emit an Astral light that is powerfully counteractive to the negative pulls of this planet.

ALUMINUM, MAGNESIUM, AND PLATINUM ARE SPACE VIBRATIONS

- Science is still not sure what these metals can do, but they do add to the higher vibrations of Universal consciousness coming through in this space age.

ACURITE, CHRYSOCOLLA, MALACHITE, AND TURQUOISE

- These have copper in them to prevent a negative attitude and can be used as an aid against glandular malfunctions.

COPPER STONES AND GEMS

AZURITE

Color and Description

A light blue to royal blue ore of copper. Opaque gemstone.

Uses and Benefits for Healing and Therapeutic Use

- Stimulates mental powers.
- Gives symptomatic relief for arthritis, liver, skin, thymus, and muscle tissue.
- Assimilation of vitamins A and E; also increases copper and zinc absorption.
- Helpful aid for muscular dystrophy.
- Improves psychic abilities.
- A valuable aid to meditation.
- Increases dream states and capacity for Astral projection.
- Helps in cases of lack of discipline and hyperkinetic behavior.

CHRYSOCOLLA

Color and Description

Similar to turquoise in color, greenish aqua, electric blue.

Use and Benefits for Healing and Therapeutic Use

- Calcification such as arthritic conditions.
- A good musical charm for singers and musicians.
- Calms emotional stress.
- Tranquilizes nervous tension.
- Improves clarity of dreams, an aid to meditation.
- Works on a higher spiral of evolvement.
- Works well in the higher force fields and dimensions of the Trinity, causing a reactive vibratory concussion up to the highest planes of consciousness.
- Can sometimes ring in your ears and feel hot to the touch.
- Can balance the higher body with the lower body, expanding the sixth sense.
- Facilitates clear seeing on the Astral levels for the neophyte.

- Carries the planetary influence of Uranus as it cleanses the forces of the subconscious mind that may block the development of either the personality or emotional maturity.
- Stimulates the throat and lungs. (Blue stimulates these areas.)
- Works well absorbing the toxins out of cancer patients especially along with blue quartz. Roll them over affected areas.

Tips

Sleep with chrysocolla tucked under your pillow at night for a good night's sleep if you battle with insomnia.

MALACHITE

Color and Description

Bright blue green gemstone with a lighter green eye-shaped form within. A secondary copper ore used for human development.

Use and Benefits for Healing and Therapeutic Use

- Used as a protection from evil, especially as a talisman.
- Wards off undesirable business associations.
- Prevents infection.
- Promotes sleep.
- Aids fertility.
- Stimulates and strengthens clear vision and insight (the physical and inner eyes of man) as it aligns the crown center and the pineal and pituitary bodies, and becomes a Divine balancer for emotional imbalance.
- Helps kidneys, head, pancreas, and spleen, and increases lactation.

Miscellaneous

- Use for meditation as you go into time and space. Has a negative and a positive charge as it is a powerful copper source and can even be utilized for good interaction and relationships with others.
- Averts faintness, relieves cramps, cardiac pain, cancerous tumors, colic, infection, leukemia, rheumatism, and can help ulcers ease up. Also helps gastric complaints involving nervous tension.

• Wear high on the neck for vertigo or to protect from danger of living near a nuclear power plant or storage facility. Keep lots of chunks of malachite in the house.

TURQUOISE

Color and Description

Blue to green and sometimes includes all the shades between sky blue and deepest green. Semipolished and rough. Composed of copper, aluminum phosphate, and iron. Subject to color change when wearer is in need of mental relaxation.

Use and Benefits for Healing and Therapeutic Use

• Turquoise is a stone of friendship.
• Calms emotions and relaxes the body. Influenced by a Venus moon that keeps updating its healing frequencies. Also keeps your soul from clinging to past memories.
• Acts as a soul-cheerer and has prosperity consciousness to stimulate the mind to business action.
• Helpful for eye conditions such as cataracts.
• Used as a protective gemstone. If you are accident prone, it protects against falls and accidents.
• Improves a person's vibes (only if it is used with silver) and restores a healthy mental attitude.

Miscellaneous

• A favorite talisman of the American Indian. Acts as a relay station and unifying stone that puts the spirit in touch with the forces of Mother Earth. Atlantean cultures gave this stone life and breath from energies of the Earth and sky.
• Improves meditation.
• A master healer indeed as it enhances the color spectrum of the Universe.
• Turquoise strengthens the entire anatomy and is an aid for all diseases, including making all nutrients better absorbed and all subtle bodies aligned.
• General tissue regenerates and is stimulated.
• Helps, too, with nutrient-deficient diseases such as anorexia nervosa.

- Helps circulatory flow.
- A pollutant protector and can be worn anywhere on body.
- Works faster on the physical body than most others—choose whichever color feels better for you: green or blue (communication promoters).

TALISMANS AND AMULETS

An *amulet* is a charm worn around the neck as a remedy or protection against negativity. It consists of stones or metals arranged in a particular order that can protect the owner from calamities.

Talismans are for healing and well-being; they work through the application and wearing of their energies. They are magical powers (stones and metals) to keep anything negative away. A talisman can be a ring, stone, neck piece, or arm band.

QUICK RESCUE TREATMENTS

Sapphires

SORE THROAT OR ANY THROAT AILMENT:

- Wear a necklace of sapphires or blue semiprecious stones against the throat. Blue is the color of the throat Chakra.

Orange Sardonyx or Amber

ASTHMA:

- Wear a pendant of orange sardonyx or amber next to the skin, or a red silk ribbon on left wrist.

RHEUMATISM OR ARTHRITIS IN HAND:

- Wear rings or orange sardonyx or amber. Also, blue sapphires on the fingers will help.

RHEUMATISM:

Rheumatism is an accumulation of wastes including uric acid. If you flood the body with red light you can dissolve crystalized energy in the joints which has resulted from malfunctioning kidneys.

Wear a red scarf around the neck for colds. Red increases the blood cells.

When taking light treatment, patient lies flat on back upon a bed. Red light is projected first upon the soles of the feet, then ankles, calves, knees, thighs (5 minutes on each location).

Yellow Opal

HEARTBURN:

• Wear a pendant of yellow opal on chest, exposing gem to the skin.

Yellow Jasper

MENSTRUAL PROBLEMS:

• A yellow jasper pendant on a chain, worn directly on the skin, will help with period regularity.

Emerald

LIVER PROBLEMS:

• An emerald worn around the neck at base of throat will help heal eyes and liver.

Moonstone

ARTHRITIS, LEG AND ARM PAIN:

• A moonstone pendant worn day and night on a fourteen-karat gold chain will alleviate dull arthritic pain in joints.

Ruby

HEARTBREAK:

• A ruby will heal the heart if used as an amulet worn on top of the physical heart.

OTHER TALISMANS AND AMULETS

| Agate | • Can protect owner from calamities. |
| Agate (Carnelian) | • Wear on heart Chakra to strengthen meridians of body to treat anorexia nervosa patients. |

- Produces an increase in the nutrient-absorption properties in the intestinal tract.
- Amplify carnelian by placing it inside a cone form and exposing it to red light for ten minutes.

Amber
- When worn around the neck it helps to fight respiratory diseases and infection.

Amber (Yellow)
- Helps keep one on the physical level as it has a grounded energy field.

Amethyst
- This stone can work to control the body's temperament as it can be used for serenity and has a strengthening action. When worn around the neck it can act as a kind of laser beam, with its power being absorbed into your breathing to thus control energy blocks in the body. This color's wave length or band of atoms oscillates a purple spectrum that creates an energy flow.
- Can be worn anywhere on the body as it stimulates the meridians and the individual's acupressure points. Test it on the brow and the thymus gland.

Aquamarine
- Balances out imbalances. Can filter in good energy to an individual's cells if charged frequently for eight to twenty-four hours in direct sunlight. Put on a bed of copper to increase its power.

Beryl
- Quickens the intellect and cures laziness.

Bloodstone
- Protects against negativity especially when under hypnosis and you feel negative energy directed to you. A physical healer and mental balancer.
- *Bloodstone and pearl combination*: Can send out a cure for healing vibrations in the body to quicken the pace. Especially good for checking bleed-

ing problems and hemorrhaging. Capitalizes on calcium in the body.

Copper
- *Copper bracelet*: Can be good for arthritis or rheumatism.
- *Copper earrings*: Prevent sciatica and balance emotions.

Coral
- Use red coral to rub around gum inflictions, upper respiratory infections, and as a protection against sterility and impotency. Also aids and relieves voice ailments.

Chrysocolla
- Research is presently under way with this stone and metaphysicians are seeing the use of this stone to protect against cancer-cell buildup.
- It is the author's belief that this stone, worn around the neck, has potential properties for treatment against cancer, especially that of karmic origin. It can counteract the body's calcifications such as arthritis. A definite healing tool when worn with a programmed crystal. It filters up the mental strata of the auric field via the solar plexus and helps alleviate personal guilt and fears. It also breaks up emotional congestions.

Cat's Eye (Tiger's Eye)
- As an amulet for psychic protection.

Citrine
- *Yellow only*: A direct stimulant to man's mental bodies and serves as an aid to open the higher mental, as a bridge, from the lower mental up to the intuitive levels of the mind. A stimulator, not a generator.
- Reduces fears.
- Helps man to obtain spiritual growth.
- Stimulates general healing (heart, liver, kidney, and muscles).

Crystals
- *Rose or pink*: Mellows the emotional and the heart centers. It strengthens

love energy as you feel and think of Universal love. It promotes these vibrations of the Universe with glowing inner serenity.

Emerald • If this amulet is worn by a Taurus or Libra at the base of the neck, it can reflect light to the wearer that fits the zodiac capacity. It can attune them to a frequency that helps their mental set and emotional attachments. Especially effective.

Garnet • Use this gem as a radio set to communicate with guides in the Universe. It will pull into your mind space-age thinking and can work with the individual's orbital field or inspiration and helps to raise levels of being.

Jasper (Red) • Especially effective when worn around the waist. Absorbs clogged material in livers and bile ducts. Adds an energy stimulus that enters through the solar plexus and sacral force centers.

Lapis Lazuli • This royal blue stone, cut as a pyramid and worn around the throat and neck areas, will activate the higher intuitive frequencies. It bestows the gift of increased sensitivity to the higher vibrations of the solar system. Good for deep meditational practices, especially when put up to the third eye for spiritual attunement. Also good when altered state energies are needed for our physical knowledge. Lapis, in this triangular shape, is extremely powerful to open our psychic channels.

Malachite • When it is worn on the physical body it can stimulate the optic nerve, causing the visual producing chromosomes of the body as well as aiding the functions of the pancreas and spleen.

- Wear for vertigo or around nuclear power plants.

Malachite-Azurite Combo
- Affects the mental thought processes and decreases illusions on the mental levels. It benefits the crown and brow centers as it allows a mental flow to decrystalize mental habit patterns that are outgrown. For this influence, you need to wear them together.

Moonstone
- Helps with mild endocrine imbalances in females and can clear the lymphatics when in a congested or blocked condition.

Pearl
- If applied to stomach area, increases understanding in financial affairs.

Peridot
- Calms and balances the physical organism; can dispel fears, guilts, melancholy, or depression, and counteracts negative emotions. Protects from enchantments and illusion. Gives wearer foresight and eloquence. Has added power when set in gold. The darkness of life's troubles and physical burdens stay away and cannot come through you, as it gives an uplifting feeling.

Rhodochrosite
- To be worn by individuals to heal the negative aspects of their mental and physical stress. This direct flow of energy immediately helps the wearer to direct the energy of stress into new reconditioning for their mental outlook and attitude. Helps with detachment for those drawn into toxic depressions.
- To amplify energies and activate with a positive force field, it should be made with *pink gold*. Your problems will be clarified, and with the help of your physical practitioner, you will have a greater potential for movement, better health and understanding, and a peaceful inner growth.

Ruby	• Sends bursts of colored flame in all directions as it works with a fiery person's energy and auric field. Gives an individual revelations for what we feel, think, see, or hear; helps perceive a new meaning of life for us.
	• Opens the energy of all the Chakras if programmed to do so and keeps energies in a vibrant, even state. All the self-attributes come true on a physical level as well. If applied to the area of the heart meridian, or heart Chakra, it focuses the energy concerning distress and aids the individual in learning how to give and receive love.
Sodalite	• For physical deficiencies within the glands emphasizing the metabolism. Controls the manufacture of insulin. (Works similarly to lapis but on a denser scale.)
Topaz	• Source of physical strength, especially for women. Useful in the treatment of tension headaches.

RUBIES, EMERALDS, AND SAPPHIRES

Put together as a triad, if capped, and worn on chain around the neck, brings out the higher power of one who is truly on a path of completion. Make a triangular configuration of these three stones and set in gold.

Ruby—Works with the heart and emotional magnification.
Emerald—Activates lungs and breath, and aids equilibrium.
Sapphires—Stimulates brain and intuition.

*All the above gems work in harmony together.

MINERALS

There are minerals that work as talismans to steady the head and brain cells for increased mental energy.

Lace Agate

Agates can protect the wearer from calamities and can be used to treat schizophrenia. If one holds the stone to his head, it can pull out turbulent energy like a magnet.

Celestite

Works with migraine headaches. Pulls negative energy like a magnet away from the body. Used in love rituals and healing. Promotes sleep, dreams, friendship, growth, fertility, and spirituality.

Talc

Soft white/gray material. Put in sunlight first to store energy. Creates a whirlwind of spiraling energy to clear out deposits of anger and restraint. Talc is made into powder by pulverizing it. An alteration product of magnesium. Makes negative energy rise more quickly. Good for migraine headaches if talc is held where pain is. *Note*: Also can be capped on a chain to be worn close to head. Using talc will enhance past life therapies. Good for treatments using hypnotic processes. Releases past life talents so they can be understood and worked through.

Prehnite

Calcium-aluminum silicate; a light green or greenish white crystal mineral. Scientists use this when working with people who take lithium. When prehnite is placed on the Crown Chakra (top of head) it works instantaneously. The pain energy goes downward, the sinuses clear as it moves to the throat, and some people can see their inner organs or Etheric and physical bodies. It has ultrasonic sound in it as it replaces cells. It acts as a regulator and neutralizer and has hydrogen content. Activates the pineal gland (sensory organ) in the brain of all vertebrates to open the crown activity. Acts also as a source of light power coming in from above space dimensions as an aid to repair damaged body cells. Replaces new radioactive molecular structure of the body. As it comes down and through to the physical body, it relieves and removes old rancid energy and transmutes it to a new frequency.

Lepidolite Mica

An ore of lithium; six-sided, silvery, pink to lilac. Integrates the Etheric body into the physical on the *mental plane* to blend and bring cheer into you as an antidepressant. Has the ability to reverse negative energy and negative thought patterns as it balances all Chakras. Specifically helps to open the heart center as it will expand and open you up. Helps as an activator and intensifier to refine energy. Good also for mental illness. If placed on top of the head, this rock should work immediately. It can be better than a tranquilizer!

Note: This mineral has quartz and pink tourmaline in it, and comes from Palo Alto, California.

Author's Note: Caution should be used as this chapter was channeled from space frequencies.

Miscellaneous

• An *armlet* made of gold will be a source of vitality and strengthener for energies of the wearer.
• A *silver and lead armlet* can be helpful for liver trouble.
• *Copper conductor energy talisman*: If stones of azurite, chrysocolla, malachite, and turquoise are put together, they can prevent a negative attitude problem and act as an aid for gland functions.

QUESTIONS TO PONDER

Q. Have you ever wondered why certain talismans or amulets work for some and not others?
A. It is due to the spiritual level of attainment and the cycle of an individual's existence at a given time in the cosmos.
Q. What about the notion that young children have problems of their own?
A. Children have an innate sense of knowing what is good for them. Why not let these children go into a gem shop. They

will surely attract to them the energies that they need by picking and choosing all the healing agents. Chances are their choices will work well.

GEMSTONES OF THE BIBLE

THE BREASTPLATE OF AARON AMULET

The Breastplate of the High Priest contains the twelve original stones as described in the Bible (Exodus 28). It has been referred to as having great powers and being a most effective talisman. The twelve stones represent the twelve tribes, and are placed in the exact position as in the original breastplate.

They are: emerald, peridot, agate, onyx, beryl, lapis lazuli, topaz or citrine, amethyst, garnet, carnelian, crystal, and green jasper or jade.

The combination of these twelve stones was known by the ancients to harness energy and bring power to the wearer. You can have one made for you by a jeweler. It can help with certain ritualistic practices.

The Breastplate of Aaron was crafted into a metal with the stones of the Bible's vibrations put into it. It consists of the gemstones used by scholars to incorporate all twelve energy emanations for healing and as a talisman for luck, love, success, wisdom, health, and protective empowered energies. Wear around the neck as the vibrations of healing will produce a force field on the physical body. Carry it in your pocket or place it under your pillow at night to receive balanced energy and comfort for a restful nights sleep. Represents and pulls in the vibrations of the Zodiac as well (all twelve signs) to bring one into the celestial and higher realms of New Age thinking.

This breastplate was worn at times by the priests who stood in communion with God. It served to amplify consciousness, and to obtain knowledge of prophecy with greater discernment and clarity. It amplified the piezo-electric effect of the stones on the metal when worn against the skin. The nature of stress on each individual was seen by the higher acidic properties of the skin tissue. Such stress caused some of the gemstones to lose their brilliance but also served as a healing force that would work on them.

GEMSTONE HEALING

GEMS CAN BE USED AS MEDICINES

Start with a clean, clear bowl. I use about a sixteen-ounce size. This amount can be cut in half depending on how many glass storage bottles you can fill from it with an eye dropper. Sterilize both first with hot water. Leave for about five to ten minutes before you pour water out. It is best to use distilled water for your own gem elixirs. Some people use spring water. That can also be okay.

The mineral you have chosen to put into the water should be cleaned and be a natural one. Size is not important. The purity of the stone is. The gemstones should be placed under the Sun's rays for from a full two hours to two weeks.

Keep your thoughts on a high level as you feel inner clarity and calm while preparing the solution. Place gem in the center of the water. Place a quartz that you have prayed over next to the stone you are using.

Make a white oaktag or cardboard pyramid to fit around the

jar or container you are using. It will keep it dark and charge the
elixir. Put a dash of brandy in the solution to keep it longer.
Keep it under the pyramid for one week.

To amplify gemstones, expose to rising Sun at least two hours
(life force is heightened). Meditate on the gem as in a prayer to
your higher self.

At the end of the week, the gem is removed, washed in water,
and stored away. Those gemstones that work best are listed below.

Amber

This stone is used as medicine for stomach pains and stomach
ailments.

Amethyst

Amethyst is a high-quality stone. Put the stone into a clear glass
bottle containing two parts distilled or spring water and one part
regular grain alcohol. Cover, cap, and charge in *maximum* sunlight for six hours total. An internal remedy for parasites, as its
ultraviolet rays help and it hastens receptivity and a person's
transmutational state of being.

Chrysocolla

Use a clean gem that has been cleansed in kosher or sea salt
water overnight. Then it is rinsed and placed in a Pyrex pan of
boiling distilled water. Put the mineral into the water while it is
cooling. Store in amber-colored glass. The charged solution will
counteract bodily calcifications and tend to eradicate them.

Emerald

This gem should be cleansed in a mixture of water and alcohol
that is simmered down until a tincture has evolved. (Two parts
spring water to one part 180-proof grain alcohol.) Bring to a boil
and simmer in a glass pot with cover for thirty minutes. When
cooled, pour into a clear glass bottle that has been sterilized. Put
into bright sunlight for five hours. Then put in a green glass
stoppered container. Put two to four drops under the tongue. It is
used as an earthly balancer on our physical, mental, and emotional levels. A tonic as an internal stabilizer and tranquilizer for
seeing our true realities.

Lapis Lazuli

Lapis is very cleansing and can open up many channels. It is a physic to the mind. Can remove stored toxins. This elixir aligns the body.

Note: The above are some that the author has worked with. You might want to use others. Simply read the section on gemstones to choose those for your use. These above have been most effective.

MAKE YOUR MEDICINE BAGS
OR POUCHES

Some people wear a personal crystal hung around their necks on a chain. This amulet can serve as protection against anything negative coming at you. It can also heal and stimulate the crystalline structure within your body, depending on how and where you place it.

It has come to me by Divine sources, that in the making of medicine bags you can utilize the power of all the gemstones that you need as indicated in the previous pages. Place chips and pieces in a soft velvet pouch. The color of the pouch selected would be your choice or preference depending on the color energy you feel you need. Make sure each pouch you make has at least one crystal in it, as crystals are used as the center of power, a power object. They energize your body to its full potency and boost the energies of the other stones selected. They contain life, and are used as a catalyst, as a "live rock," and awaken all the others collected.

You can wear a pouch around your neck, keep it in your pocket or attaché case, by your nightstand, and so on. Keep in mind that it carries a force field of power of at least three feet around you.

I would suggest selecting some breastplate stones, especially sard, agate, chrysolite, peridot, garnet, amethyst, jasper, onyx, beryl, emerald, sapphire, lapis, and some crystal as a starter. These will be used as a tool to reflect your inner brain's light and as a healer.

Remember to clean off all negative vibrations from the stones—wherever they were before—by soaking them overnight in salt water first.

12

Crystals

QUARTZ CRYSTALS

Quartz crystal is the sacred mineral, the healer of the mind and planet, the nugget that raises the level of our souls.

Today's physicists have affirmed that many things exist not only in matter but in energy. Crystals are one of those things that exist as energy as well as matter. Crystals have either a positive or a negative charge with high rates of vibrations, since they come from such areas as mines, caves, grounds, rivers, streams, or mountains. Because of their high energy, crystals can amplify, store, transform, focus, and transfer energy. That is why they work in areas of communication such as computers, lasers, audiotechnology, electrical signals, audiovisual equipment, microcircuits, and so on. As tools for technology, crystals transform electricity into radio and TV broadcast signals and are used in computers for memory banks.

In our private world, crystals can be used to modify our negative and positive emotions by energizing or healing our bodies. They also give us energy to increase our concentration and our powers of visualization. If you place a crystal over your third eye (behind your forehead) you can listen to your inner voice and quickly calm yourself.

I suggest that people who are beginning to utilize the power of crystals work with their right-brain energy—this intuitive capacity increases and expands with everyday application of crystal energy.

Ultimately, relying on the right brain can help increase wisdom and instinct. As Westerners, we have relied much on the left-brain activities of logical, linear, goal-oriented thinking. With the use of crystals we can expand our right-brain thinking, leaving us open to our intuitive capacities. Quartz, with its energy, amplifies and transmits the energy of our minds.

Quartz appears to be light or water transformed into solid matter. It is the only natural transparency we can hold in our hands. In selecting one, choose the one that draws you to it. You will be attracted to the harmony and effect it has on your body.

If we use crystals along with our own thoughts, through meditation, through prayer, we can focus and give energy to anyone in anyplace we desire to heal or otherwise make well. We can heal a loved one or help sell a house. We can communicate telepathically. We can even learn to speak with Angels and Masters, but that means we must first learn how to listen and create the means to hear. As the crystal helps put you in a state of altered consciousness, you can direct the crystal of your choice, which I will teach you to program, to awaken the physical body to balance and repair itself.

You can also use crystals to expand your own personhood, as a tool for mind expansion, if you will—for self-transformation and actualization—so you are working only on your higher self. If you meditate upon a crystal, it is the voice of your higher self that is reflected back at you. The crystal serves as a tool to help you see yourself. In time, you won't even need the crystal to see your truest self—in time, you can put the crystal aside, for its knowledge will have become a part of you.

Throughout this chapter, keep in mind that I am not trying to make scientific explanations for why crystals work the way they do. I am simply trying to make you aware, for your personal use, of a simple mineral we have rediscovered, one we can pocket, adorn ourselves with, or even sleep with under our pillows. My purpose in this chapter is to help you explore the practical uses of these tools for mind and energy expansion.

None of the techniques you will find here are meant to be substitutes for the medical or other healing professions. They are meant only to augment the natural healing of our mental, emotional, physical, and spiritual balances.

These windows of solidified light can be transformed into the highest energy, and the quartz can then serve as a stepping stone—a rainbow bridge from the Earth to the celestial realms, the realms of Universal mind, the mind of Father of the Universe.

CHOOSING A CRYSTAL

Love it, be attracted to it. It should shine above all others in front of you. In fact, it should vibrate in front of you and ask to be purchased. This instant inner rapport will make it your personal tool. An inner awareness will make it signal to you as it stands out in the crowd. It will be harmonious and will blend with your energies.

See how far you can hold your crystal away from you and still feel its vibrations. A half-inch crystal projects an energy field up to about three feet.

The best way to get a crystal is to receive it as a gift.

CLEARING AND CLEANSING

Some crystals have other people's thought forms and negative emotions already in them. If you use crystals for your own aura cleansing or if you use them for healing purposes, it is wise to cleanse them frequently to unlock the grief, anger, sadness, or other impurities trapped in the crystals.

There are many different methods of cleansing, but all methods I know use either salt water, spring water, or sea salt.

This is the method I use: Place stones in a bowl of water with at least two tablespoons of coarse salt (kosher) for twenty-four hours. It cleans them of negative influences. Dry in sunlight or near a plant to give them a whiff of nature. *Do not* let anyone else handle them.

If a crystal has been used for healing, it can be purified by circling it through sage smoke seven times counterclockwise. It is best to keep at least one crystal for personal use and several for healing and sharing with friends. (See Indian smudging techniques, p. 221.)

PROGRAMMING

Programming is important because it enhances your crystal's energy, which comes back to you.

Colors and music are the easiest vehicles both singly and in combination to use to program your crystal. Single tones or specific chords of music can be coded in crystal sound. Color serves also as a fundamental energy and can be used for programming.

Place the crystal on top of your stereo speaker or perhaps nearby while you are chanting. Your voice or another's can be programmed for the sound and vibration needed. It will be helpful for energies also to be captured in certain outdoor places—near a river, woods, trees, waterfall, or any aromatic environment.

Snowstorms or thunderstorms can be coded, too, or a strange weather phenomenon. All of these aspects of life, programmed into your crystal, serve as enhancement. Remember, once it has been programmed, a crystal processes incoming energies and sends these signals into you. So you see, crystals serve as transmission tools. You can create your own "eight-track tape," if you desire.

HOW IT WORKS

Hold the crystal in your hand.
Program it to be cleared.
See yourself sitting in a purple spinning top.
See a white background behind you.
Take your particular problem and create a thought form.
Put the thought form into the crystal.
Keep it there as an energy will be produced.
The answers will come through crystal energy.

DISSOLVING OLD PROGRAMS

Once the crystal has taken in the energy, you no longer need the programs in it. First, with prayer and a lot of intent, ask it to be blank. Do so by cleansing in salt water again and charge it in sunlight. After it has been cleared, cleansed, and everything "erased," proceed to reprogram.

ADVANCED PROGRAMMING

Scientists now studying thought photography believe a crystal or
system of crystals can be a clue to understanding this phenomenon. Crystals, they say, are subject to mind-brain energy patterns
and if nurtured into specific geometric shapes the prisms could
likely be tuned to the mental frequency range of certain individuals.

Try these methods of advanced programming once attuned to
your own crystal. Try to image the waves in a crystal as an
imploding tornado of light in a greenhouse.

- Focus your thoughts while holding the crystal to be programmed.
  Imagine a white laser beam coming out of your third eye into
  the crystal. This energy will feed back into your consciousness. Stare at the crystal, looking for a place for the beam of
  your thoughts to penetrate.
- See if you can put a mental picture into your quartz, or create
  an image and hold it steady in your mind as you interact with
  this crystalline matrix.
- Take a deep breath and exhale while you are imaging into
  crystal. Programming involves pure intention. Hold the crystal
  in your hands and blow your thoughts into it (do this three
  times). The crystal will retain all your needs. However, it is
  best to use this program for a specific purpose.

PRAYER FOR THE PROGRAMMING
OF POSITIVE ENERGY

Begin by saying the following prayer over a crystal to imprint the
energy of good after you have washed and cleansed it.

> I accept the Divine form of Divinity with the use of this
>   crystal, to be used, utilized within my conscious world,
>   and the consciousness of the Universal mind of the ethers
>   beyond time and space.
> I accept in using this form of energy the truths of I am that I
>   am and all of God's attunement to the highest form and
>   for the forces of good, leaving out any interference of
>   negative law.
> I ask only the law of my master Elohim to be invoked. [You
>   can substitute any name for your highest power.]
> So Be It!

POINTERS ABOUT CRYSTALS

Crystals are used as centers of power, as power objects that maximize your full potency. They contain life-giving properties and can be used as a catalyst to project the soul to the other worlds as "live rocks." The seven stones of importance are diamond or clear quartz, sapphire, jasper, emerald, topaz, ruby, and amethyst (this purple quartz is a highly prized and influential stone with abilities to endow the wearer with quick intelligence and invulnerability in battle).

As discussed in the chapter on gems, some breastplate stones include: sard, agate, chrysolite, garnet, amethyst, jasper, onyx, beryl, emerald, topaz, sapphire, and diamond.

Amethyst, jasper, onyx, and *agate* are of the quartz family and are the power wands of alchemists. The specific placement of these minerals creates a complex code pattern of vibrations to perform certain priestly functions. The physical crystal is a tool to reflect the inner brain's light. Again, understand that quartz is an inexhaustible cosmic transmission of pure white light the mind, manifestation, and radiance of the Father of the Cosmos.

Because crystals receive, transmit, and amplify human intention, we should use crystals only when in a clear state of mind. When not in use, crystals should be kept on an altar or in a medicine pouch covered by cloth or deerskin.

Program a color in your crystal to increase your vitality. Chant soul sound around crystals to activate them. Bring them up and make them sing.

Before you work or heal with it, clear it if it is dull and lacks vitality.

If crystals are misused, they may spontaneously crack or disappear.

Abrasions and marks are indicative of nature's creation and in no way diminish the value and effectiveness of your crystal.

- *Single terminated* crystals have one point with natural facets. The energy flow of the crystal runs from the bottom, where it enters, up through and out the point.
- *Double terminated* crystals have two points, one on each end. The energy comes and goes in both directions, as in a battery.

- When used in jewelry always set crystals so that the circulation of energy flow works for your body to increase the body's rate of vibration.
- To feel the crystal's vibrational field, rub both your hands together vigorously for about a minute (producing a lot of heat). Open your hands to feel the sensitivity, then blow on them to feel a sensation. Then touch the point of your crystal to the center of your palm and pull the crystal up a couple of inches or so and make a circular movement over your palm. You will soon feel its energy. See how far away you can still feel the sensation of activity in your palm. Run it over you about six inches from your body and feel the extraordinary surge of power that the crystal energy produces.
- When you put a crystal in your left palm it brings in energy. If you feel "hyper," hold it in your right hand and the crystal will pull out chaotic energy. For some people, this is reversed.
- When you need an all-over balancing, put your hands out in front of you, both holding similar hand-size crystals pointed in the same direction. Then ask guidance for a flow of energy (and try to see it as a golden light) to come through your Crown Chakra down the neck and shoulders into your arms.
- Quartz crystals' vibratory rate can be manipulated with a mantra, sound, color visualization, saying positive affirmations, and breathing.
- To aid thought vibrations, hold a crystal in your left hand while you think happy, peaceful thoughts and what you need to be healed.
- Feel peace and contentment, experience this heightened feeling, take a deep breath, and blow into your crystal as you exhale.
- Imagine the crystal vibrating more and more while you try each step and enter into it each feeling, each sound, each thought that can lift you higher and higher. The crystal will store all this information and keep it until you clear it or erase it all.
- Next, point the crystal toward your heart. Imagine your body breathing into it for a healing. Peaceful energy enters your heart from the quartz. Breathe long and deep. On the in breath, more of the energy enters your body. Carry it with you.
- Gaze into the crystal, close your eyes, and place the crystal between the brows over the third eye while lying on your back.

Drive the blockages out of you by waving the crystal or by circling it over the affected part of your body.

CATEGORIES OF CRYSTALS— THE ONES MOST POPULARLY REFERRED TO

1. HEALING CRYSTALS. Many of these have specialized capabilities because of their electromagnetic field. They help to get rid of our negativity and imbalance, clear out our system, and absorb the toxins. We can surround our bodies with them in such a way that we can absorb bad energy from different places of the body. We must continually clear these crystals, however, so we do not put the bad energy back into us.

2. ENERGY CRYSTALS. These are programmed crystals. When activated they have a long, strong energy output. We call them "fire crystals," as they have undergone an alchemical process by passing through an interdimensional doorway. There is a DNA grid structure in the crystal (remember, quartz is *alive!*). The spiral molecular structure of quartz interfaces with the tiny seed blueprint of creation—"DNA." The genes of select molecules grow on them, enhancing the fire crystal's function.

3. ATTUNEMENT CRYSTALS. These serve as "tuning forks" of a special frequency and attune you to another person's vibrancy level. They are helpful in meditation and contain specific harmonics of life.

4. POWER RODS. These can amplify thought forms and initiate changes through a laserlike beam or ray.

5. DEVIC CRYSTALS. Shamans use these tools to keep grounded in one spot. They can be used to recharge and ground yourself into your higher self. They also have interdimensional-communication properties.

6. LIBRARY CRYSTALS. These can store a great amount of information. You can store a lot of knowledge in crystals of this type to code information for someone or to tune in to them for a library of information where you might store memories or thoughts.

7. ENERGY RODS. You can use these to focus awareness into your aura and awaken specific levels of the mind. They're like "cosmic batteries" to release stored energy.

8. SINGING OR TUNING CRYSTALS. These are "tuning forks" to be used as healing and attunement agents. They have the energy to respecialize and send to an area for a specific purpose.
9. SURGERY CRYSTALS. White light and thought are sent in from the operator for special psychic surgery. These crystals change and rearrange the atoms and molecules in you through your thoughts for a healing.
10. VISION CRYSTALS. These work with the frequency of the third eye Chakra and increase the abilities of your inner "sight" to amplify your own power.

You must learn to utilize all your crystals and play with them. They are your friends. You will soon see which ones fall into which categories. There are only a few experts who can tell you which ones work for what. I have found the most effective way to tell is either through their different look, shape, or feel. You will find that each one has different properties from the others. Certainly meditation and holding each one in your hand, or meditating with each one touching your third eye, will get results.

COLOR VARIATIONS OF QUARTZ AND USAGE

PINK QUARTZ

Various shades of pink; sometimes called rose quartz.

Usage

• Has a calming effect on the heart center as a love stone.
• If used correctly, can have a calming effect on the physical heart; especially important for advanced healers who choose this instead of using clear quartz for heart problems. Helps irregular-heartbeat problems.
• Increases feeling of self-worth and love.
• Relates well to the kidneys.
• Used in conjunction with breathing a pink ray into the nostrils for skin rejuvenation and to reduce wrinkles. It gives the wearer a soft complexion.

• You might say this particular shade acts as a softener and yet does not weaken the great intensity of energy that these crystals produce. Some practitioners use them to heal cases of advanced disease where there is great sensitivity of the tissue.

Miscellaneous

• Good for calming children, particularly hyperactive ones.

SMOKY QUARTZ

Cloudy, brownish color, as it is exposed to the radiation in the ground; sometimes grayish.

Usage

• Stands for transitions and centeredness. A grounder and strengthener used to eliminate distortions in people's vibrations. It opens vibrations, and allows them to feel truth coming from the source. Used to increase the clarity of communication.
• Acts as a synthesizer, magnetic, and purifier of energy together with the attributes of regular quartz; hooks the physical impurities of the body into the mental to lift and filter as a strainer.
• A good deterrent against parasites.

Miscellaneous

• Good for children who are severely brain-damaged and riddled with anxiety to stay here on Earth and not out of the body all of the time.

RED RUBY CRYSTAL (RED QUARTZ)

Usage

• This crystal maintains the vibrational balance of vibrations here on Earth. It works with the polarity and the fields of energy to develop one's growth on this planet.

YELLOW QUARTZ OR
CITRINE (YELLOWISH)

Usage

• This quartz expands mental clarity and awakens the mind to greater thoughts. It can relieve pain and transmit sound waves to connect with your loved ones if put under your loved ones' pillows to make them believe and raise their spiritual consciousness.

• An all-around healer that aids in the stimulation of food absorption.

• Back in the Atlantean era, it was utilized as a focal point of energy, especially to those being trained as mediums in the healing temples. This advanced energy was used in mind control and is good for the administering of hypnosis, as you can attune yourself to a magnetic transference of energy to shift the levels of consciousness in you.

• These golden or yellow crystals are also used for diagnosing physical ailments. They can be passed over the general area of the body and when the color tone changes it shows where there is a distortion of vibrations and where the ailment inside of the body lies. The body's charge corresponds to the change in the crystal's color.

• It helps heal spreading infections such as blood diseases and cancer, especially when great power is needed. Use for only a short period of time. Not designed for spiritual growth alone.

AMETHYST CRYSTAL

Light to dark shades of purple and violet (see also Chapter 11).

Usage

• It operates as an atomic cell as its radiations come from a cosmic source.

• Brings integration between three healing systems of the body—physical, mental, and emotional and spiritual—as it raises the vibrational capacities so one is truly a sensitive.

• While held in the hands in the practice of meditation, it clears out unwanted forces and centers you to reach higher frequencies.

A HOW-TO ON QUICK CLEARING

1. Hold the crystal in your hands and pray to open up God's light to penetrate the crystal.
2. Hold the crystal in cold running tap water while visualizing God's light entering it for about sixty seconds.
3. Blow love into the crystal and as you are doing so ask to release any negative energy. Repeat at least five times.

LONG-TERM CLEARING

This process will pull up and out any loose static or rampant energies surrounding your crystal's auric field.

1. I find the sea or ocean best for long-term clearing.
2. Place the crystal overnight in salt water (kosher or coarse salt).
3. Pack the crystal in dry coarse salt for forty-eight hours.
4. Bury the crystal under the ground for seven days.
5. Wash the crystal under any cold running water (and see white light going into it for sixty seconds).

CHARGING AND ACTIVATING

After the above, the methods I find the most effective are:

1. Place the crystal in outdoor sunlight (begin before noon) for twenty-four hours so it is also exposed to the moonlight as well as two dawns.
2. Place the crystal in sunlight between 10:00 A.M. and 12:30 P.M. in a circulating foot bath. Use enough water so that they are completely immersed.
3. Set a ring or a circle with other crystals around the crystal to be charged and activated. Use twelve in all, the thirteenth being the crystal you want charged. All the points of the circle should be facing inward, all circling the one you want activated (the twelve also representing the signs of the Zodiac). *Now* imagine a white light lighting up the twelve, making a complete circle. Leave for thirty minutes, as it will be highly intensified.

4. You can also leave crystals in a power spot, such as by a waterfall, ocean, or mountaintop.

ON CARRYING THEM AND
WEARING THEM

If one keeps quartz on him for a month, it will serve to stabilize and balance the human aura and become attuned to one's own vibrations. Quartz crystals keep our frequencies steady. They absorb all the imbalances. It will help to program them so that other people's energy systems don't bother you. Quartz is responsible for the bioelectromagnetism of all our energy spectrums. It picks up negative influences by pulling these negative influences into the crystalline structure before they become processed through a person's aura.

This can be done by carrying crystals in a pouch, pocket, or on a chain (wear a pendant over the heart Chakra). Sleeping with them under your pillow each night can also be very effective.

- The thymus gland is one of the body's major stress centers. A crystal worn in that area will help the heart Chakra function (see Chapter 15). When faced upward, it will serve to generate more vitality and uplift. Double-terminated crystals will serve both these aspects.
- When a crystal is worn or placed on the body, its extremely high rate of vibration will energize the wearer by increasing the body's rate of vibration.
- Wear your personal crystal hung around your neck. It heals and stimulates the crystalline structure within your body.

OTHER CRYSTAL-CLEAR FACTS

Crystals can be used for:
- Charging and vitalizing water
- Study of plant communication
- Balancing and stabilizing human energy
- Bringing wisdom and clarity in dreams
- Recording spiritual history
- If prayed over, they can develop a luminous quality or be used in rituals.

- Esoterically, the quartz crystal increases the awareness of fire and light within one's own body.
- Every crystal should be invested with a prayer to use for the good of mankind. Try this method:

When charging a crystal, hold it in your hand and charge it with breath. Draw the breath and hold (inhale), and then let it out through your nostrils suddenly (sniff out forcibly). This puts a vibration into the crystal and it will continue to oscillate according to your note. Now you can use this crystal to communicate with other persons through their "subtle bodies."

Once you've put the crystal around your neck, charge it again. Focus on your "witness area"—by the thymus gland between the shoulders—about four and a half inches down from the throat. We witness our being there. As we breathe in and out, the energy field expands and contracts. We manifest ourselves with our breath, with our being. Connect by rotating the crystal counterclockwise, penetrating the aura and the Etheric body. When that is done, you become one with the individual and can communicate. If you wish with his or her soul, you are at a soul vibration.

For healing, by charging the crystal with your own life energy, you can penetrate the aura. Draw your breath to find the person's need. You will communicate this nonverbally; the vibrations do the rest of the work.

INDIAN TECHNIQUES

SMUDGING

Put some sage, cedar, or sweetgrass in an abalone shell and light a match to it, fanning or blowing on it to create lots of smoke. Then move your crystal through the smoke or fan or blow the smoke over the crystal until it either physically looks or feels clear. This technique exorcises a room of bad vibrations. Sunlight and running water energizes the crystal.

Herkimer diamond quartz found in New York State is revered as a "dream crystal." Indians will wave it through sage smoke while praying for a healing dream and place the Herkimer either underneath the pillow or by the bedside. In the dream world, quartz can psychologically integrate the subconscious state. Crystals represent expanded awareness, the light that illuminates the depths of the unconscious. Used as a "dream talisman," they can give you affirmation of your spiritual progress. Place your crystal in a medicine pouch where it evokes the presence and guidance of the dream spirits in everyday waking life.

COMPLETE CRYSTAL HEALING:
FOR RELAXATION AND SMOOTHING OUT
YOUR BODY'S ENERGY FLOW

You will need thirteen crystals for this healing (for balance):

   10 quartz crystals approximately same size for both sides of you
    2 generators (larger crystals)
    1 crystal for wand (your choice)

1. Set up your twelve crystals to the configuration of the person you are healing. Use five of the same size crystals on one side, five on the other approximately of the same size. The person's hands should be on top of the third crystal down while he is lying on his back. Then put a large generator crystal over the top of his head and one large generator at the bottom of his feet.
2. Before the person to be healed goes into the crystal bed on the floor, seal in the force field (seven times) counterclockwise with your crystal wand. When he is in crystal formation, seal in by using your wand (seven times) clockwise.
3. Make your prayer for the good of all, and always surround you and the person you are balancing with white light. Touch the sick person's collar bone to send in the energies for transformation for a minute or so. This will remove insecurities and balance the person first.
4. Open the person's Crown Chakra by starting a counterclockwise circular motion above his head (about three to four inches over) three times.
5. Draw energy down from head to feet. Ruffle energy field with your thirteenth crystal. Send white light into crystals and have the person lie in this bed for ten to fifteen minutes. This will flood the system and concentrate energy all over. (You can energize yourself, by the way, by lying inside the crystal bed—though not in the middle of the healing!)

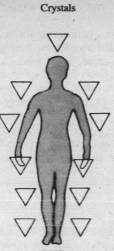

6. After ten to fifteen minutes the sick person should emerge. *Remember* to close his Crown Chakra as in closing a jar the opposite way that you opened it. Use exaggerated movements.

- You can heal best with crystals of amethyst, rose quartz, smoky quartz, tourmaline, beryl, and corundum.
- Read up on stones and healing by themselves or in conjunction with crystals.

HOW CRYSTALS WORK FOR YOU

TO SELL YOUR HOUSE

Crystals are better than baking bread in the oven to sell your home. They give it "buy me" appeal.

Method

Put one single-terminated crystal in each of the four main corners of your house when you wish the house to feel good and look wholesome to the looker. Place the four crystals with points facing into the rooms. In your mind's eye see and create a circle of white light going from point to point (seven times) as if the room were lit up like a neon light. Then, set the conditions through prayer that the sale of your home be in the best interest to seller and buyer.

UNDER CAR HOOD AND GAS LINE

A double-terminated crystal taped to the *gas line* will increase gas mileage. *Under the car hood* a crystal pointed toward the motor will help for a smoother engine performance.

CRYSTALS AROUND BABY'S CRIB
WILL HELP HIM/HER TO SLEEP OR PUT TO SLEEP

Do not use *physical* crystals for this treatment. Before baby gets into the crib, say a prayer for the comfort of your baby and *visualize* seven crystals surrounding the crib. Close in the force field (seven times), asking for white light to surround it. Now, put the baby in the crib and set the conditions for the care of your child.

CRYSTALS ON ANIMALS

Buy a collar and put a very small crystal on it, then program your needs. Good for the animal's protection—in case it gets lost, it can find its way home; also good for its health.

CRYSTALS FOR CONTACTING SPACESHIP

Choose the one you feel is most likely connected to space or a spacecraft. Program for same. Maybe you will see one that is close by the Earth. You may see a ship shape in the crystal. It might be an actual ship that is receiving your message.

CRYSTALS FOR PLANTS

Rose quartz pieces work well. Buy them by the pound and sprinkle around (no more than three) the plant, or use clear quartz and place three in a triangle facing into plant. Water the same way and program for the healing of them. A little love and music put into them will help to program.

LEADED CRYSTAL VERSUS QUARTZ

Leaded crystal has no healing power.

HOW TO PROGRAM CRYSTALS TO SING

Use only three in different sizes and shapes. Sing into them. Your voice will serve as a "tuning fork," and when you enter the room they are in, listen as they will sing for you. This will clear and energize you.

BATHTUB ENERGIZER

While bathwater is running full force, place six crystals in the tub. If it is not too uncomfortable, lie on them till the tub is filled up, then push them to the side while you do a few breathing exercises together with arm and leg movements. This will balance your sensitivity and help to clear energy blocks.

MAKING LOVE IS FUN IN A CRYSTAL BED

When you wish to, try making love in a crystal bed. You and your beloved will be totally unified. Put twelve single-terminated crystals under the mattress, all pointed toward head or foot of bed. Use a thirteenth crystal as a wand in your hand and close in circle with white light (seven times). See page 226.

HEAL YOUR SCATTERED ENERGY WITH CRYSTAL

Sit for at least five minutes a day with three crystals: two under the balls of your feet and one resting on your navel. This will create a triangulation from the navel through the lower half of your body.

Exercise will help you alleviate scattered energy or any shocks to the body that have altered your thoughts or actions. It grounds you on the Physical Plane and clears out and energizes your mind.

GO INTO YOUR CRYSTAL SANCTUARY . . .
IT'S AMAZING!

Imagine yourself shrinking down to the size of the crystal and entering it through an invisible doorway. The crystal will become your sanctuary, your laboratory for spiritual work.

It is a friend and helper.

13

Healings and Emergency Cleansings

Cast no shadows on me, dear Lord
Allow thy energies to come through me
Wistful as it may be as I am in need of your love and
    protection
Guide me through any uncalming storms and deliver me on
    thy doorstep for a healing
Fill the flame of my desires to aid mankind and eliminate any
    conscious thought that deters my vision
Fill me up with your knowledge, wisdom, guidance, and love
    so I can best serve you
As I am your earthly disciple and servant!

HEALING

PSY-CHIC: *adj.*—lying outside the sphere of physical science or knowledge: immaterial, moral, or spiritual in origin
or force.

        —WEBSTER'S NINTH NEW COLLEGIATE DICTIONARY

Sickness is the most common way to discharge fate. Most of us
seem to accept our illnesses and treating them is becoming more
and more expensive. Especially since we seem to be experienc-

ing more severe and intractable problems today more than ever before. People seem to expect to solve the problems of health in a simple way. How long will it be before people begin to grasp the fact that while we accept all the answers to our illnesses, we do nothing about it!

We can trace modern medicine back to Hippocrates (400 B.C.), who followed the God of healing. Priests then healed the sick through rituals, use of magical gemstones, and by chanting. From their point of view, illness was always connected with guilt. The rituals allowed the patient to repent and change his ways. When Hippocrates turned away from this tradition, he also turned away from the concept of ''accepting'' illness.

Medicine has concerned itself only with the *treatment* of illness and its symptoms, without touching on the sick man himself. We must begin by isolating the problem and treat where it has affected us in our physical body. By not accepting it, we treat it!

I do not encourage anyone to turn away from a physician and use a ''do-it-yourself kit.'' Our medicine *does* provide necessary help. I believe we can benefit by looking at things not on the level of mere cures of symptoms but the healing of the total person.

To heal is to make whole, and it takes place on a level that is unknown to medical science. If we can understand the state of being we will be in harmony with our problem. Only when we can say yes to it can the problem reverse itself and be terminated. Only if a man is sick can he be made whole. Without illness there is no healing. Without all of these things we would not have a closer understanding of life. To struggle against something means we are not in accord with it or reconciled to it. We can, perhaps, trace this back to our unconscious fears. When society can accept medicine only and is unwilling to take responsibility for people and their illnesses, it is unable to change fate.

Remember, we all experience symptoms. They signal that something is amiss. We can learn how to work with these signals, we can be healed.

As our race grows more and more sensitive to all our changing conditions, it needs to understand our bodies' physical, mental, and emotional conditions and needs.

We do not always have to learn to live with pain, as some doctors tell us, although we should *always* go to a physician if we are in difficulty or need a diagnosis. Often, both a medical doctor and a qualified psychic healer or metaphysician or holistic practitioner can be beneficial and work in sync with each other. However, sometimes the drugs prescribed can work adversely on the flow and chemistry of the body. The subconscious mind attuned with our physical body may tell us that something is not right.

Under the right conditions, a psychic or spiritual healer can effect a beneficial healing for almost any type of physical or emotional ailment. Call it Prana, God, life force, or good energy—the healer works with an invisible force that people can feel. It comes from God, or from the cosmos. The healer is merely the interceptor of these energies and the channel through which they flow.

A healer may not have to be specifically physical with you. Psychic energy can be transferred or induced thousands of miles away. Such is the power of thought and energy placement. You can send a flooded area of white light anywhere you wish it to go and with seriousness and intent for goodwill it can appear anywhere you wish it to be.

Some healers say disease is self-generated and self-inflicted, due to anger and pent-up emotions. A healer who "lays on hands" can usually be effective if a person is ready to be healed or cured. They will try to remove the symptoms and usually be able to tell you the causes of it. Holding on to fear and anger results in illness. The deeper we hold on, the more severe the illness. Vanquishing inner poisons may be released by one word—*forgiveness*.

Psychic healing certainly is not new. It has been performed by priests and medicine men in Indian, Atlantean, Egyptian, and Greek cultures, to name a few. It is merely being pooled together at this time from both Eastern and Western cultures, from all races and all religions. It all adds up to the same words—God or cosmic energy.

The human parts of the body and its nervous system were designed to have long life. The Bible reveals this to be so, but who among us has ever taken the time to evaluate these possibilities? But healing does not always produce miraculous or cure-all results. The process of healing is often unpredictable and a mystery. Sometimes people discover that while they went to a healer for one problem they find another part of the body has been healed. Perhaps the body might not at once have been restored to health, but the conditions that led to the illness may have.

Many healers and channels are awakening now and have come into their abilities after a severe illness, a near-death experience, or perhaps after facing undue emotional pain and trauma in their lives. Many awaken in their mid-thirties and later. It's an emotionally liberated time to begin their mission. They become transforming powers of God. **All the healers I have talked with agree that their clients should be under a doctor's care.** Most feel that along with the medical diagnosis, though, they can concentrate their energies on the place that will do the most good. If you are frightened to consult with a healer, don't be: the worst that could possibly happen is . . . nothing, zap, no results!

Be aware of the charlatans and phonies that lurk around, especially one who tells you he guarantees the healing. A healer guarantees nothing. Most don't know if it will work or what will happen. If it is not God's will, then nothing can be done, or perhaps it is your will that is blocking it. Your release consent *is* necessary.

The practices of spiritual cleansing through alchemical processes are described here. The ways to use your own God-given power through thought, prayer, and psychic-concentrated energy, in tune with your needs, are listed, though not necessarily in proper sequence or order. How can one describe for another the conditions they live with or live under? Or know exactly which type of treatment is needed? We must all make our own choices, according to our own needs.

There are also suggested treatments for psychic emergencies. Some of them are included here. I hope you will find that learning through transformation of the physical and inner bodies can flush out stifled negative energy and replenish our systems with our life's force.

BASIC HEALING PRAYERS

GOD'S UNIVERSE

In the *center*
In perfect balance and led by the light.

The light of God surrounds us. The love of God enfolds us,
     the Power of God protects us, the Presence of God
     watches over us, wherever we are, God is.
So Be It.

— Unity Prayer

The Our Father (see Chapter 9)
The Twenty-third Psalm of David (The Lord is my shepherd)

Carry these prayers (if you don't know them by heart) on little
index cards. I say them aloud or silently; they work the same. I
sometimes say them in between cleansing processes. You must
take care of yourself first, or you cannot be effective in your
work.

THE USE AND APPLICATION
OF COLOR FOR HEALING PRACTICES

Colors help us connect to the vibrations of the Universe and we
can use them to aid and heal ourselves and others. We can
channel these color agents to the physical body with positive
results as they are high frequencies of light.

Color vibrations uplift and heal our minds as well as our
bodies and emotions. Apply these colors in your mind, emanate
the color rays from the area of your third eye and down into your
hands, and "see" your hands turn the color of the healing ray.
Then, apply the color you need to yourself or for another by
imagining it touching the area you are treating.

PINK RAY—This has spiritual vibrations for all-over health,
     conditioning, and body toning. If you are allergic to a
     certain food, send the pink ray down into the affected areas,
     as it will help with certain allergies in the air around you as
     well. Pink is a nerve organizer, too, and helps you feel
     centered. Pink is the Universal color of love. Your body
     regenerates when you use pink.
BRIGHT RUBY OR DEEP RED RAY—This can be effective
     for bladder and liver infections and aids the circulatory
     system.
FUCHSIA RAY—This color will regenerate the whole Etheric
     body system. Pull this ray into your Crown Chakra (see

Chapter 15) and imagine the color fuchsia streaked with silver dust running through your body as it filters down to your throat, heart, and chest centers. This color will fill you with vital energy and will mingle with your bloodstream to renew your strength. After doing the above, for renewed extra power, try the following:

1. For physical healings, envision a circle of white light about six inches above head (a halo).
2. Picture a light green ray of light pouring down through the halo as a flowing stream of liquid coming into your Crown Chakra and continuing through all of your other six Chakras (forehead, throat, heart, solar plexus, spleen, and base). (See Chapter 15.)

VIOLET RAY—This color can penetrate anything in existence and can be used, for example, to break up congestion or even a blocked thought. Violet is the healer of the soul.

PURPLE RAY—This can cut through pain and numb it. This ray can be used to accept the condition of the body, even if the disease is of a terminal nature, and bring clarity of mind and peace to the sufferer.

DARK BLUE RAY—Use this ray to treat degenerative diseases. Releases the deep and heavy pain that accompanies advanced physical and spiritual disease.

EMERALD GREEN WITH DASH OF BLUE RAY—This is a very high healing color.

GREEN RAY—Swab the body as if you had large pieces of cotton dipped in green paint. This is for an all-over healing on the physical, emotional, and spiritual levels. Green balances the Chakras depending on various gradations of this healing color.

YELLOW GREEN RAY—This is a high ray for spiritual energy systems.

PALE GREEN RAY—Use this ray to clear out breathing problems and respiratory conditions.

YELLOW RAY—To clear the mind of heaviness, apply the color yellow to stimulate the wind (like a trade wind, use the ray slow and easy). The ray works on headaches, stomach and intestinal problems, and can ease the anxieties others feel. As you disperse the yellow ray, appeal to the intellect of the sufferer rather than to his intuitive feelings.

He will more easily accept the ray's power as he grows and learns.

BRIGHT ORANGE RAY—For vim and vigor; also aids the lower body, intestines, liver, and pancreas. Is useful for breaking up colds and phlegm.

PERSIMMON/BURNT ORANGE RAY— Use to treat advanced disease of stomach; kidney and liver infections can also be treated with this color. Ulcers, skin disorders, and blotches benefit, too.

WHITE RAY—If in doubt about what color to use, the white light is the Ray of the Father. It can heal any condition.

GOLD RAY—This is the highest color, closest to frequencies and vibrations of the Universe. Gold has the power to raise your vibrations and be magnetic.

SILVER RAY—Represents the moon. Silver prevents schizophrenia and also brings out your intuitive side, but don't overdo it! Too much silver can attract paranoia and anger. Promotes self-improvement. Balances the central nerve network.

COPPER RAY—Prevents negative attitude. Improves glandular functions.

HEALING WITH PURPLE

There is not a place on the body that cannot be healed or touched with psychic energy. If you think of and concentrate on a *deep purple color,* you will find that this particular color acts as a carrier or transmitter for healing thought forms.

When you are getting ready to heal:

1. Make your energy perfectly still and prepare yourself, body and soul, for healing.
2. Your mind should bring forth pictures of the way you want the healing to be. Picture this in the windows of your mind and heal everyone or everything within the range of those "pictures."
3. Raise your arms up toward the Universe to connect with your highest spirit general (God, Jesus, or highest spirit guide). Your index finger is pointed upward, with your other hand sending energy to the person you wish to heal.

4. As you are pointing at the person you are healing, pray for a circle of light to be brought into form over the specific area that needs healing. Pray also for the circle to be filled and let it flow with your thoughts. A simple rearrangement of cells of the body will begin. As you concentrate on that energy, direct your breathing into it and into yourself; the pressure will affect you both.

5. Positive healing light can eliminate pain and disease. Thought is all-important. Disease cells have a foreboding feeling. They also have a black and gray aura and a sad sound. Your thoughts of purple and white light have a happy vibrating sound and can go through anything and change the cells. The atom flow can reach the grayness and disintegrate it into a golden color for well-being.

Everybody has a different sound, so be attuned to this. Sometimes you may need to feel the pulse to feel the flow and sound of the body and to know where there is an adjustment needed. Your thumb or finger will feel the pulse so you can drive out pain with purple.

Notes:

1. **Always put yourself in white light before you heal**, to set up your shields. This prevents any of the negativity from the person you are healing from bouncing back into you.

2. A prayer is helpful and usually should be invoked beforehand. (See Chapter 9.)

3. Always make sure the person wants to be healed. *Ask* beforehand.

HOW TO GET RID OF A HAZE
BOTH INSIDE AND OUT:
RED AND VIOLET COMBO FOR RELEASE
OF NEGATIVE GASES

1. Use both *red* and *violet* in your mind's eye as you visualize a red and violet flame. These two colors are consuming fires that will burn out negative body gases.

2. Ask for and imagine your Crown Chakra opening and see both colors, as a flame, enter and go through your crown and pull it through the body. (See Chapter 15.)

3. Remain still and silent until you feel this is done. Close your Crown Chakra.

   - When you speak or visualize color, you experience energy waves. This twin flame combo is very powerful. Use it with caution for *extreme emergencies* when your Chakras feel dirty, your insides gummy, or filled to the brim with invisible or physical negativity.

HEALING TO CLEAN OUT YOUR VIBRATIONS BY THE USE OF COLOR, CRYSTALS, AND SOUND

1. Say a Universal prayer. Send for your higher spiritual guide.
2. See yourself walking down a path, walking on seven different-colored stones of the color ray's spectrum (primary colors). Make sure the path is a sturdy one and feel the energy of each color you walk on.
3. After you finish your walk, visualize a golden or white pyramid. Walk in and the door will automatically shut. You will stand in the center of this pyramid in total darkness (You may experience a cold, chilly feeling. It's possible after the energizing of the color ray stones.)
4. Turn counterclockwise in the darkness making three complete circles. When you have finished, look for a pinpoint dot of light where you are standing. Let yourself be drawn closer and closer to the light. Watch it become larger as you begin to walk through a beam or room of absolute brightness. *(You have entered into God's dimension of light.)*
5. Ask the guide who is with you to lead you to a healing room filled with crystals of every color you can imagine. *This is a crystal healing room, one that has been used in Atlantis.*
6. As you are walking past crystals of every size, color, and dimension, some covering floor to ceiling, some on the ceiling, some on the floor, hear the sound of these vibrating crystals as you pass. Each one has a song, a tone, all different from each other. They sing and cover every sound possible. **Caution:** *Don't stay too long,* as energies may get you overdosed.
7. To get back to the present, notice a blue or pink ray. Choose whichever one you feel the need for. When you have walked

toward it, stand underneath this beam of light and *ask* for the *return* of all your bodies intact and in perfect order. (Your subconscious will see that this is done.) Ask, too, that you return to where you started out before you left on your trip.

SAY THIS PRAYER:
 I am in the center of God's Universe
 In perfect balance and led by the light
 So Be It!

EXPLANATION:
This is an ancient Atlantean method of body attunement via the usage of very powerful energies used in the Atlantean age in the "Temples of Healing." It's a modern approach for the balancing of all four bodies within and without for the irrigation and *clearing* of your Chakra system.

POLARIZE YOURSELF

When you are in bed and you can sense the force of the flow more easily. If you lie down with your head to the north, you can be in line with the polar energies. Then you will feel yourself becoming a part of the Earth's rhythm and you will mentally float.

If you learn to float you will experience *no illness, no upsets,* and be able to *let down your guard.*

Close your eyes and put your hands in front of you. A black coolness comes in and settles in a heaviness. Learn to experience the vibrations of relaxation.

WALKING INTO OTHER PEOPLE'S FORCE FIELDS

Keep your consuming fire going . . .
Your own and no one else's that you come in contact with . . .
Learn how to handle it . . .
It's a matter of life . . . or . . .

Unfortunately, we live in an environment that is unbelievably polluted. Our planet shows only the outer physical effects of pollution. We get sick from other people's pollution. We need to live in this state of awareness. Avoid dirty auras. Watch out for the energies of those people who are part of witch covens or occult groups.

Sometimes you cannot avoid taking on the load, but you can learn to avoid it so that you do not get wiped out. Practice and concentration are necessary. Use the thought energy, notice who controls your thoughts. Is it you or is it the pollution you come in contact with?

ANGELS CAN HEAL, AS WELL AS YOU, THROUGH YOUR AURA

Angels are not human, they are not people, they are energy! High Angels come to us as colors, sparks (fireflies), or balls of light. They bring us wisdom and illuminate us. The Angel worlds are in one vibration and our world is in another vibration or frequency. When they want to communicate, they will come into our dreams, through a medium or Clairvoyant, or through a white light. It can sound like electricity crackling or a shock. They can light up a room as they translate as light.

When you are ill, invoke the aid of an Angel. Your aura is disturbed when you are ill; the colors are dark, giving off sick impulses. If you can stimulate the areas of illness, you too can change your body's energy as well.

The healing of the future is working with the electrical body, the physical body, and the aura. Why not use the power of the color rays as you work with your Angel?

USING A PHILOSOPHER'S STONE TO GAIN WISDOM AND KNOWLEDGE

1. Put palm Chakras on armrests of chair, similar to a throne. Feel the lights of energies energizing your palms with light (chair represents the "hot seat of knowledge").
2. Put your feet up on a stone (philosopher's stone). Good for your Etheric or energy body.
3. While you are now sitting in this reality with your hands resting on your armed living- or dining-room chair, be aware of the energies in your hands as well as your feet as they pull in the energies of your philosopher's stone.

4. Seal in your energies after finishing prayers asking for insight
   and wisdom, and seal it with a greenish gold and violet light
   surrounding you as a halo. It will revitalize your force field
   and hold for a good three-day period of enlightenment.

Philosopher—Represents all the esoteric teachings there are.
Stone—Has all of Earth's healing properties in it.
Feet—Pertain to the understanding of man.

FOR TRAPPED NEGATIVE ENERGY AND
REVITALIZING YOUR FORCE FIELD

- See a white cylinder (visualize).
- Put yourself into it. Image your whole body.
- Breathe in seven times. Breathe out seven times.

Visualize your Crown Chakra opening and work white light
down each Chakra, letting in spiritual energy to each center.

Breathe out negative air. Pull in lavender air (see it happening)
through color visualization. Think it.

Concentrate on *caduceus energy* (visualize cobras at bottom
of spine; the Hippocratic symbol of snakes entwined). The
Kundalini center, the lower spine disc, will then begin to
activate.

Put a magnet overhead (through thought) and draw out any
trapped negative energy. Visualize . . . and ask this to be
done!

Now, coat blue color in the throat. Imagine dipping a paint
brush into a can of blue paint (painting your throat). Imagine
yourself sitting on a throne wearing a white gown, your throat
a beautiful blue. Sit back, watch yourself, and view yourself
sparkling as silver dust falls downward. Stay in this position for
five minutes before going back to normal activities.

Note: The throat center is the gateway to clairvoyance. It
serves as an energy station. Upper respiratory areas will be
cleansed. It is painted blue because blue is the throat Chakra
color.

This exercise especially helps trapped energy move from the
heart up to the head. Clears head and throat pains.

BLACK AND WHITE SILHOUETTE EXERCISE

Try the following exercise to keep negative thought forms from forming and to rid yourself of negative thoughts:

1. Create an image of your body as you view it mentally in front of you.
2. See your whole body in total darkness or visualize yourself being all black.
3. Imagine a white light coming in and down through the top of your head. It is coming in very white.
4. See the white light pushing down the black energy as it creeps through your head, down your body, and push it, push it again as the white creeps down, causing the black negativity to leave through both your legs.
5. Make sure it finishes eliminating all the black in your feet and toes. *Now see yourself totally in brilliant white light.*

Thoughts can heal you. Proper thinking produces an electrical impulse in the brain. It goes throughout a person's body to produce the manifestation that the brain thought is sending. Happy and angry thoughts can be measured.

Analyze your thoughts. Substitute good thoughts for the bad, and if you find it hard to do that, say:

I am filled with healing light (three times).
I am whole (three times).
I am healthy (three times).

CLEANSINGS

FOR CLEANSING YOUR ENERGIES AND AURA THROUGH THE WINDMILL EFFECT

• With perpetual motion
• For quick and fast relief

EXPLANATION:
You may need movement to speed up impurities or negative energies you have come into contact with. Each spoke of light is like the speed of sound. With the power of thought you transcend time and space and rid yourself of rancid energies from the

Earth Plane. It serves as a gravity force to bring the alchemical process from the Universal energies into you.

1. Create the image of a windmill inside you.
2. See it being put in the center of your heart. Image it, as it will act as a generator, a motion to cleanse and purify your energies or to pull as if by force that stuck or negative energy out of all of your Chakras. Imagine it moving at a faster speed turning counterclockwise.
3. Watch it grow bigger and bigger as it rotates. Each spoke on the windmill is bright energizing light as it moves as though by gravitational force faster and faster.

You say, while you are erecting this in your mind's eye:

I call on God, the protector of my energy
I ask that He set up a force field of light as a windmill
to keep my aura cleansed and protected.

This should be said at the end of the thought projections as this will set the conditions in place and keep you safe for a while.

FOR BALANCING YOUR ENERGIES
IN AIR, ON LAND, AND AT SEA
(Nausea in Motion)

To balance your energies in air, on land, or at sea, put yourself in a white spiral cone. Hold hands extended out to imaginary white walls, palms against wall.

For safety in flight or at sea, envision your plane or boat wrapped in a cocoon of white light. In case of air turbulence or rough seas, command the energies of the light to be balanced for you and all those traveling with you.

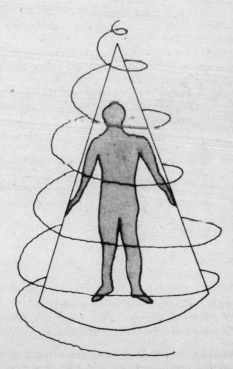

FOR HEALING OF CIGARETTE ABUSE

Put cigarettes in white light to rid yourself of hacking cough and
fear of disease.

Envision tobacco leaves to be celery leaves.

FOR GROUP HEALINGS

PHYSICAL HEALING

1. Have a glass of clear water in the room on a piece of furniture
   to absorb and pull in bad energies.
2. Have the group breathe deeply and slowly through their
   mouths three times to build up Prana energy and clear out
   toxic energies. (See Chapter 8).
3. Each person in the group rubs his or her wrists and palms
   briskly to increase the circulation and cause heat to be used
   for the energy needed in healing.
4. The group is instructed to close their eyes and place their
   hands in front of them, palms facing them, and to focus their
   psychic energy and desires to heal, into the palms of their
   hands until hands become hot.
5. Each member of the group is then instructed to place hot
   hands on forehead, face, and head of the person seated next
   to them.
6. Proceed with other healing techniques described in this
   chapter.

MENTAL HEALING

1. The leader looks into the subject's eyes and tunes in to the
   condition of mind and emotions.
2. The leader then talks to the subject and evaluates his or
   her karmic condition. This is accomplished by conversing
   about the subject's state of being. The leader must try to tune
   in to the inner levels of the subject's subsconscious mind
   and soul.
3. Past lives should be searched and mentally asked questions in
   order to determine the causes of problems existing in present
   time and present life.

4. The major causes of present illnesses and psychological blocks are usually due to religious guilts from past lives. Determine what these are.

SPIRITUAL HEALING

Protect yourself with white light and Prayer of Protection (see Chapter 9) before doing a healing with others. Ask if they want to be healed. Then, concentrate on a ray of white light projected from your third eye into the eyes of the person you are to heal. Then ask the God force to come through if the person is to receive the healing.

The performer raises his level of consciousness by tuning up his vibrations through meditation, breathing deeply, or chanting AUM (three times).

VERY EFFECTIVE HEALING
FOR HIGH BLOOD PRESSURE

TOOLS:
Three mineral stones: paradox, peridot, emerald (buy them at a museum shop or lapidary store).

• These stones have the properties to lower the high voltage of the body's energy rate and distribute energy evenly throughout the body.

CAUTION:
If the person you want to help doubts this method, proceed with care!

EXERCISE 1

Hold your blue and green stones in your hands and breathe into your nostrils the feelings and colors of these three stones. As you are in the process of doing this, visualize the color violet going into the energies of the three stones in your hand.

Empty yourself—take a deep, deep breath. Take another whole breath in. Do not hold it. Breathe a little less deeply (three times). This will clear and center you.

Activate and energize your stones in crystal spring water overnight to clear out any unwanted negative energy.

The green and blue stones will work through the brain and circulatory system. Breathe all three colors into your system (blue, green, and violet), then put the stones to your lips as you breathe, keeping all these colors in your mind's eye. Gradually feel all these colored energies spiraling around or twirling around your body (head to toe) as a rainbow and focus on this blue, green, violet twirling flag of a rainbow for ten seconds.

EXERCISE 2

Purchase and use *mother of pearl, amethyst, garnet,* and *alexandrite*. Hold all of these stones in your palm (cleansed, of course). Walk toward a tree and step on a tree trunk or root of the tree, as the energy of the tree will ground you and clear out all unwanted energies. Your feet should feel as if they are being pulled down into the Earth. Breathe the energies through your nostrils and through your body.

Now, put a shield around you. You do this by simply visualizing a sheet of pure cotton covering you from head to toe. It will serve as a magnet for excitement and help with the lowering of body temperature.

Note: Alternate these two regularly and **keep doing what your doctor says.** In no way will it do anything but speed up your recovery.

When high blood pressure exists, all the "excitement" forces and centers of the bodies are overtaxed and generate too high an energy. This causes the body's excretions to go out of balance. The energy of these stones works for you to clear out and balance all the passages of blood through the heart and circulatory system. Stones act as agents to pull this accelerating force through you and harmonize with the rest of your system. (see Chapter 11.) You should carry the stones of the treatment you have chosen in a pouch *on your person*.

Some people find that these methods augment the help they are receiving from their doctor. Some find this method works by itself. **Always check with your doctor when augmenting his treatment.**

If you doubt it, don't try it!

HOW TO HEAL HOT FLASHES

This exercise helps to get rid of hot flashes brought on by menopause or ovarian surgery.

TOOLS FOR TRANSFORMATION:
Only a red stone will do (red sea glass, ruby, or any bright red stone).

STEPS

1. Hold the stone in your hands and allow it to pick up your vibrations as you clear your mind.
2. Bring it up to your lips and inhale through your nostrils the color's energy and vibrations. Then exhale the color through your mouth.
3. As you inhale, picture little red wheels going through your entire body, following the path of your blood. As you inhale the color of the red stone it will balance you with your body heat, which breaks up estrogen.
4. When you feel a hot flash coming on, breathe in those little red wheels and watch them circulate through your whole body. Activate red wheels whenever you need to, as they will act in unison with your body and give you balance throughout your system.
5. Visualize, then, the whole body radiating red equally to give you an even flow. (Red works like a body thermostat.)

Note: If you have a heavy menstrual flow, try taping this red stone on the area of your ovaries, or put the stone into a pouch directly over the affected area. It will help the cramping and extraneous flow to subside.

MALE MENOPAUSE:
RED, WHITE, AND BLUE METHOD

INGREDIENTS:
One Herkimer diamond.
Used to flush out toxins from system and eliminate depression in menopausal men.

1. Hold a *Herkimer diamond in your hand. Empower it by projecting a white light to glow inside of it.
2. Mentally put on a bathrobe of light (picture a lounging robe).
3. Visualize a twelve-inch phonograph record the color of royal blue and balance this disc on top of your head. See the record start to rotate in a clockwise motion, using your head as a turntable.
4. See your bare feet standing ankle high in a *bright red sea* of water.

---

*Herkimer diamonds are from the mineral kingdom of quartz and are considered magical stones. They contain an electrifying energy that is good for transformation. American Indians used this stone to help with their dreams and altered states of being. (See Chapter 11.)

14

The Left-Hand Path: The Dark Side and Evil

"Ghandi said,
the enemy is not always wrong."
Every individual has the potential
to discover the light within himself.

The Moon is in the center of the Universe
It is malefic and creates energies of illusion, disgust and
    despair
Purgatory is one that stands neither under light nor darkness
but is in the hands of God on a Physical Plane.

Try as I might to put my thoughts down on this chapter without sounding like a doomsayer or some sort of weirdo with a crucifix in one hand and a stake in the other, I can't seem to make the subject of dark forces sound light.

It's simple, really. We are all subject to the forces of energy and some of them are evil. We must learn to defend ourselves, to hurl back the negative forces of those who want to possess us or control us or harm us for their own evil purposes. In this chapter, I will teach you how to build your psychic self-defense system, how to hurl evil back or put up a shield so that it does not penetrate your soul.

I don't want to speak too much of evil, except to say that you know it's out there and we will all, always, be tested. Spelled backward, it is "live" energy. Evil is a counterpart of God and all positivity. We do need to be exposed to the dark side, whether it be physical or in a spirit body, in order to achieve the proper balance to move the many steps forward to meet with our higher self or to our spiritual higher vibrational levels. We must be exposed to learn! Never shrink back with fear. We must meet it head on or keep ourselves closed in a vigil of awareness. By our being constantly tested by the negative side (which is used as a counterbalance for our growth), even though temporarily side-tracked, we do come back to "rightfully" choose a new direction, get ourselves back on a new growth course. This path eventually leads us to a level of higher vibrations.

Negativity runs the other way, as it cannot break through this shield of light. Making a decision on how to handle negativity gives us a choice. From that moment on, what and how we choose ends our test period and puts us on the path we are to follow—whether it is higher or lower. Remember this: Love is the answer to combat evil. It is love alone that can overcome the evil barriers of violence and aggression. It is love that can help us to perceive that selfishness and manipulation are evil. Love can displace our lust for possessions. Love broadens our understanding so that we can see that it is better to give than to receive. Love helps us to help those around us who may be floundering on their spiritual path.

We know that we are all standing amid negative force fields all around us. We are receivers and senders of energy and we must learn to give out positive energy and to hurl back evil energy that is sent to us, to repel it with love, or to put up our psychic shield and defend against it. We must learn, too, that we must never misuse the energy of God's power. It is not through force but *will* that we can extinguish these evil energies.

God is infinite. Evil is short-lived.

Your *circle of protection* is your white light. It gives you protection from *unknown* entities, protection from evil or negativities. By giving out too much help from your own energy systems, your aura can become depleted and broken. Any broken line in an aura is an easy mark or way for anything seen or unseen (spirit as well as people) to break through your force field. Your own health is, therefore, at stake! It breaks down your immune system barriers and through psychic attack permits illness to get inside you.

Reinforce your aura by demanding (mentally) and commanding this attack to *stop*, to go back to the source it came from. Then *ask* your higher self, your God-self, and higher power to seal and close off your aura with a band of *golden light*.

IF SOMEONE PUTS A SPELL ON YOU OR SOMEONE ELSE, OR YOU FEEL YOU ARE BEING HAUNTED

1. Get his picture or write his name on a piece of paper.
2. Light a white candle and say this prayer: "Let evil return to evil." (Say this three times.)
3. Burn the picture or paper completely. Make sure it burns completely. Burn it until it is nothing but black ashes. This will remove the curse.

TO RID YOURSELF OF SOMEONE WHO WON'T TAKE NO FOR AN ANSWER: TRAP DOOR DISASSOCIATION/DUMBWAITER SYSTEM OF RELEASE

This is good to know if you have felt plagued by people who won't take *no* for an answer, refuse to get lost, and refuse the *exit door* of your life. After many trials and tribulations and asking them politely to get out of your life, they leave you no choice but to resort to "legal" methods of removal of their energies . . . *forever*.

- All of the following must be done as a ritualistic process before beginning:

1. Pray to your higher powers. Ask that they fill your vibrations with love.
2. Mentally don your ceremonial gown or robe of Light. *Note to alchemists:* Red robe and a brilliant vibrant blue gown makes purple gold edges. Imagine this.
3. Mentally put on a headpiece consisting of gold made to look like a crossbar (from temple to temple) with filigree work in it.

4. See the person you want erased from your life in a black light (black absorbs all energies) with a red color in back of him (red is the color of primordial energy).
5. See the darkish figure of the person you are exorcising *standing on a trap door* with a lever on the side of it to which you have control. Perhaps you may think of him standing in a police line-up with the lever near you to pull.
6. Now light your white candle as you call in your spirit guides for assistance.
7. Repeat this incantantation three times:

I wish to erase [*person's name*] from my memory bank. That is the memory bank of [*my name*].

Also, I wish to rid any thought forms from any of the controlling entities that surround [*friend's name*] that negatively influence him.

I release all thought forms and vibrations that associate myself [*your name*] with [*person's name*] and again I release the entities that control and influence him or her.

I wish this to be immediately carried out and to remain in power indefinitely. Thank you.

So Be It!

Amen

Note: It may take a while for the cycle to rid yourself of this being on all levels, but with patience and positive thought of action it will be done. For extreme cases, repeat the process once more eight days later after sunset.

HOW TO GET RID OF A PLAYFUL HOUSE GUEST—OOPS, HOUSE GHOST!

• Paint the house. Remove all the old wallpaper—it holds thoughts. Ghosts that are thought forms don't like red, so think about choosing it when ghosts seem strongest.
• Strong, loud music, especially rock and roll, should be played loudly for a period of three days.
• Burn sandalwood incense for one week. This is a good purifier.
• Ghosts do not like strong light or sunshine. Flood the house with light and lots of sunshine.

If the above methods do not work, bring in a spiritualist medium. They can speak to the ghosts through their thoughts and find out why they are there or what they want. They will tell them how to leave and travel on.

Ghosts are thought forms that attach themselves to the area they have lived in or perhaps died in. Their thoughts are so strong, they linger on, so much so that their energies have crystalized into a habit. You have to release the thought form.

There have been many reports of old mansions, castles, or estates where people hear some clatter, chains banging together, or pots and pans crashing. They can't see anyone, but that energy habit (ghost) is still hanging around. Pray for the ghost to go into the light!

FOR RELUCTANT SPIRITS
WHO ARE EARTHBOUND

Adapted from Banishing Evil, *by Jonathan Parker*

1. Fill a bowl with coarse salt and concentrate on it while you are starting to concentrate on an inner stillness.
2. Say a prayer of protection to set the conditions of safety in place. Remember to use your white light.
3. Take four or five deep, deep breaths and ask for energy to be put into your hands. *Will* it there. They should start feeling hot and have a tingly sensation.
4. Place the palms of your hands about nine inches over the bowl of salt.
5. *Say:*

   • My hands are the energies of GOD.
   • I free these energies into this bowl of salt.
   • I *command*, so it will be done.
   • I *command* this to be released so it will burn and repel all undesirable things not with God on all planes of existence.

6. Feel your God energy flowing through you into the salt and release these energies into it.
   The salt is now charged.

   Imagine your hand to be a knife. Pass this knife across your forehead—down your stomach—and *will* the connections to the salt to be cut. You do not want to remain attached to anything.

   Now you are ready for your dehaunting. The salt will stay charged for a long time.

Sprinkle the salt around the house in every room, especially in corners. It will repel negative influences as long as it is there. Utilize the salt after sunset (the rays burn some Astral entities and won't leave the house). Leave some doors and windows open. Take some deep breaths to fortify your own aura with energy, and also to keep anything negative away from you.

Keep sprinkling salt every few feet into the closets, behind and under furniture, and say: *"I command all negative entities to burn or leave!"* In each room you go into, or perhaps whatever room is filled with these Astral things, stand in the center of the room and visualize a white light emanating from your body and filling the entire room with white light, dissolving all negative things.

Fill yourself with pink and spread the pink outward and ask that the house be filled with *love*. If you would prefer to ask your spirit guides or Guardian Angels for assistance, you can do so.

Another way to perform this dehaunting is to imagine the wind coming in (you are actually asking for the energy of the Universe to help you). You might open the windows if that helps stimulate your imagination. Ask the wind to flow through you into the salt in the room.

HOW TO EXORCISE A HOTEL OR MOTEL ROOM

Adapted from Banishing Evil *by Jonathan Parker*

Use the dehaunting technique on p. 251. It's especially important that you dehaunt. Thousands of vibrations have slept here, and no doubt some of them were very negative. Rake through your bed to lift this negativity and cleanse. (Do so by compelling your hands to lift the negative energy. Hands act as a rake.)

1. Fill a cup with water or holy water.
2. Make passes with your hands as if you had a knife in them and start from the head of the bed to the foot.
3. When you feel the energies being broken and lifting, take your cup or glass of water and command these energies to go into this receptacle. Say the command three times.
4. Keep this at the foot of the bed.
5. Later, you will throw it away as you do not want to keep any receptacle that is negative.

6. Stand on the side of the bed with hands aimed toward the head and imagine energy coming out of your fingertips from top to bottom. As you get to the foot of the bed, flick your hands as if they had water on them. Flick them downward toward the cup of water as you say: *"I find this energy in that water."* Do this at least four or five times to strip the bed of its negative energies.

Now take the water and either throw it outside or dump it down the toilet and throw away the cup. Then, standing at the foot of the bed, turn your palms toward the bed and channel energy from the Universe through your body, out of your hands, and fill the bed with love energy. Visualize a beautiful pink aura all around your bed and fill it with love. *Will* that anyone who lies on the bed will be filled with live energy. Be sure to cut that psychic connection between you and the bed.

PSYCHIC ATTACK

If you feel you are being attacked by either seen or unseen things, say *"Anyone attempting to reach me in a negative way will reach the Universal mind,"* or: *"I will that anyone trying to read my mind for selfish purposes will reach the Universal mind."*

You can generate a white energy sphere from your solar plexus region to expand it so that it fills your aura. Then will all negativity to be dissolved by the energy sphere.

SYMPTOMS OF PSYCHIC ATTACK

1. *Discordant influences* in the material world:

• The relationship always goes wrong
• Financial difficulties
• General instabilities
• Fighting with everyone

2. *Intellectual capacity.* Blocked, always uncertain, can't ever make up your mind, mental wandering, no control of emotions or reactions to other people.

3. *Unhealthy condition of physical body.* Sudden skin eruptions, film or clouding over the eyes (especially when you check with a physician and he finds nothing wrong).

4. *Blockage of finding spiritual or psychotherapeutic help*. When you know you desire assistance and help and everything blocks your progress in getting there, prayer doesn't help, there is no peace or serenity . . . only thoughts of self-destruction.
5. *Feelings of negativity*. Trends of thought run to causing fights, bitterness toward other people, total hatred, total jealousy, total pride and vanity.

REVERSE 'EM

FIRST: Know for sure who or what's attacking you.
SECOND: The boomerang effect goes into play—what you give out, comes back.

- Prepare for a calm frame of mind—relax all your muscles.
- Fix your gaze on the most distant point visible to you.
- Take a deep breath, hold it, and then let it out with a loud explosive sound as though you were expelling the negative energy itself. Take your next deep breath as though the air for it were coming from that distant point you set your gaze on. Repeat.
- As you have inhaled a third time from the distant point—see in your mind's eye the person from whom the attack is coming. Feel the negation being drawn to you with each breath you inhale. Then exhale as before with a short, explosive sound. This time, as you exhale with an *explosive* sound, it should be as guttural as possible. See the negativity being sent back to the distant point and back to the person from whom it came.

The key is the strength of your visualization and concentrated sound of rejection that comes as you exhaled. You want to include the entire power of your physical, emotional, mental, and spiritual self to impel the negativity right back to its source. Don't allow any deviation.

PSYCHIC DEFENSES AND SHIELDS

1. When afraid, always think of a white light as your protection.
2. Say a prayer and ask for protection as you put up your shields. Praying is good, as it lifts your vibrations, attracts higher entities, teachers, and such.

3. Don't think, just hum. Whistle a song or sing to yourself, as it will pull you together. It will, in effect, tune you up.
4. Meditation helps your psychic defenses. The mind becomes calm and you become stronger.
5. When challenged, breathe deeply.
6. Be careful whom you help. If you are not, you can be pulled down and energy will be drained. Never pity anyone. They are suffering because they have certain lessons to learn, they have a certain Karma. Having feelings and considerations is all right, but be careful of feeling sympathy. People may take you into their vibrations and all of yours will close off. Put yourself in a "tube of white light" and close off your solar plexus (stomach area) if you feel overwhelmed by a person making a bid for your sympathy.
7. On the other side of the coin, you can tune up your own energy by being near someone who is already developed. Your aura will tap into his or her aura. You will feel the power, you will accelerate upward and feel high.
8. Physical exercise will help. Walk a lot, don't sit for hours without moving. Keep everything inside you circulating.
9. Focus on a white candle. Pray into it. You will feel aware of higher worlds. It is a spiritual focusing. If you need something better, *ask for it. Ask* and you will *receive.*
10. *Food* vitalizes your energies. Eating is a necessary force for the human body.
11. Sleep will make you reach higher levels. You must get enough sleep.
12. Be careful of hypnosis. You should be careful of anyone who speaks in a soft manner, especially a monotone voice that makes you feel as if you would like to fall asleep. Salesmen use this technique to sell things, as does anyone who wants to talk you into something. If you raise your voice, or snap your fingers three times, you will create a shock and break the spell. A cough will also break any spell.

EMERGENCY PSYCHIC SELF-DEFENSE

If you are positive you are the victim of psychic attack, use these self-defense methods:

1. Breathe deeply three times.
2. Say a prayer of protection.
3. Stand erect, arms at sides.
4. Visualize an intense blue light coming down into your body.
   Be aware of another intense circle of white light above your
   head.
5. With your inner vision, see the white ball growing intensely
   brighter and larger, staying there, but some of the white light
   is running down. Bring this down too so that its aura fits and
   merges with the blue and it runs outside the intense blue light.
6. As you are now aware of these two color images, see the
   white globe again over your head sending down glittery silver
   sparkles flooding your aura and at the same time permeating
   and coming vibrantly through you.

REINFORCEMENTS OF THIS ENERGY

For the remainder of the day imagine sign symbols on your third
eye or brow, such as a Star of David, a cross, a pentagram, or a
crescent. Even a dancing girl can be a symbol if it makes you
happy. The sign should be visualized in the same brilliant blue
light if you feel an impending danger.

HOW TO RID THE BODY OF NAUSEA
FROM NEGATIVE ENERGY

In a hospital waiting room, lecture hall, restaurant, or any place
a lot of people gather or congregate, you may want to:

1. Breathe in color (inhale white and pink through each nostril).
2. Exhale the color blue.

• Be sure to protect yourself and other people from expelled
  negative energy by placing yourself in a protective light before
  you work. I like to imagine a clear amethyst light.

HOW TO RID YOURSELF
OF NEGATIVE THOUGHT FORMS

• Stop and confront your thought forms.
• Destroy them!

• They are parts of yourself that need to go so you can become a more healthy self.

EXAMPLES:
• Use an imaginary "zap gun" on them.
• See the thought become a cheese and watch it melt.
• Use an imaginary wand, rod, arrow, sling, or rock to destroy your thoughts; dynamite can be effective too.

RESTAURANTS NEED EXORCISMS TOO . . . NEW AND OLD

Q. Why do they keep changing hands?
Q. Are people reluctant to go into them to eat?
Q. Is the ambiance creepy, is it dark, does it feel dirty?

Wood needs cleaning and prayer.
Salt must be sprinkled around.
Vibrations should be lifted by chants (sound and candle rituals).
Perhaps a flowing water fountain stocked with fish and crystals would help. (Fish could grow, too.)
Try having garlic in bags in all the corners (you won't smell it if the air is cleared out by your spiritual cleansings).
A huge quartz programmed crystal will help to absorb negativity.

VAMPIRES

PSYCHIC SAPPERS AND VAMPIRES

Sappers are those people who generally, unknowingly "sap" energy from other people via their auras. Some sappers deliberately behave this way. I have studied some of them knowingly manipulating other people's energy and force fields. It is an act of ungodliness. Following is a blueprint on how to detect sappers of both kinds and how to stop them from bleeding your aura.

How do you recognize a sapper? Sappers do not have an especially determined energy of their own. They drain from others at first by simply demanding attention. Nice, sensitive people are easy victims, as they always are too nice *not* to give anyone their attention. They are easy marks. Family as well as close friends make it all the easier as you are supposed to love them and give them your attention first and foremost. If you don't, guilt attacks.

A sapper refuses to be guided into a state of independence. He gathers his strength only by feeding on the poor unfortunates who do their own work. He finds he cannot release himself wholeheartedly in some activity and always needs to be within eyesight or hearing of one or some of the people he truly thinks are marvelous.

If you slowly stop giving your attention little by little, maybe he will have to find the answers for himself. If not, know you are doing someone less good by allowing yourself to be used this way. Try explaining how he can work out his own problems. At the same time, put up your *shields!*

HOW TO PROTECT YOURSELF FROM SAPPERS AND VAMPIRES

This general method will apply when you feel your energies drained by another person.

1. Wrap yourself in a bluish purple light, almost like a cocoon.
2. Place a white cylinder around you and make sure you are inside it.
3. Surround yourself in a *pink mist* or fog of pink light.

FOR AN ATTACK ON YOUR FREE WILL

1. Face your opponent, eyeball to eyeball.
2. Ask your higher power mentally for protection against evil or wrongdoers and surround your aura head to toe with a brilliant white light.
3. You will begin to emanate a ray of brilliant iridescent white light, an intense one, from your third eye into his and continue until he begins to squirm or move away. (He will definitely be dazzled.)

FOR USE AGAINST A SAPPER

1. Repeat numbers 1 and 2 as above, but after a shot of brilliant white light, start to change the emanation to a rosy glow.

Discount number 3. *Instead*, from the third eye send out a blue ray (this will calm them down).

All three of these methods will protect your energy, sympathy, and vulnerability.

HOW TO PROTECT YOUR AURA
FROM THE SIMPLY SELFISH PERSON

Here's what you do with the simply selfish person or an innocent child who tries to drain your energy:

1. Enter a still state and say these words: *"No one can draw off my energy. I am shielded by the white light of God, which completely surrounds me and blocks them."*
2. Sick people unknowingly do this to strengthen themselves. Try to hold their left hands with your right hand if you can. Know you are channeling the flow of God's energy from the ethers into them to strengthen and heal them.

For children's rotten attitudes and tantrums, lovingly hold the child in an embrace and will the two of you to be surrounded by pure white light. Create the thought in your mind surrounding the two of you in light, then spin the light around you both clockwise in the northern hemisphere and counterclockwise in the southern hemisphere, and *will* that pure light energy to dissolve and disintegrate all negativity and fixation in and around the child. Hold the white light in your vision around you both for a while, then send a radiant pink light of love energy from your solar plexus area and ask for this low light to fill the child, casting out all fears.

You can also use this for pets who get ill or angry if their masters leave them.

Always remember to disengage yourself from the person you have contacted by mentally cutting a "cord" with gold scissors.

POSSESSIONS

- Stuttering
- Schizophrenia
- Manic depressive illness

Possession occurs when earthbound spirits do not realize that they have died and intense emotional feelings keep them attached to the Earth Plane. They can possess sensitive persons, live in their houses, and get inside of them. In some cases it is believed that epilepsy is due to possession. People can become possessed at birth (although it is not common). Spirits can enter a person during an emotional outburst. Some possession symptoms are: twitching, particularly when a person is trying to relax; a person who stares blankly without much of a memory may be possessed; those suffering from multiple personalities, suicidal tendencies, or who have had their energy totally drained.

Those possessed can speak languages other than the ones they know. They may become clairvoyant or experience voice changes. A person who becomes possessed usually has severe complexes of hate, fear, and guilt. Someone near them has died and they can strongly will the person to return, to come back. Possessors are trapped on this plane and cannot reach the higher levels. They are in between planes. Maybe someone put an "evil eye" on them and they were too weak to fight back.

Antidote: Careful with this one. If you are not strong enough yourself, enlist the help of several strong and highly developed spiritual beings.

1. Always, always, say the Our Father (three times).
2. Take many, many deep breaths to fortify and fill your aura with brilliant light and command a white bright light to shine over you.
3. *Say:*

   I am a white light [three times]. Surround me, white light, and shield my aura against any negative attacks. I am wrapped with this robe of light and love from the Universe of harmony. I will this white light to dissolve all and any negativity hurled at me. Surround me, all enlightened Masters, and we command all entities to be part in love. Go to God for enlightenment. I free them from me so they may advance and I am free. So Be It.

POSSESSION VERSUS OBSESSION

Possession means that a being has been invaded by an evil or discarnate spirit. It is an *external* force of energies that enters the body of a soul, a form of ownership and actual occupancy of a being. It is forced in by a soul who has no particular reason for being or living a life of surety. They can, therefore, be induced and swayed by a physical weakness, drugs, alcohol, or by a nervous disorder.

Obsession is *internal* as spirit fills the mind completely and occupies the thoughts, directing them to one thing. Obsession is a complete domination of the mind by one idea: a fixed idea. We self-obsess when we turn our own energies against ourselves.

We have to find a balance rather than create our own hells. We do everything to ourselves, we are not victims of God or other people. We alone create the reasons for our own states of being.

DRUGS

Psychic faculties are open to curses when you take drugs because they loose the girders of the mind and give it a temporary of consciousness. It is okay to unleash the mind for leaving character and personality development through the slow ripening practice of mind training and meditation, but drugs are a disastrous means of development.

For the highly sensitive soul, experimenting with drugs can be disastrous for the Chakra system. It can open the subtler planes of existence to the experimenter and should be avoided—you never know what will walk in through those subtle open doors. Fright could cause a sensitive soul to totally freak out. Indeed, many spirit possessions do occur when the body's psychic shield is lowered due to drugs. These spirits can make suggestions that can make it impossible for you to get back to the Physical Plane. A lowered vitality leaves an open gate to invasion and your Earth trip could be over before you accomplish your life's mission.

AREAS OF SPIRIT POLLUTION

You may want to avoid some bars in rough neighborhoods; cemeteries; houses near cemeteries; some old houses.

There are many earthbound spirits around. They may have died but are still attached to the Earth or perhaps to some people due to intense love, hate, or fear.

Some people I have spoken to think it is cute to have spirits live at home with them, but you should understand that if a spirit is earthbound, it is due to a lot of negativity in his life on Earth.

You will know if you are in an area of spirit pollution when you feel chills, intense heat, experience lots of sneezing, or feel a tightening of the throat.

CURSES

THE COMMON TYPE

This is when a person is angry or jealous of you, is upset, and thinks negative thoughts about you. If you've been cursed this way, you may suffer from sickness, accidents, losing things or hurting yourself, bad luck, the "evil eye," or perhaps have had a death prayer said over you. **Say the Antidote.**

UNCOMMON

This is when a black magician conjurs up a dark ritual at midnight against you. Keep deep breathing for an hour. This will be the cure as you say the Antidote.

ANTIDOTE

Say over and over again:

- I am love.
- I am a white light.
- I am harmony.
- I am peace—come to me.

(Say it with feeling and meaning.)

MENTAL CLEARING

Rid yourself of negative suggestion. Don't give any curse power. Doubt must go; fear brings it to you.

Know that nothing negative can have any effect whatsoever unless you accept it. You give it power if you believe it. You must be totally convinced that nothing evil can happen unless you give it power through belief. Get to the root of the curse, or negative systems will return. Mentally clear yourself of these energies and then fill yourself to the brim with love, harmony, and peace.

PROTECTING YOUR HOME

The basic cleansing begins with a burning white candle, fresh flowers (I am partial to white ones), and an open-topped container of water. Also, the saying of The Lord's Prayer.

I go through the house room by room, saying The Lord's Prayer. If I stumble or forget, I begin again until it is perfect and I keep repeating until the room feels right.

Always, before you begin any such process, do your prayers of protection (see Chapter 9).

Understand, too, that *exorcism* will work only if your energy is significantly stronger than the energy of the entity you want to exorcise.

Chanting the negative energies out is more effective at times than prayers, as it sets up a vibrating field that connects to the rhythm of the unseen entity. As you continue to chant and shield your vibrations (with light), the entity suddenly finds he has to fight off your vibration and you have dominion and an advantage over him or her.

ARTIFACTS FOR PURIFYING AND CLEANSING YOUR HOME

- Gemstones
- Candles
- Water
- Scents and incense
- Metals
- Music
- Smudging

USE OF THE BIBLE

The Bible is not simply a book to be kept on a bookshelf. It's funny that it is probably one of the only things that never gets stolen from hotel rooms or homes. It contains the books of recorded facts and scriptures to help mankind understand the transformation and energies of God. It is a history book and has an energy all its own. The "written word" is the vital importance and words have energy. When it's opened, the power seeps out and causes an energy vibration that brings forth the messages of life. When you utilize the Bible for safety, usually by reading it, an intense vibration is set up. You need to control and incorporate these energies for your cleansings and purifying.

The *use of candles* brings forth the essence of light. Each color has a sound and vibration all its own. The wax is usually a pure energy, while the fire and flame activates all. It is the mastery of light.

HOW TO CLEANSE YOUR ROOM OR HOUSE
OF NEGATIVE SPIRITS

• White Candle
• Prayer
• Bible

When doing a single room, light incense and leave it on a table. Walk around the room in a counterclockwise circle with an open Bible in your hand, saying The Lord's Prayer until your circles get smaller and smaller as you find yourself making a vortex or a spiral of energies in the middle of the room. If the furniture in the room does not allow this usage of space while you move about the room, imagine if the furniture were not there, and move until you continue physically walking into all the empty spaces. (This allows a flooding of higher energies or positive spirits to come through.)

Now, light your white candle. Hold it in your right hand, the Bible in your left. Stand as much as possible in the center of the room and say: "I call on God's protection. In the center of God's light I stand! Nothing less than God's perfection can touch me where I am. I command all discarnate and incarnate spirits to rise up and leave this room." Sense now a giant fan the size of the whole ceiling starting to rotate as the white light you now stand in stretches up from the room to the ceiling, opening up and letting the skies open up. See or feel the spirit forms draw into the light and through the rotating fan to make them rise up quicker and out through the roof. Then say: "I send all of you into God's light of protection. Go in the name of peace and love toward the light as I command thee."

PRAYERS IN FRONT OF THE CANDLE

White Candle

Always use a white candle for purity and protection. Always use white when you are not sure what to use. For general purposes and to pray to the higher forces.

Red Candle

Red is for an activating force and general energizer. Use to rid yourself of sickness.

Good for one-night stands If you feel alone and need to attract someone highly sexual, maybe your desired mate, it will activate your sexual energy. *Caution:* Be careful how you use this one. You may attract someone very negative who seems okay, or perhaps a negative source.

Rosy Pink Candle

Pink candles are for a loving, peaceful vibration of love. They can be used to attract love for yourself and to get the one you love. It can be very romantic having a rosy pink candle lit when you and your partner are together. Use pink for your creativity energy. This one will inspire you to pen it, paint it, write it, or create it! Use red and white at the same time with the pink to stimulate your creative process even more.

Purple or Violet Candle

These are high spiritual colors for healing and attunement. They aid in development of your psyche and all your energy centers and Chakras to clear up so you can be in tune with your God energies. (Use to pray for your development.)

Blue Candle

The energies of the blue contain the properties of healing depression and moodiness. Aids calmness, helps in finding your true love and filling the need and desire for a true commitment, whether it is friend or lover. Also helps to bring a feeling of peace.

Green Candle

Use for money, too, but mostly for your healing energies (of an emotional nature), lost friend, romance, or lover. This color attracts your finding of lost items. It is good for healing and peace and helps to attract money.

Orange Candle

Helps you find quick solutions to problems. If you want to get something and get it fast, light one. For protection while traveling in car, plane, train, or boat. It is a quick communication candle if you want fast answers.

Black Candle

The force field it carries is awesome and powerful unless you el in total control of your energies. For dire, extreme emergen-_ies. **After you use this, always light up a white candle** to absorb everything negative. Then _is_ard both after use. Prefera-ly use purple—it can be more easily used as well as effective the above purposes.

The color black is always associated with black magic or negative forces directed to and at you. For ridding your physical body of unwanted tumors or skin eruptions (boils, warts, or some unsightly growth). A black candle can eradicate an evil force or any dark energies coming at you, trying to destroy or obstruct your good deeds. Prayers to the higher energies are to be alerted first, praying that you want good energy coming in and laying to rest the negative obstructions coming at you. Remember, clean the residue of that darkness by lighting a white candle alongside of it while working. Then, light another white one and ask for any leftover negative debris to be gone.

Caution: Use only for God-like purposes—then use a white candle to clear away energy debris.

Always light a white candle after using any other color candle.

FOR BURN-OUT:
THE SACRED FLAME RITUAL

A healing force from the Temple of Isis in Egypt

This exercise is an exorcism that can rid your body of the demons of unwanted conditions you no longer need to hold on to and unrealistic desires you have been harboring within, blocking the flow of good energy. This ritual can eliminate the tensions of fear, torment, or any discord you are holding on to in your life. This ritual can help your soul clean up and release old thought forms, fears, obsessions, or blocked communication with friends, neighbors, partners, or loved ones. It can burn away and alleviate the angers within, whatever form they take. Burning old, unwanted feelings or negative desires in fire can purify you of obsessions of sickness and banish the lower feelings such as jealousy or hatred so that your consciousness can be elevated and you can reach a higher state. When you use this ritual faithfully and burn away unwanted desires, they do not come back.

INGREDIENTS FOR RITUAL PROCESS

- Bible
- Prayers
- Water
- Incense (sandalwood)
- Three candles (white, purple, green)
- Ashtray, white paper, pen
- Piece of orange paper, cut into a circle

RITUAL PROCESS

1. Open the Bible in front of you. Light a white candle and keep it directly in front of you.
2. Start burning sandalwood incense while you are doing this flame ceremony.
3. Gather up the purple and green candles. Stack them together to the left side of you with a glass of clear, clean water next to the two candles, and light them, too.
4. Make sure the ashtray is large enough for burning paper. Take one sheet of white paper and pen. Put pencil to your right side. You are now ready to begin!

While all the energies are available to you at your table desk, sit in silence for five minutes to absorb these energies filling into the room. (Keep a window open slightly.) Say your protection prayers (see Chapter 9).

Begin to write down on the white paper your desires, such evil be gone, negative energies remove yourself now from physical, emotional, or mental bodies, and so on.

This paper will be burned in the ashtray at the end of ritual, thereby removing all obstructions preventing your flow good.

List all your desires i.e., removal of a problem, a person, get a new home or apartment, need of money, to get money back from someone, whatever. Think strong thoughts of what want or what your needs are. Then put the paper in the flame the white candle and burn it in ashtray (you can also use an urn) and recite the following ritual prayer:

I call on the Divine keeper of my energies and the Divine my keeper of the Sacred Flame to bring me fulfillment of my desires and dreams.

I ask these higher forces of the light to remove any entities and spirits that block my flow of goodness love.

I ask the flame to burn away objections or obstructions on levels of life and consciousness, on all realms in world or other worlds.

I recognize the energies of the Golden Light and Kingdom Life to bring to form and illuminate the darkness in body and mind so I can tune in to the Universal mind perfect good and in perfect order, bring and fill me the fulfillment of these dreams and desires.

My flame and desire rise to bring my needs to the throne thy mercy and grace, and as it descends, the ashes hate, sickness, poverty, worry, limitation, loneliness depression, failure, and fear have left me and I am free to feel these truths of infinite peace, infinite love, infinite abundance, and the infinite freedom of release can be reached.

So Be It!

End this prayer by re-igniting the white paper in the white candle's flame. Burn it in the ashtray. Once it's burned, ignite the circular piece of orange paper (orange clears out all residue energies) in the white candle's flame. Finish the burning in the ashtray and say: "My dreams and desires have all ascended to the throngs of thy mercy and grace as it is granted."

DANGERS OF DABBLING: THE HOWS AND HOW-TO'S

• Crystal ball
• Pendulum/Dowsing
• Ouija board
• Psychometry
• Automatic writing and typing

All of the tools of self help I have listed deal directly with spirit communication on other levels or planes. There are various other tools or vehicles utilized, such as astrology and Tarot cards, or other decks of cards, but I will not concern myself with them now. These "tools" can and will come in handy when working with energy vibrations attuning you with a "spirit personality" that might happen to be around. Concentration, complete honesty, and a positive, sincere attitude are needed, so that discarnate spirits of the lower worlds do not enter into your sphere of existence or influence unless you yourself dabble in those "black art" areas. Negative spirits generate a hypnotic spell over you and also lower the room's temperature. Stop immediately if this happens to you. Positive ones give warmth and glow.

Always start with a clear idea of what you have in mind. Do not play with spirits. Use them for help, wisdom, and knowledge. With earnestness, a good heart, and a healthy mind, we should expect to get good results.

As you begin to have some success on your way, you will become more attuned and sensitive as you begin to make communication. (See "Using Your Spirit Guide as a Co-therapist," p. 66.)

Some days are not good days to "dabble." When you experience fear, perhaps something in your thought process is not right; the wise man utilizes this time to put these practices on hold. It is a way your spirit guide may be warning you that it is not the right time to connect, as there are negative influences around that can cause you alarm or fright. True mystical aware-

ness makes us react and think about the experiences we have, so
we know when something should be pursued or stopped. It
comes in hunches or flashes. The impression can be vague or
distinct. Dwell on positive thoughts. Vibrations get built up on
good thoughts as you prepare to question your guides. By consciously submitting those mental questions, one by one, to spirits, you will be led to make the right choices and move gracefully
in the right direction.

CRYSTAL BALL GAZING
(CRYSTALLOMANCY)

We still use crystal balls today as they were used in ancient
times. No one knows how long crystal gazing has been in use,
but it was thought to be popular in Egypt six thousand years
before the Christian era. Before that, people did their readings at
calm lakes and used the lakes' reflections to achieve desired
results. The third eye is the power of energy utilized to see
beyond. The water or crystal is a reflector of energy and is used
together with the third eye being opened. Those who are awakened find the answers they are seeking.

Crystals have been found within the ruins of many lost civilizations. Indian tribes used them; so did the Atlanteans, who also
utilized this energy to the hilt. Anyone who honestly desires to
develop the mental power necessary to learn the secrets of crystal
grazing for divination can do so by following a few rather simple
procedures.

1. One must obtain a good clear crystal, very well shaped, and
   with no disturbing shadows. It needs to be at least the size of
   an orange. The larger ones are better as they have a larger
   viewing space.
2. You can hold a crystal in your hands, or place it on a table or
   pedestal. It should, if held, be held away from the gazer, so
   that no reflections or shadowy areas are noticed.
3. A black velvet cloth should be underneath to avoid physical
   contact with the crystal. This is because condensation is
   produced by perspiration.
4. A vessel of fire is suggested on the left of you. Try sprinkling
   acacia perfume oil into the fire to induce psychic awakening
   to the gazer.

5. Now say your protection prayers and use your white light as you call on the higher entities for assistance.

Bless me, O Lord, and sanctify my fire as I ask this fire to be blessed and raise the aromas of this from the heavens so no false enemy or evil may come into me. Raise my consciousness from the worlds of the light by the powers of the light. [Now, you can add the name of your highest power, or God, Jehovah, Elohim, or say, through our Lord Jesus Christ, Amen.]

Remember, rituals are always involved. It makes everything go smoothly and you can always expect good results.

Hints:

Before using your ball, warm it next to your body to attach it to your vibrations. Be in seclusion, undisturbed.

Some say the best way to gaze into a crystal ball is with a light emitted from a candle and in moonlight. Some succeed in broad daylight. Ancient practitioners believed that the worst times were from 10:00 P.M. till 2:00 A.M., as too many undesirable spirits were out then.

Initial attempts are often unsuccessful. Concentration on the crystal ball should last no more than five minutes, the first two or three times of gazing. Sit back and learn to relax completely.

1. Look into the crystal ball for a hopeful picture to reveal itself. Perhaps you won't see it but will feel it or feel you are seeing it.
2. Don't be discouraged if these visions you wish to see don't appear on command.
3. Don't allow anyone else to touch your crystal ball *ever*.
4. You can cleanse it with warm soapsuds but only the owner can do this. Dry with a chamois or velvet cloth.
5. Use the crystal ball when you get more experienced in these matters, possibly at the same time of day for each use (for best results).

Clouds of white inside of it are good omens. When impressions do appear, visions in the background indicate something in the remote past or future. Visions in the forefront denote the present or immediate future. Black clouds are unpleasant events. If the cloudiness is orange, yellow, or red, it warns of impending danger, illness, trouble, grief, deception, or slander. Purple, green, or blue is a good and certain omen of upcoming happiness and good times ahead. If clouds are seen descending, the answer is "no" to any and all questions. When clouds move to the left, it means the reading is at its end. If clouds move to the right, the presence of spiritual beings is announced. When a vision appears to the gazer's right-hand side, it is considered to be symbolic; to the left-hand side, it is a representation of something real. Project good thoughts through its constant use and build a reservoir of mental power.

Good luck!

DOWSING SECRETS / PENDULUM

The medium used is psychic energy. A pendulum can be bought or made in a variety of ways. Essentially it is a thread or cord with a weight at the end of it. This cord, thread, or chain should be from five to ten inches in length and not heavy. A metal coin, a piece of wood or plastic, a piece of crystal, a ball with a hole in it, or a ring would be effective for the weight. A weight of an ounce or less would suffice, just as long as the object hanging from your chain or cord is balanced.

You need to hold this chain or whatever between your index finger and thumb as motionless as possible and at the same time tense your muscles as best you can without permitting the inevitable vibration that comes from too much tension. As you hold the end of the chain, put into prayer what your needs are, if it's water you're looking for, or answers to questions. Ask your question either silently or out loud. The pendulum may move in a circular manner or, if the answers to your questions will be "yes" or "no," back and forth. You will then need to establish a "no" or "yes" answer. From this point on you are set. Concentrate your energies on answers to each individual question but do establish when you ask each time which plane of understanding you need answers to. Is it physical, mental, or spiritual? Your energies will do the rest.

Dowsing—the search for water—is sometimes called radiesthesia. This is an ancient practice. Many believe it acts on certain nerve impulses and sends messages from the conscious or subconscious mind. They assume everything emits radiation, and as it does so, a type of current flows through the hand. Try the same or different parts of the day to use your pendulum. The energy emitted from it will be more effective when you are relaxed and in an even state. (Some people dowse holding a forked branch—experiment!)

You can try using it over foods and/or vitamins and ask it for information about you and others. When you do this it may gyrate clockwise if the food is not okay for you or counterclockwise if the food is okay. Or, perhaps it may go back and forth. Get to work establishing your energy for sure and test it out. Get some quick answers, then as the day progresses, see if the event happens as described or does not. You can also use this means of divination to hold a pendulum over the physical body of another to see what area may need some attention or care.

Always be honest with your pendulum. Game playing is a no-no, such as asking questions you already know the answers to. Be serious when you go about dabbling.

PLANCHETTE OR OUIJA BOARD

This is a means of automatic writing often treated as a parlor game. It consists of a hard board with numbers and letters on it and a place for "yes" and "no." The surface of the board is quite smooth to facilitate an easy motion by the "planchette." One end of the planchette is pointed to rest over the various letters or numbers that are selected in answer to your questions. The planchette stops at various letters to spell out the answer to the question. Ouija will do better if two people operate it by each placing one hand lightly on the planchette, facing each other across the table. This increases the supply of psychic energy. *Again* . . . say prayers before starting. I believe this to be a lower form of psychic energy as it attracts many levels of beings in answer to your call.

Clear this up beforehand. Ask which guide is speaking, get the name, and ask if they are in God's light. You will get a "yes" or a "no." By Universal Law the answer to this question must be the God truth. Then ask how many entities you are working with. Establish a rapport with them. Say again, "I call in my or our higher spirit forces of the light emanating from God energy." Your emotional and mental attitudes can make this change, and a lower being who has gotten inside your force field will leave. You can attract discarnate intelligences or the minds of living persons who have temporarily wandered away from their bodies. Maybe they will be in a deep sleep, on alcohol or drugs, *or* maybe contact is with the mind of someone who has died and crossed over.

Be careful to raise the level of your consciousness. Automatic writing is quicker and Ouija is a short-sighted means. Using it, you do not develop your promising inner abilities properly. It's real "bugga-bugga" stuff and better left to the tearoom.

PSYCHOMETRY

Takes:

- Concentration
- Visualizing (forming mental pictures)

The steps to follow:

1. Take a lock of hair, hanky, ribbon, or ring belonging to someone else.
2. Press it lightly against your forehead, and close your eyes.
3. Assume a receptive and passive state.
4. Say, *"I will,"* and begin to visualize the past history of the object.
5. Wait for the impressions.
6. Have patience to wait for it to unfold.

Psychometry is a means by which you can pick up vibrations from an article or lock of hair belonging to another and read into it the person it belongs to. Vibrations are the energies that do not wear off a thing even when you become its new owner. That is, *unless* you carefully cleanse all other energy belonging to the previous owner with prayer, salt, or sea water or spring water soaked for several days. (You could put the article into dry salt covered for a quick cleansing overnight so you do not feel you have ruined the article.)

AUTOMATIC WRITING / TYPING

This can usually be accomplished by a person with a well-developed medium ability, under instruction from an unseen guide. Many who are developed in this manner do not even know they are. There are thousands of people out there who have this ability. It can be taught, and susceptibility to external power of this sort can be increased. Your hands can be guided by an intelligence superior to your own. Psychic mental energy does come to us via a highly developed source of spirit. If you are highly developed, with sound mind and character, this may be for you. If not, be careful with this—it can lead to severe mental confusion.

INSTRUCTIONS:

1. Always bathe before any automatic-writing session. You will be cleansing yourself physically of impurities that may be clinging to you but a symbolical spiritual cleansing takes place too, before you subject yourself to a new influence.
2. Sit where you will be left undisturbed.
3. When you are clear, calm and cool mentally, take three deep breaths. Let each one out very slowly.
4. Take a pen or pencil in your hand and place it on the top line of the blank pad before you. See that your arm is comfortable. More likely you will get no response the first time out. The rule of thumb is that if nothing happens after at least five to six times of trying, set it aside for a period of a year until you feel the conditions of your life have changed for the positive.
5. If your hand starts to write, it could be nonsense or serious material. If nonsense, stop immediately. It will be a poor connection of spirit from a very low-grade entity.

The sample principle applies, too, with your typewriter as you hold your hands over the keys to begin.

Remember:

Always set the conditions of your safety through prayer before beginning.

SOME OTHER MEANS
OF DIVINATION (SOME NOT SO OFFBEAT
AND USED REGULARLY)

AEROMANCY—The divination of the future from the air skies. This goes beyond the range of weather prognostications and concentrates upon cloud shapes, comets, spectral formations, and other phenomena not normally visible in the heavens.

ALCHEMY—The science of transmuting the base mentals into gold or silver with the aid of a mysterious psychic substance termed the ''philsopher's stone.'' Alchemists claim to prolong human life indefinitely by means of a secret life elixir.

ALEUROMANCY—This requires slips with answers to questions that are rolled in balls of dough and baked. These are mixed up and one is chosen at random and presumably will be fulfilled. Our modern-day fortune cookies derive from this ancient ritual.

ASTRAGYROMANCY—This was divination with dice bearing letters and numbers. It has developed into the modern fortune-telling by dice.

ASTROLOGY—The ancient science of the stars was basically a form of divination as persons who could foretell changes in the heavens were capable of predicting the smaller affairs of mankind. It has been used well and continues to be an asset and tool for our understanding of ourselves and others.

AUGURY—To interpret the future based on various signs and omens.

AUSTROMANCY—Divination by the study of the winds. The Indians used this means quite well.

"BUMPOLOGY"—A popular nickname for phrenology; deals in head formations and is a modern form of psychic science to interpret conditions of the body.

CHIROGNOMY—The study of trails through general hand information.

CHROMANCY—Divination from the lines of a person's hands.

GELOSCOPY—The art of divination from the tone of a person's laughter.

GRAPHOLOGY—The analysis of character through one's handwriting.

NUMEROLOGY—Of ancient origin, a modern form of information which uses names and dates to interpret vital information about an individual's traits.

OCULOMANCY—A form of divination from the eyes. A higher form, called iridology, is used to determine the health of an individual.

ONEIROMANCY—The interpretation of dreams.

OOMANTIA AND OOSCOPY—Divination by using eggs to determine a reading.

PALMISTRY—A most interesting art in psychic sciences. The "language of the hand" interprets knowledge for the student of this art.

TEA LEAVES—For the foretelling of future events. Tea is used as it acts as a point of concentration for reader. Teacup grinds do form various images and pictures in the cup. All of us can see them if we let our minds go.

CHAIN LETTERS; TERRORISM; GROUP NEGATIVE ENERGY

Oh, those glorious bits of fear that arrive by mail from various parts of the globe. If only they didn't have handwritten envelopes, maybe we would throw them out unopened as junk mail. Once opened, they can make your eyes pop out of your head as they grab you mentally or pull on your insides emotionally. *They* are chain letters. In short, they "prey" on your weak spots. They are contrived by salespeople who excel in hype of a low-caliber vibration. The biggest problem is that you're taken in by very unevolved individuals who do not know how to work with the Laws of Prosperity.

Scams of this sort can be quick-money schemes that appear to give you better odds than the lottery from people who do not have the creativity to make their own money. Many of them are vampires, sappers who blame their lives and conditions on others, not accepting their own weaknesses. Lack of character and laziness are the main reasons for their problems. These terrorist letters come in waves and can skyrocket as pyramid rackets have. The first ten people in line may prosper, but are you ever among the first ten unless you start it yourself? And if you *are* one of the first ten, are you guilty of profiting from an immoral scam?

These plagues always come when your luck is down, appear in your most economically and practically depressed moments, and say, "Mail this out within three days or your dog will die, the pin in your left leg will fall out, not to mention your teeth! Better yet . . . your money and bank book will disappear if . . ."

Can you be guaranteed anything in life? Who but you or God controls your prosperity cycles? As the letter sits opened on your kitchen counter paranoia sets in. Over a period of time, you keep glancing at it, wondering what to do. You think maybe you should throw it into the garbage, but—oh, that fear!

The written word is as powerful as the writer's psychic energy. Typewritten, the psychic energy is transmitted by the force applied on the keys. This is not always apparent if the key faces are badly worn or the ribbon is in need of replacement, as it can arouse a field of energy or a field of thought that can be extremely negative.

Most chain letters state the following:

"Give someone else your luck."

"Find what you have lost."

"Money will come to you within four days after you receive this letter."

"You can win the lottery in ten days."

"Wrap a dollar in a blank piece of paper and send it to the first name on the list."

"For Women Only, to get the money for something specific. Within ten days you will be $10,000 richer."

"Saint Jude says, it works!"

"A missionary from South Africa says, 'You will get a surprise.' "

My summation: It's a good way to get a mailing list, and Saint Jude, the "Patron Saint of the Impossible," doesn't operate this way.

PART FOUR

—

SHAPING
THE FUTURE

15

Chakras and Body Systems

With eyes to see
Ears to hear
Depths to explore
Tuned into higher frequencies
New vision tomorrow
In the physical Expression!

ON OUR CHAKRAS

We store information in our tissues and in our extremities or the bones and bony parts of our bodies. When we give the body a sudden blow or impact, that blow is stored in the tissues, and bone damage also serves as information that sends a message to the brain. The tissues do heal and bone reknits, but our organs trigger the memory, if not whole, of any incident or accident from an injury to our brain, too. It is called an "energy block." When an organ suffers and we feel pain, we know something is wrong, but our rational minds cannot identify the problem so we use an X ray. A qualified metaphysician can, with the use of healing crystals and other healing agents, go into that energy block and pump enough energy into the afflicted areas with the use and knowledge of the Universal mind to pump enough energy into the area and open that blocked dam so energy again begins to flow and heal. The creator or creative mind (Universal mind) works in coordination with our brain cells to allow healing to happen more quickly. For those not familiar with theosophical terminology, I shall attempt to explain how our souls and bodies work.

Man *is* a soul and owns a body, several bodies in fact. The physical form certainly is made up of a complexity called "matter." Students of medicine are familiar with its bewildering complexities. Our spinal column is our life force center. Everything springs from a center in the spinal cord. It is almost always to these centers of the spine that the Hindu books refer when they speak of the Chakras. In any case, an Etheric stem of external energy connects this root in the spine with the internal Chakra. This starts a process where an energy force from the spinal cord or column can meet with each and every Chakra in turn and work with the other bodies inside our physical selves. It certainly is a "marriage of life" that helps with our vitality and interlocks with some of our respective molecules and atoms. It results in our personal magnetism and flows alongside the nerves of the body. The Chakras extend energy to the aura, giving it depth, texture, and color due to the biological and metabolic activities that are going on.

Man develops his physical body by exercising it. So does man develop his emotional or so-termed *Astral* body by the exercise of his emotions, and his mental body by the exercise of his mind. We think of our emotions and our thoughts as products of our physical organism. They are not.

These subtle bodies are "garments of the soul" and help us to function and act as central balance points for the gravitational fields of Earth when there needs to be an integration of mind and matter. We do exist at this center. As you are developing knowledge and experiencing a new and fascinating world opening before you, this stage of development may provide some answers. Bringing our more "subtle bodies" into the light may aid in the understanding of our unseen bodies, which teach us that our minds and emotions may open us to the healing of ourselves.

When we look at a *human* body with our physical eyes we see a *human* physical body. What we cannot see with our physical vision is that contained in our physical body there are three other bodies that are invisible to human vision.

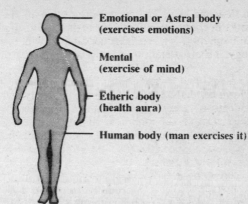

Emotional or Astral body
(exercises emotions)

Mental
(exercise of mind)

Etheric body
(health aura)

Human body (man exercises it)

Each body is a universe unto itself but must act in connection to form a galaxy that is a whole person.

A medical textbook available at any library can quickly give you a general idea of the physical organs that make up the physical body. Each organ has a different function and responds to the Law of Energy, which is *all* energy. Energy responds in direct proportion to its cosmic cycle and the strength with which you are causing it to act for you.

The world is made up of energy, which is found in a substance called ether. In the Universe, we have energy, matter, motion. *Matter* is energy at a specific rate of vibration that becomes what we identify it to be. *Motion* is more than *movement*. It is aggression. Without motion, matter disintegrates.

Now we will look at the invisible bodies. The main function of the *Etheric body* is to absorb energy from the ether via the magnetic attraction between the energy and the Etheric body. This same energy is distributed to the other bodies through *psychic* (invisible to the human eye) nerve centers called *Chakras*.

The *Etheric body* then electrifies this energy and sends it to the other bodies via the magnetic electrical process.

The *mental body* is basically designed to function with mind through the brain.

The *emotional body* is designed to experience and develop human feelings. Feelings are longer lasting and a good deal truer than emotions, which mean a sudden explosion of energy. Feel-

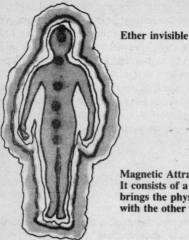

Ether invisible

Magnetic Attraction (AURA)
It consists of a magnet that
brings the physical body together
with the other three bodies.

ings relate to the soul, while emotions tend to relate to the cruder
appetites of humanity.

When we breathe we are recreating the motion of the sea, the
ebb and flow of tides. Every energy can be influenced by forces
that we are not aware of. This is why people who need to think
in concrete terms should create a mental picture that has as many
details as possible.

Etheric body. The vital field called the "health aura" is a
silvery haze extending a few inches beyond the skin. Some can
see it when they squint and are unfocused in a half-light so that
the outer parts of the retina come into play; some use straight
clairvoyance. It looks opaque. It is a vital aura that consists of an
interwoven mesh of streams of light or three-dimensional energy
and has a form. It is similar to an alternating electrical current
entering the system at the head and at the opposite end of the
spine. The circular currents act like the lymphatic system, which
is in effect a reservoir of chemical food for the body. Its Etheric
counterpart is an accumulation of potential vital energy for the
whole system.

Mental body (Astral body). A flood of emotion does not
greatly affect the mental body though for a time it may make it
almost impossible for any activity from the mental body to come

through into the physical brain. Because the Astral body, which acts as a bridge between the mental body and the brain, vibrates at a rate incapable of conveying anything that is not in harmony with it, it makes sensations possible and serves as a bridge between mind and physical matter. It acts as an independent vehicle of consciousness and action.

If we touch into the center or core of a person's body, we will find that energy is sent throughout his body system through the spine. All energy is generated there. Correct breathing helps these separate particles of energy not to get stuck and rejuvenates the body and body cells from storing unused energy. Laughter releases energy, while crying and fear stifle it, till the mind is clouded in darkness and the bodies suffer. By learning to relax, you are allowing some of the blocked systems to separate to create a balancing energy to obtain a level of balance for the bodies' correct functioning ability.

Our bodies consist of two basic structures, interior and exterior. The interior consists of molecules and microscopic atoms that float through the system and make up the chemical and physical composition of the body form. The exterior is a "cover-all" for all that occurs inside and reproduces what is created inside a person's soul. Examples: nervousness inside creates broken skin capillaries, pimples, blemishes, marks. When damage occurs to the interior body, it shows on the exterior.

Man is a soul and owns more than one body. When he is sufficiently evolved he can utilize all of these bodies. Every time we think, we work with our *mental body*. When we feel and utilize our emotions, we use our *emotional body*. The Etheric body electrifies all the other bodies and serves as a magnet to bring the physical together with the other three. It is an invisible part of the physical used as a vehicle through which our energy flows for our vitality to keep the body alive and our aura in good chemical shape.

The Chakras or force centers are the points of connection at which energy flows from one vehicle or body of a man to another. When persons are clairvoyant or highly developed, they may see these saucerlike depressions or vortices. They have a brilliant color wheel and are perpetually rotating and always flowing with what we call the primary force. That force is sevenfold in its nature as we have seven of those discs or wheels that operate inside the physical body. With an undeveloped

METAPHYSICAL AND PHYSICAL CORRESPONDENCE OF THE CHAKRA SYSTEM

Spinal Chakra/Physical & Sympathetic Correspondences of the Body System

PINEAL
(not recognized as endocrine)
Information/Telepathy/Pure

PITUITARY carotid, caveinous and post-nasal ganglion

CROWN
last chakra to
be awakened
(undulation all its own)
(path of spiritual
advancement)

THYROID AND PARATHYROID
The laryngeal/
pharyngeal plexus

BROW OF THIRD—EYE
on the brow
(modification of energy
clairvoyance)

THYMUS
over the heart
(8th cervical–plexus,
cardiac, pulmonary
coronary, etc.)

THROAT
Clairaudience

ADRENALS
(dual)

PANCREAS
(dual)

HEART
Over heart
(inner identity,
purpose)

ADRENALS
over navel
(8th thoracic–hepatic,
gastric, etc.)

SOLAR PLEXUS
(over navel)
radiations of
personal well—being

over spleen
1st lumbar
(not recognized as
endocrine)

SPLEEN
(specialization
of vitality)
left side of body

SACRUM, PROSTATE, GONADS, ETC.
at base of spine
4th sacral plexus
coccygeal

ROOT
(vitality &
life force)

being, they rotate in a sluggish motion, just doing what is necessary for the life force they need, but no more. In a more evolved man, they glow and pulsate with living light so energy of a more creative or scientific nature is activated.

CHAKRA CLEANSING, BALANCING, AND ACTIVATING

STEP 1. BEGIN WITH A GROUND EXERCISE

A. Sit in a straight-backed chair and enter into a still state for at least three minutes. Visualize the chair you are sitting in removed to the outside with you sitting facing a large oak tree or other large tree. Always use the same tree in your mind. While facing the tree see that your shoes are off and feet are on top of a large root popping up from the ground surface, your feet flat on top of the root. Ask this tree to give you permission to utilize the Earth's energy into you (the Mother in each spirit will see that this is done).

Mentally, pull out and up the flowing energy from deep inside the Earth to go into the roots of that tree and see the energy entering up through the middle of your feet. Feel its pulsations, set the conditions. Now it will enter through your being to keep you grounded and provide the energies that it contains for your revitalizing. Begin to see or feel a current of this Earth energy or white light running upward through your entire body, feet, leg, and each Chakra in turn: base, spleen, solar plexus, heart, throat, brow, and coming out through your crown, going straight up as far as you can imagine like a rod of light.

B. Slowly come back to this reality in the chair you started in, take a deep, deep breath, and relax.

STEP 2.

A. Stay on your chair, close your eyes. Know that the current of white light is flowing through you because of the grounding exercise, and the energy is running through.

B. Visualize now a shaft of white light descending through the sky, hovering around the top of your head (Crown Chakra), building up in intensity. Permit it now to go through all your major Chakras in turn. You have now perpetuated the rhythmic flow of new energies to start.

Begin and pause at your solar plexus Chakra, the seat or place of your emotional nature or state, and see the color *violet* coming out from the white light pouring into that area. Watch the churning of that Chakra disc cleansing and pulling dark specks of negativity out of it and watch the negativity return and flow into the white light. *Command* that Chakra to be cleansed of your negativity (or another's, for that matter, clinging to you), to dissolve into the stream of white light and vanish.

Pause mentally now . . . at the adrenal Chakra or spleen center. See a *red* flow filling that Chakra in a brilliant blaze of red and rose alternately pouring in from the stream of white light energy. Mentally order that unwanted negativity or energy banished into the descending stream and flow of white light. Watch it wash away and dissolve.

At the Root or Base Chakra, see the color *dark violet* (almost *black* mixed with *light purple* flecks) and command that center to be free of any unwanted energies or anyone else's energy systems to be detached from you. See it going into the stream of white light. Feel the merging at this point of the Earth energies coming up and the skies' energies above that come down. Feel your system activating alive as a cable connection or loop through you.

Pause at each point longer if you feel the area afflicted. Know that whenever you pause, this cleansing goes on as the energy keeps flowing.

At your *heart Chakra* now, see a beautiful *golden yellow* light. See the flow of *white light* pulling out any unwanted connection with other people's energy systems, being pulled out from the circulating disc of the yellow golden light as it spins like a top into the stream of white light. Command that the heart center be cleansed and that all negativity is washed and dissolved away.

Go to the hollow of your *throat Chakra* and watch the pouring ray of *emerald green* filling and sustaining a circular motion there, too. As you see the stream of white light again, say, "Cleansing be done, clear away the debris of uneasiness," and wash the toxins of negativity into the white light.

Move to the *brow* or *third eye* area next and watch a *silver* plate appear swirling and pulling. Command the area to be cleansed and balanced into that stream of white light.

Last, but not least, the *crown* or *top of your head*. Imagine the ray to be of *violet and yellow* lifting out the darkness and confusion inside you—those unnecessary energies or other people's energies disorienting you will be pulled upward and out with a ray of white light coming from a *white star* about nine inches above your head. This is called your transpersonal point and it is usually a good starting place for any meditation period, especially if interpersonal issues of any kind are involved.

Breathe deeply in a relaxed quiet pattern now as you once again go over your body from toe to transpersonal point, working your way upward until you feel assured that any leftover blackness of negative thought forms or patterns have left you. Bring it up into that star as the star above your head is dissolving away all debris and matter, washing and cleansing all. Gather all your energies upward and hold them there by deep, deep breathing.

Now . . . as you release those energies from the star into you, see the *stardust* of *golden* specks of light wash like raindrops over your entire body, energizing and cleansing all of you once again.

Finish your cleansing and balancing meditation now by *shielding* your space, in the Universe, your light by the light above by establishing a cocoon of white light around your whole body as if to enclose it by this cocoon or room of protection.

Notes: If you do not have time to go through the above exercises and need instant help or relief in any part or area of your body in dire need or distress, put a ring or band of white radiant energizing light in a complete circle around any Chakra or area you feel is vulnerable or in discomfort. Mentally command it to stay there until it is healed within that circle and it shall be done.

LETTING OUT EXCESS NEGATIVE ENERGY THROUGH YOUR CHAKRAS

Use this exercise to open your Crown Chakra for healing by letting out excess energy for your health.

1. Surround the individual you are healing in white light. Call in your highest power and say the following prayer (person being healed should do this, too):

I am in the center of God's Universe
In perfect balance and led by the Light.
So Be It!

2. Say, "I open [*person's name*] Crown Chakra for this healing to let out all excess energy or negative energy" (bad energy will rise up and out). (To open the Crown Chakra, mentally make the motion as if your hands were unscrewing a jar over the top of your head.)

CHAKRA BREATHING RITUAL

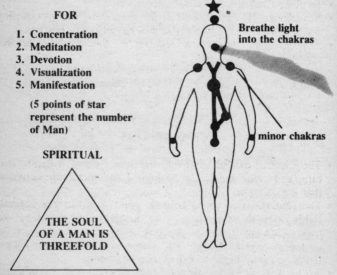

FOR

1. Concentration
2. Meditation
3. Devotion
4. Visualization
5. Manifestation

(5 points of star represent the number of Man)

Breathe light into the chakras

minor chakras

SPIRITUAL

THE SOUL
OF A MAN IS
THREEFOLD

MENTAL   **PHYSICAL**

Visualize a *five–pointed star* above your head (called the transpersonal point). *Think* of the correspondence color of each chakra in turn (head to foot) as you breathe in the light from the *white star* about 9 inches above your head working your way down. *Breathe* slowly into the nostrils alternately within the natural rhythm of your breathing system to carry the flow of energies throughout system. Concentrate on each color in turn and on your exhalations. Your breathing out the color as well as in will give you added strength and stamina.

3. Stand in back of the individual while you are doing this. Touch the inside of his collarbone to center him (hands on shoulder wells) and to put into him your energies of transformation. You will be balancing his upper-body Chakras.

4. When you have felt enough energy transmitted into him and you are not depleted, stop! Now close the Crown Chakra by a clockwise motion over the top of the head. This seals in the energy.

5. Surround yourself as well as the person you are healing covered in white light.

NOTES:

• To open Chakras, use a counterclockwise motion.
• To close Chakras, use a clockwise motion.
• Never open all the Chakras at the same time without closing and sealing them all in, or you will have Chakra burnout.
• If you happen to pass an accident on the street, close that person's Crown Chakra.
• Balancing by placing hands helps the body to attune itself on both sides. It can help to clear your Chakra system.

CHAKRA AIDS

• The Chakras extend energy to the aura, giving it depth, texture, and color due to the biological and metabolic activities that are going on.
• The Chakras are central balance points for the gravitational fields of Earth when there is an integration of the mind and mass. This then becomes psychokinetics. The Chakras are the centers of psychokinetics. When there is an alignment of these fields you may begin to experience levitation.
• An hour of sleep will balance each Chakra. Three hours will balance the upper three and it will then help to balance the lower four main Chakras in the body. Oversleeping activates the muscular structure that can overload energies.
• Each Chakra vibrates at a different frequency. *Yellow* helps the emotional body, soothing the nervous system. It merges with the corresponding Chakra that is green (yellowish green helps the healing process).
• Gemstones can help to balance the Chakras. Use them.

ABSORPTION COLOR RAYS OF VITALITY

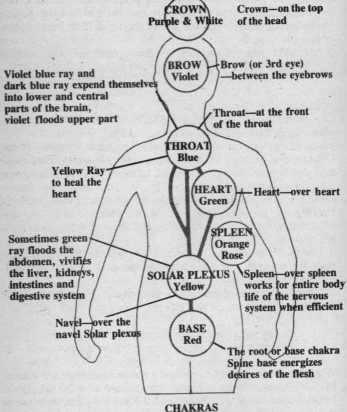

CROWN
Purple & White

Crown—on the top
of the head

BROW
Violet

Brow (or 3rd eye)
—between the eyebrows

Violet blue ray and
dark blue ray expend themselves
into lower and central
parts of the brain,
violet floods upper part

Throat—at the front
of the throat

THROAT
Blue

Yellow Ray
to heal the
heart

HEART
Green

Heart—over heart

SPLEEN
Orange
Rose

Sometimes green
ray floods the
abdomen, vivifies
the liver, kidneys,
intestines and
digestive system

SOLAR PLEXUS
Yellow

Spleen—over spleen
works for entire body
life of the nervous
system when efficient

Navel—over the
navel Solar plexus

BASE
Red

The root or base chakra
Spine base energizes
desires of the flesh

CHAKRAS
—THE SPIRITUAL CENTERS OF MAN—
THE GATEWAY TO A HIGHER STATE OF AWARENESS!!

LEARN TO CENTER YOURSELF

As you sit with your eyes closed in a meditative state, take three deep breaths. Visualize and feel your meditation circle of light around you (white light) and your heart Chakra at its center (visualize a brilliant yellow light). See and feel a warm golden glowing flow of unconditional love coming in from the Universe with a warm gentle ray flowing in and out of your heart Chakra coming from the Golden Sun Universe and all the other stars of the Universe (energies of gold and pink rays of light).

Picture yourself in the center of the Zodiac's circle, with all of the twelve houses surrounding you (see illustration). Allow your heart Chakra (give it permission) to fill up with *pink* light and radiate that feeling with compassion and unconditional love for yourself. Project this love outward from you into the Universe, going to each of the ten planets (Jupiter, Mars, Venus, Pluto, Uranus, Sun, Moon, Mercury, Mars, and Neptune). Feel those energies in turn coming in from the energies of those planets into your own astrological houses. Really feel compassion and acceptance for yourself. Then, visualize and feel this glowing sunlight flowing out through each part of your life as you feel also compassion for others there as well. Suffuse it throughout your entire being.

Use this exercise at any time and in any place that you feel the need for strength, courage, or centeredness. It is also an excellent way to close a meditation period.

Your *Energy* receptacle is in your chest. Your *power* is in your third eye area.

THE UNDERSTANDING OF YOUR
THIRD EYE (THE ALL-SEEING ONE)

When the sixth Chakra is opened, a man begins to see things. Maybe clouds of color, visions, waking and unwakened sights, feelings about people, places, and things. This center between the eyebrows is connected with sight in another way beyond our physical seeing. We then begin to examine and magnify our potential expanding consciousness, to see beyond our reality. The full arousing of this brings about clairvoyance. For the ordinary person it lies dormant until man has made a definite moral commitment to himself for this development to continue or until his will is strong enough to control his thoughts with purity in his heart to open himself to himself and to others. The Clairvoyant is simply a person who can develop within him- or herself the power to respond to another out of a *need* (what the soul must have to mature), to enable himself to see more of the world around him than can those of a limited perception.

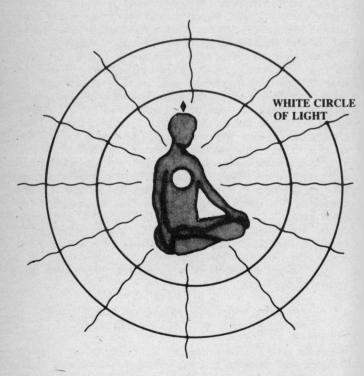

WHITE CIRCLE OF LIGHT

A WORD ABOUT THE PITUITARY GLAND (MASTER GLAND)

The third eye is equivalent to the pituitary gland. It transforms the colors of the light rays into revitalizing energies to rebuild those centers that are lacking in energy to reinforce the energies being created within each gland. It also reinforces vibrations to the adrenal glands. If the individual applies himself physically, mentally, and spiritually, when in meditation with the creative force, healing will be possible.

16

Awaken the Genie Within: Your Personal World of Dreams

Caught adrift with no place to row
Only our dreams to guide us through the coming seas of
    oblivion and confusion . . .
I see it, feel it now—blending into my being—
My eyes see, lips reveal the splendor of yesterday,
    replenishing now in abundance with no place to go,
    run or hide—
I stand still, open to it all . . . feeling the essence of
    the seasons recycling . . .
Pull me beyond—over the caverns of my lost hopes—
    leaving my fears behind and beyond
Drawn to a new plateau of commiserating with the oneness
    of it all—forever everlasting
Only the stars to guide me

MAY 8, 1984

We all dream. In fact, we can't live without our dreams! We dream lying down, sitting up, standing, we may dream in any position or any place, in sunlight or at night. It may take seconds, minutes, even hours. Some people do it more than others; some remember their dreams, some don't.

All the ancient empires had their theories about dreams. Scientists, philosophers, and psychics all try to reason with and understand them. But does anybody really know why we sleep and dream? Are dreams our unconscious mental thoughts during sleep? Are they a third state of being, the others being waking and sleeping?

Each night, we go up and down through four sleep stages several times:

STAGE 1: As we drift off to sleep our brain waves are small and erratic. (Beta) (fourteen to twenty-eight brain wave frequency).

STAGE 2: The brain starts changing. We toss and turn (Alpha) (seven to fourteen—a healthier place to be).

STAGE 3: Our sleep is sounder and brain waves slower (Theta) (four to seven).

STAGE 4: Deepest and heaviest stage sleep (Delta). Marked by slow brain waves, a drop of body temperatures and a lower pulse rate. If you are very tired you will spend a lot of time in this stage.

After a time in stage 4, we go into reverse. We don't awaken but we enter a REM (rapid eye movement) stage, in which brain waves are short and erratic, and eyes dart back and forth.

Sleep is a kind of a battery recharge. It allows the body to rebuild and replace used cells. Internal biological clocks control the amount of sleep we need.

The first dream is short, only a few minutes long, but later dreams can extend to twenty to forty minutes each. You spend at least two hours a night dreaming. The long, involved dreams occur in the last third of a night's sleep, toward morning. The last dream can often be remembered and captured. It is the dream you can harvest each day.

Most people cannot function in the darkness. So we switch off at night and dream. We sleep, some believe, in order to dream. My own feelings are that we are always awake and never do sleep as we know it. We live and work through day and night and can even remember through our so-called sleep states. Every night our thinking during the REM period, the illogical, emotional, and very high visual right brain is almost freed from the rational left brain. It results in a flood of images and feelings, which we call dreams. The sleeping mind works every minute. The mind does its homework at night while you sleep. The dream mind is a great artist; it creates paintings and stories. The dream is our voyage and exploration to our inner worlds, our travel into an altered consciousness.

The dream is the actual experience of the mind, body and soul. Since I do not work with dreams much, nor am I an authority, I am here only to let you know what my guides tell me about them so you can start to keep a journal and help to understand your progress in your thinking and feeling patterns of life.

There are three types of dreams:

1. They can be *symbols* that form the language of our dream life—connected to us in our daily or conscious life. You may think of them as spiritual, a link with higher self or consciousness.

2. *Psychological* dreams only tell us the truth of what we really could have done with our logical reasoning minds. Also we may get some helpful needed information about some other person. It is like a telepathic dream experience. Or, working out our "*reasoning* world" that we live in. Maybe our rational mind helps us connect with ourselves during dreams.

3. *Precognitive* or warning dreams tell what may happen in the future or are warnings made up by the subconscious mind to match some fear that we consciously hold. We should not ignore this type of dream. First decide if you are frightened by your own fears and worries before you decide it is in the future.

   The subconscious always trys to take over and strike a balance with the conscious, as it awakens the opposite extreme in our waking life. It may also tell us the outcome of our future lives and show us the way to make happen what *we think* impossible.

You will begin to learn now to interpret all the symbols. Once we find out what the symbols represent, we can receive the messages. Dreams are a wonderful tool for your learning experience. The real importance of dream interpretations is to make you aware of your real feelings and make you understand the positive input or conclusions. Don't try to figure out what it all means—work with it and do something about it!

Remember, dreams are not an accidental byproduct of sleep but perhaps the very *purpose* of sleep. Sleep helps to blend new learning with old. When sleeping, our brains do what computer do. When not sending or receiving messages from the outside world, they are very busy tidying up our memories—processing new data with old, relabeling files, and getting rid of outdated information.

In dreams, we rehearse things of importance to us in our daily activities. We organize them into our thinking process. The human brain has more images and data in it than there are atoms in the Universe. The brain programs and organizes automatically; if we put in positive thought, it updates the information and our memory gets richer and more diverse.

Alcohol, barbiturates, tranquilizers, and other drugs frustrate this experience and interfere with the dream process. Hallucination may leave us in a permanent state of confusion, both awake and sleeping. Without dreams, there would not be a merging with new or old experience. It is essential for the normal living of life.

Call on your "dream genie"—your unconscious dual personality—who gets up and travels out of you when you are sleeping.

PROGRAM YOUR DREAMS

1. Keeping a dream journal is helpful in keeping tabs on your life.
2. Before you go to sleep, tell yourself to remember your dreams Visualize yourself putting them in a glass of water by your bedside. Drink the water on rising, and while you sit at the edge of your bed recall and write them down.
3. Perhaps you might want to program your crystal to help or perhaps tuck it under your pillow.
4. Keep a notebook or cassette by your bed and wake yourself up to catch the dreams. This works well. If you get out of bed you are liable to miss them. Some say it is best to lie there quietly while recalling a dream, as motion sometimes makes them disappear.
5. Every morning jot down some of the dreams you remember.
6. Make a chart to record your dreams as an aid to understand unexpressed emotions. At first they might not make much sense, but work with them a little while and you will begin to find their meanings. First try a literal translation. Second, a psychological interpretation, then a symbolic spiritual one.

Example: You have missed a bus, plane, or train (maybe you are afraid that life is passing you by). Your timing is off, giving you a warning. Notice your expression in the dream. Were you glad or sad?

7. Set your alarm ten minutes earlier than usual. You may wake up in the middle of a dream. The last dream is usually right before normal waking hours.

DREAMS ARE THE KEY
TO YOUR MIND

What's going on in your brain and body? If you understand your dreams you will understand yourself, as the mind controls your external life. As it processes the information that makes you anxious, you can therefore understand and analyze, thereby overcoming anxiety-provoking events and people.

DREAMS ARE
OFTEN ABOUT CONFLICTS

Love and hate
Life and death
Freedom and security
Right and wrong
Masculine and feminine aspects of yourself

They tell us about our basic needs, desires, and fears, some of which we may be unaware. Allow them to come . . . ask for them and you will learn to welcome those fears and tensions.

Often dreams about other people are reflections of yourself in different states of being. What your fears are or what you would like to be or achieve is often reflected in your dreams. Precognitive dreams, however, are different.

DREAMS WITH THE
USE OF UNIVERSAL SYMBOLS AND
THEIR MEANINGS

HOUSE—Your house of thought, the way you think. *You* or your inner body of feelings.

APARTMENT HOUSE—Means you have so many ways of thinking that you can't get yourself to fix on one room of thought. Your mind is always diversified . . . you can't concentrate on one thing. You take too much in, or perhaps you can think big. (See how the rest of your dream takes form.)

FUTURISTIC HOUSE—Means that you are thinking ahead, you are of the space age, not of the Earth's thinking. You are aware now you must go forward without fear. You have a calling.

MODERN HOUSE—Means you are living in this time, truly in the present.

OLD HOUSE—Means you are living in the past, you are hung up on the past, where you have been happy or sad. It is a past life or a part of the past. In this life it has some meaning as a connection to new thoughts as well. Put this together with the dreams of people who are or have been in your life. Answers will come.

HOUSE IN NEED OF REPAIR—Your mind is in trouble, you don't want to change, or you need to change your habits and thinking. You must clean up your act, physically, mentally, and emotionally. Do it now.

HOUSE IN THE PROCESS OF REPAIR—Means you are trying to improve your thinking and change your outlook. Everything is in the works of progress. These dreams can return again and you will begin to see the changes.

**OTHER FLOORS ARE DIFFERENT
LEVELS OF YOUR MIND**

FLOORS—The levels of your thinking.

GROUND FLOOR—The foundation of your thinking or what you are or where your consciousness is. Part of the solid rebuilding structure of your life.

CRACKS OR HOLES ON THE FLOOR—Means you need to repair your ways of thinking, they are not that solid, you need adjustment, and should consciously work until the holes have been mended.

STONE FLOOR—Stone is a symbol for a solid mind and also solid emotions. It means it is hard for you to change as you are fixed in your thinking and difficult to penetrate.

WOODEN FLOOR—In symbology is spelled "would" and means willpower. You have a desire or will to do it. The need to balance Earth and yourself for revitalization. You can also bend and blend into the planet. A stabilization balance to keep you grounded.

BASEMENT—Always your subconcious. If you continuously dream of going into the basement, it means you are an introvert and have a need to live inside yourself in order to find your reality. You do not want anyone to know who you are and are hiding something.

STAIRS—Like the ladder of Jacob. According to the direction of the stairs—if the stairs go up, then you are going toward higher teachings, or higher floors, or floors of the house of your mind. Stairs going up also means that your way of thinking is coming up to the conscious mind, because "up" in a dream means the conscious mind, "down" in a dream means going toward the subconscious mind, and any of the floors below the foundation such as basement or subbasement are levels of the subconscious mind.

ELEVATOR—Where your conscious level is. Good for re-evaluation. You are in a hurry to find your direction, to get someplace. Is the elevator going up or down? "Up" means you intend to achieve great heights. "Down" means uncertainty.

FLYING IN THE SKY—Means your subconscious mind or a large part of your thinking remembers being in other worlds in which you were an energy form or a mental form before you were a physical being. Your mind is space-oriented, trying to ascend to the higher worlds or Angel worlds, being a space being or a space person. You are also free of your physical body and ready to transcend your ways of thought.

INVOLVED WITH THE GROUND—Means your mind is very physical, your mind is very Earth-oriented. It means if you are looking at the physical you are focused on Earth and materialistic patterns, on things that have three-dimensional form.

MODERN AIRPLANE—A vehicle always represents you. It isn't that you are in the plane, it is that you *are* the plane. If you see a jet going up higher and higher, it means that your mind has the power of reaching great heights—you are capable of soaring high above the conscious level of this planet. If you see it go down you are not able to cope.

OLD AIRPLANE—Means that a part of your mind remembers that you were a being from another world once but the memory has become so lost through time and many life-times that the memory is dim or not that well defined or secure. Your mind can't remember that without fear or pain, so you put in an old form so you do not feel the fear or pain.

BOAT—Exploring mind and slow thinker. You need to take time out to explore your emotions and put it all in shipboard compartments efficiently in your mind. It is an emotional "container."

SHIP—This is you. If you see an ocean liner that is magnificent, this is you. This is your ego, this is the power of your identity, you are an ocean liner because you are a powerful being, you could not be an ocean liner unless you had many, many lives, unless you are a very old soul. You are steering into new emotional waters of feeling—very powerful, and strong enough to navigate the waters.

OLD CAR—Need to possess things of value on Earth and keep very traditional traits. No wish to change.

NEW CAR—Need to keep up with the times of automation. To put your gears in shape to reorganize your life for a new purpose. The need for change from where you have been. It is your new self and your vehicle for success.

HORSE—If it is a beautiful race horse, you are capable of competition, you are capable of winning or being a leader, you are capable of being out in front, your emotions and your mind believe that you can win, that you can run, that you can race. You have a lot of energy, you have a lot of faith in yourself to enter the human race and to be a winner or leader and to succeed in something. You are becoming streamlined.

PLOW HORSE—You are hung up on your own problems and all you think is that you are a servant who can never be a winner, who can never be a leader because your mission is to be a servant, a slave. You are trudging through life, digging in the mud.

DENTIST—He is pulling out one of your teeth. Teeth in a dream are always thought patterns. If you dream that your teeth have got to go, it means that you have done a lot of bad thinking. If there is a need for a bridge, it means that they are bridging or welding your thoughts together. Adding teeth shows a respect for yourself and helps to beautify your ego.

FRONT TEETH—The most recent thoughts or lives that you have had. The teeth at the back give the Angels the most trouble and they may represent a nun's life or a priest or scientist. They are so deeply imbedded and give the most trouble.

FACE—A person's face in a dream is important and dramatic and very accurate symbolically. If you see the face of a person who has a straight nose (it doesn't have to be yourself), the bridge of the nose is the bridge of learning, this person is a being who is learning properly or is capable of getting direct knowledge or direct teaching. Seeing a face in a dream can mean a "phase" of learning. If the face is beautiful, then you have achieved a beautiful way of learning. If you see a *scarred face* in a dream it means you have experienced a painful phase of learning something that has traumatized you, something that has scared your being or this phase of your learning.

BEAUTIFUL FACE—It is not the face of a human, it is an Angel to show you and inspire you to beauty, in order to interest your mind in a beautiful way of learning.

BROKEN NOSE—Means that the bridge of the person's learning has been diverged, it has been damaged, it has been bent, that they do not have a straight road to learning.

OPERATION—The operation is Karma. Every organ that is cut out in a dream represents a thought that must be cut out according to your way of thinking. Notice what was operated on.

LUNG TROUBLE (or if you cannot breathe)—Means because you are resistant, there is a part of your mind that remembers being a member of a higher world—being an Angel who had the high ozone air or the heavens—and the pure, clean, healthy air of the highly vitalizing higher worlds. You are refusing to breathe this air.

HEART TROUBLE—The heart is the center of your emotions. It is the center of your emotional attitude of things. If you don't want to love, your heart will harden, it will be shielded so you will have chest pains. If you are very emotional, very involved with people, you will suffer squeezing of your heart, you will have pulsations of your heart, as if your heart is an overworked organ.

GALLBLADDER—Your conscience. When you have an abnormal way of thinking or rigidness, you will have gallbladder trouble.

FLYING

It can be a comfort to float through the air. You can release a lot of pressure. In a dream, flying can mean to be forever free of responsibility, to rise above other people, and a desire to overcome problems. It is a pleasurable experience.

PURSUING, BEING PURSUED

Are you chasing after something or someone that can never be caught? Looking for something or someone that just isn't there? Things may be particularly frustrating in your life now. Too many pressures for you. Think about it and eliminate some of these pressures.

FALLING

You are experiencing, perhaps, a fall from grace. Falling down in your work. It doesn't have to be a negative experience. Think of the free fall of parachutists and the fun they have gliding through the air. Try to change the fall to a positive experience.

LOSING OR FINDING VALUABLE THINGS

Perhaps your subconscious is trying to tell you to hold on to something you cherish.

FINDING VALUABLES

Dreams of self-worth, of satisfaction in how you are handling things. Maybe you will find something valuable.

CRIME AND PUNISHMENT

Our sense of values is the conflict. Decisions to be made in everyday life. Something also to do with religious teachings.

LOSING TEETH

Neglected your teeth lately? If not, the meanings represent many different things—for instance, a turning point in your life. Feel like biting someone or chewing someone out? An idea to chew on.

BEING NUDE

We feel somehow exposed, as though people are looking straight through us. We are vulnerable. The "don't care" attitude. The sleeping mind will capture this lovely and frightened feeling in a dream. Many people have this dream before acting in a play or speaking in public. Even professional actors sometimes experience this dream.

DEATH AND DYING

Whether it's our own, a person in our family, a friend, or a stranger, death plays a part in all our lives. Are you relieving yourself from some grief or escaping something in your life? It doesn't mean you want to stop living, but you may need to get away from something or kill off some unwelcome parts of your character. Sometimes these dreams indicate anger or a deep feeling of resentment against someone. Problems to bring out into the open, examine, and clear out.

DREAMS OF PROPHECY

Can we tell the future in our dreams? There has been no scientific proof that this is possible, although research scientists are working on ESP (extrasensory perception), telepathy (reading someone's mind), and precognition (a sense of the future). Many world leaders have believed in this: General Patton, Hitler,

Napoleon, George Washington, Alexander the Great, and Winston Churchill. So have many writers of past history, including Robert Louis Stevenson and H. G. Wells.

NIGHTMARES

Many nightmares involve pursuit. To banish them, say to yourself, "This is a dream. I can change this terrible dream into a better dream." To be able to change your dreams, you must *know* you are dreaming. You can become a more aware dreamer by:

> Remembering them, writing them down. When someone is pursuing you, turn around and say S-T-O P. Look at the pursuer and challenge it (he or she). Say *"go away"* with authority. Have yourself rescued. Ask any monster to disappear. Use your voice in the dream.

Nightmares may occur at any age. They are prevalent when we are anxious, have a sense of inadequacy, or have experienced great distress or trauma, such as the death of a loved person in the family. They even occur if there is a fear of an event that will take place in the future. As we outgrow our fears or overcome them, they leave. Experiences buried in our inner minds can take years to come out. Children, especially, have not had enough of life's experiences to tell what is real from the unreal. Nightmares are an expression of helplessness.

UNIVERSAL EARTH SYMBOLS IN DREAMS

STEEL—Means you are very strong or rigid, usually a rigid pattern.

COPPER—In dreams, copper is soft. For a mind that is inflexible, copper is a good conductor, so there is a danger. A medium is a good conductor and they are usually unprotected, without shields, so you can pick up things of danger, such as thoughts of spirits or vibrations.

MOUNTAIN—Notice if it's a hill, mound, or flat-topped mountain. Perhaps it is very steep, pointed, and one of high elevation. See if you just view it, climbing up or coming down. Indicates changes of mood, elevations, power, or ascending to new heights.

WATER—Always means knowledge. It is the waters of knowledge. If you see yourself in a ship taking an ocean cruise and you look over the railing and the water is beautiful and clear and you can see down to the bottom, it means that you have a clear mind and head. You can see and perceive the waters of your own knowledge very clearly. If the *water is muddy,* it means you have a problem. Usually an emotional problem in seeing or understanding your own thinking or the perception and reality of life itself. Emotions are always attached to water; notice the level of the water.

Angels

You can identify Angels in a dream by knowing that anyone in a dream who has a job to do, and that includes yourself, is an Angel; anybody in a dream who has a function, a specialty, or any particular thing to do, whether it is a doorman, repairman, sanitation man, a doctor, a dentist, a lawyer, a maid—anybody who has a job to do in a dream is *always* an Angel. It is always one of your Angels who is doing a job on you.

Angels have no sexual identity. They are neither male nor female. An Angel is complete in itself. It has been female for enough lives to be female and it has been male for enough lives to be male. If an Angel comes to you as a male or a female, it will come to you in the form that is most acceptable to you.

If you see two Angels in a dream and you wish to know who is the older one, in a dream *hair* denotes age. The Angel in a dream who has the longest hair—shoulder-length hair—denotes that this Angel is older, relatively, than you. The longer hair is the wiser or older being.

UNIVERSAL COLOR SYMBOLS
IN DREAMS

BLACK—Has an absence of color. Black is the unknown, the future, potential. In certain cases black means ignorance.

BLUE—In the Angel world, means ego, mental ego, and identity. It is related to the world in which there is a blue sun vibration, its own sun. Earth-world blue is the color in which Angels come to us most frequently. It is the color of motherhood or mothering where they are giving us protection or insulation, giving us assistance to help our souls evolve.

BROWN—Angel-world brown is the color of someone who is matured. Earth brown is the color of Earth, it is an Earth teaching, it represents old.

GOLD—The highest color according to frequency or vibration, gold always means wisdom. If you dream of being paid or receive gold in a dream, you are being paid in wisdom. Gold has the power to raise the vibrations and it is very powerful and very magnetic. Gold can take any vibration of any psychic.

GREEN—Has two meanings; Angel world means green is the color of growth. It means your being is eager to grow and become bigger and bigger. On an Earth level, green is the color of physical healing.

ORANGE—In Angel world, means they have a passion to help, to do work, to learn, to grow. Full of passion to be involved. The primary meaning is passion. Earth frequency is a sexual passion, sexual hunger.

PINK—Always means a new birth of wisdom, thinking, or going into a new job. Pink is the most desirable of all colors. Your mind is always thinking, regenerating.

PURPLE OR VIOLET—Has the power even more than gold to penetrate. Violet can penetrate anything in existence. If Angels or flying saucers wanted to heal a person's soul, they would beam a violet ray into the person and heal him. Violet is the healer of the soul. That is an Angel level. The Earth level of violet means to be spiritual.

RED—Means life force; blood; energy.

SILVER—Always means purification.

WHITE—Means you have completed a Karma, or a cycle of learning. White is the highest since it contains all colors in itself.

YELLOW—It is like gold, a younger state of love. It does, however, irritate the nerves.

17

The Reincarnation Process and Life Cycles

Destiny is not a matter of chance,
it is a matter of choice.

WILLIAM JENNINGS BRYAN

O Lord, keep me forever on the trail of yesterdays and
    tomorrows as time withers away
Forget me not along the byways of a storm covered by
    the dew drops of yesterday's sun
Moments of time slip in and out
Remembrance anew of some long forgotten past when we
    were one
Tempest storms are built by angered men
    resonant of their past frivolities
Synonymous are the quiet straight path
    of the brook trickling down a mountaintop
    looking in answer to the bodies of the crying below
Go along gently wavering not, resplendent
    in your cloak of armor when I am once again with you
Respect all the laws of thine covenant
    and God adieu to the adornments of tinsel
    that fades away like a ship in the night

All the world's a stage, and all the men and women
    merely players.
They have their exits and their entrances,
    and one man in his time plays many parts . . .

WILLIAM SHAKESPEARE

EVOLUTION AND
THE REINCARNATION PROCESS

What is all the talk about past lives lately? People comment about it but very few say they remember being born to another time and another place in another world. Children are closest to the reincarnation process. They can and do have recall regarding their most recent past life. If we could ask them about it up until the age of five or six, we might be startled by their answers. Unfortunately, we deprogram them. As parents, we call their past life memories stories or fantasies, or we might say they have been dreaming or have a good imagination. But if you tune in to the extreme fears children have, perhaps of going to sleep, the darkness, or whatever, and if you would take the time to question them, you might find some deep soul memories that have nothing to do with any uneasiness from their present lives. You might find them extremely truthful and not telling stories at all.

As adults, we may have recall of different places or settings that we call déjà vu. When it comes to recalling past lives or experiences of another incarnation, they may come to us as dreams or symbols. If we pursue this it can result in growth and the understanding of ourselves and even of our cosmic relationships with others. Simply put, it speeds up our spiritual awakening. If the symbolism of a past experience points out a weakness, this knowledge gives us the opportunity to rectify such a weakness and consequently to evolve the self.

However, the initiative to do so is our own responsibility and depends on our readiness. The symbolism of an experience of a past incarnation is not always immediately understood. You may puzzle over it for some time. It is best not to rationalize it, but when in meditation, wait for the intuitive flash—sudden inspirational enlightenment explaining the symbolism that will come to you. If it doesn't come to you during the first few minutes of meditation, put it aside; recall of the experience will come at a later time. Eventually, you will know it to be so. The knowing will come as a feeling of complete conviction throughout your whole being.

I am attempting in these few pages merely to help you in this life to practice the "art of living." Also, to give you the basic knowledge of life and death, and to help you realize what your destiny is. Certainly my purpose is not to change your belief system. The higher the soul evolves in each and every incarnation, the more spiritual the understanding becomes, until a perfected human state is attained. Whether you believe or do not believe, if you understand the basics of reincarnation, you will understand how to put your fears aside due to the multiple experiences we face in our lives, and you will learn that while the physical body dies, the spirit does not, and is perpetually young and immortal. We must seek to find the answers to the perfection and expansion of our souls.

The Doctrine of Reincarnation is regarded with mixed feelings by the public. I've heard some people say they believe they were Cleopatra or Mark Antony in past lives, which seems less than credible. Also, to some, the repeated pattern of returning over and over again seems distasteful, and if they *had* lived before, wouldn't they surely remember?

The question is: can we prove it? The answer is: those who have the capacity to remember past lives with their advanced faculties are truly the masters or teachers. I feel sorry for those on Earth who believe that each individual is given only one chance to prepare himself for heaven. What if he is a criminal or murderer and dies prematurely without redeeming himself— what will be his fate? Do we disappear when we die and become nonexistent? Do the thought forms of other people who survive you have a memory of you and does it disintegrate too? How do we learn? It is advisable to regard man's organism merely as a soul and a body. Do they both disappear? By seeking the truth, perhaps you will find out.

How is one born? I believe that when one chooses to be born in this physical world, the connection with another plane of existence is cut off. Nature works wisely, erasing all memory from our soul when we are incarnating again, so we can live up to our highest good and potential. Some souls can remember; most do not. Through the process called birth, a soul is transformed into a new being with a new body and personality. Since a new brain is involved, how can that brain be expected to remember impressions and events of other places that it is not concerned with now? We have to get on with a new job now, and certain lessons can be learned only while functioning in a male or a female body. Whatever the soul needs, it must acquire this time around.

When a soul has desired to be reborn into a particular family, whether it possesses a link with them from the past, or will inherit through a new union qualities that are useful or desirable, they stay around both the chosen mother and father looking for an entry. When a couple is joined in the creative act, having intercourse, a magnetic streak of energy quickens. Like lightning filled with the same moral spiritual or emotional fiber qualities of both, this energy enters into their body the most harmonious time their vibrations have met, penetrates into the father and attaches itself to the sperm while entering the mother. The father's and mother's energy vibrations are shared with the soul, while the vibrations of the mother can be shared and felt through the entire nine months of gestation.

The mother's vibrations discharge to the unborn child thoughts that greatly influence his soul. Human beings are not formed by environmental influences, certainly, but while in the mother's womb the infant does pick up on the thoughts and feelings of the mother and father. They may take on the genes but they certainly are not subjected to who their parents are or what they did. Only the emotions and feelings are tapped into.

Every time we come back into manifestation, it is like entering a battlefield. Birth is like that; death is not. The soul, when he begins to leave his mother's womb and enter into a new world, fights against fear, anxiety, limitation, doubt, and bewilderment about having made the right choice. Choosing our parents and the environment we need is what our soul must decide before it incarnates. Everything is approved by the supreme judge or the Laws and Lords of Karma. If the environment a soul chooses to come into is unhealthy for him, the soul may leave the body. This might help you to understand "stillborns." They simply change their minds after being born and, rather than live with the mistake, decide to go back to the source they came from.

When life on Earth begins, the baby is born and breathes for the first time cosmic vibrations from different planetary positions that govern the future destiny of that child. His good and bad deeds will be accounted for in the charting of his life, and also the influences and experiences he must go through. God is not unjust. Each one of us experiences or reaps the actions he has put into force. So, if you were born blind, ill or deformed, or you die young, it is the life you chose to experience this Time around. Each soul punishes himself or limits himself. Nature does it all based on Karma from previous incarnations. If this life does not work out, you can do it again.

God helps you choose the conditions under which you are living in your present life, so you can perfect your act and perform your part in the human race.

If someone is to become a millionaire in this incarnation and at the end of his journey doesn't become one, his desire to fulfill that destiny will make him a millionaire in the next incarnation. There is an endless procession of aspirations as we enter into wholeness and eventually become whole. It is through aspiration and evolution that the soul develops the possibility of realizing the highest and most fulfilling, the Divine in ourselves. The physical body does not always hear or listen to the dictates of the soul. Our physical life or expressions (all we see materialized) serve to cover up the soul's Divine purpose. That is, to reach some kind of perfection from the realization that through birth, our lives and experiences, the soul comes down again and again to Earth or other populated planets. We evolve through endless incarnations and finish up this cosmic drama so that we can perfect our act.

Nobody can compel the soul to reincarnate except the Supreme. Although the Supreme has the power, no one is compelled to do anything. One who chooses to take a conscious part in dealing with goodness knows reincarnation is absolutely necessary for those who need to serve God on this Earth. On no other planet or plane is this realization—that is, to serve humanity on Earth. A soul reincarnates only in the physical world of Earth. For a soul, Earth has the mastership quality of divinity.

The results of a past experience point out a weakness in oneself. This knowledge gives us the opportunity to rectify such a weakness and consequently to change the self. Karmic dispensation is unavoidable, inevitable. The Law of Karma is always binding.

When we enter into the inner life and develop our inner consciousness and capacity, we get recollections of our past incarnations. The urges of our feelings of our future make us want to go forward in the spiritual life with our own inner concentration. The past like a dusty road. The spiritual chariot should run in the present and future. When we look back at our past lives we find them totally different from the present. It all forms a circle, the spirals of the world, the life stream. When we think of Earth we think of a circular planet. What goes around, comes around. Can a thought die or a word of love evaporate after it has been said?

LIFE AND DEATH CYCLES
AND THE PLANE OF EXISTENCE

1. We are born with a spiritual component called our soul, which comes to us as a portion of energies from a source called God. Our physical body, flesh and bones, houses this soul. The body is utilized as a powerful motor and a source for creative potential. Our soul contains a consciousness, a subconscious, and a superconscious. There is no end to what we can do, think, become, or strive for.
2. Human life progresses in approximately seven-year cycles. We receive an infinite amount of learning in each of these time periods. We each experience our life and learn how to expand it and utilize our creative potential whether it is in physical, mental, or spiritual attitudes of growth. What we learn through each period of seven years is vital to our existence as we go through many changes in these periods of time.
3. When we leave the encumbrance of the physical body at the period called death, our soul moves to another plane of existence, where we adjust to new conditions. It is called the Astral Plane. It would be important, at the time of your loved one's leaving this Earth dimension, to pray for a period of thirty days after his or her death. The soul has departed benefits from this period and is encouraged to grow and go on to higher planes. When some of our subtle bodies leave our physical, upon death, our consciousness still functions in the after-death states as well, until we move to the next dimension.
4. The Astral Plane is a dimension above this Earth Plane where we are washed, cleansed, and purified by the help of our guardian spirit entities. The Astral body is an exact counterpart of the physical body of a person. It is composed of fine Etheric matter and it has been encased in the physical body of a person. In dreams, it can become detached and sent on long journeys and distances. Sometimes stress can do this in life.

It can travel at a speed faster than light. The Astral body exists after the death of the physical body but it disintegrates in time. That is why prayers are important to help the fragments dissolve so the soul can go on. Some people can see this body leave—that is, if the dying person desires this and wants it to be seen.

5. We continue to grow and develop in the Astral Plane until we reach a more ascended plane of existence where we are further conditioned, purified, and refined. In this ascended plane of consciousness, we are, and can transmit, the light of God-Power to those on the Earth Plane of consciousness.

   We can appear in dreams, apparitions, or in the mind's eye, so we do get a feeling that the departed ones are close. All this is true with the normal paths of death. If there is a trauma involved, as in a quick accident, drug abuse, or suicide, it takes a little longer, as these souls must be cared for differently and may not even be aware that they have crossed over.

6. Finally, we either return to the Earth Plane in future incarnations, or other dimensions and planets for either Karma or service, in order to work out our destiny. Or, we can continue on and go into a cosmic plane of consciousness where the soul returns to the God source whence it came originally.

Note: When you can understand this higher concept of what your mental power and creative mind can do, you can see how it operates in the life stream of the cosmos. Growth, harmony, healing, prosperity, success, love, originality, and creativity are yours, and you can utilize your clairvoyant understanding and psychic intuition.

Keep all of your channels clear and open, and truth will be your guide.

REINCARNATION TESTS

DEMONSTRATION: VIEW YOUR SOUL

Seeing into past lives with a candle and darkness:

We are the sum total of our past lives. Some of our past incarnations have manifested themselves in our physical bodies and under the right circumstances we can illuminate our past soul expressions. If you try, you can see your face change to reflect the different balance of atoms and molecular structure of the physical body in our former lives.

In order to illustrate this, go into a small room, perhaps the bathroom. The room should have a mirror. Stand before the mirror. Bring a candle with you and say a prayer while lighting it. Remember: Always set the conditions beforehand that *only the entities of your highest good come through and may only God shine through*. Then light the candle and set it to your left side. Shut off the light and stare into the mirror while you watch the subtle lines of your face change in proportion to other lives' countenances. You may see a beard, mustache, or hat appear, with glasses on, off, or changing. Your face may grow longer or appear to get shorter or rounder.

Warning: Watch the time! *Do not* do more than ten minutes at a sitting. Otherwise you can slip into too deep an Alpha level for you to feel comfortable.

TECHNIQUE FOR SEEING INTO
PAST LIVES: FOR ONE

1. Be relaxed and calm.
2. Charge yourself with psychic energy (take five deep breaths—hold each one for the count of 10, then exhale slowly over the count of 15).
3. Set up a large mirror, at least ten inches by twenty-two, on a table or desk and sit on a straight-backed chair. Make sure you are alone. Extinguish all light in the room except for a single white candle placed to the left of the mirror.
4. Look in the mirror and say to yourself "I would like to see what I looked like in one of my previous lives."
5. Relax your body and strain your eyes a bit to look into your eyes in the mirror. Squinting is okay. You will see a little clouding at first. You may see a shimmering ripple—which is an indication of active psychic energy of the vibrations of chemical crystals in the air itself. You will see the changes.

Do not prolong more than ten minutes.

TECHNIQUE FOR SEEING INTO
PAST LIVES: FOR TWO

1. Reduce the lighting to a single shaded lamp or candle placed in your line of vision to the left of you, if you are first going to study another.
2. Both of you take your energizing breaths.
3. Say aloud, "I would like to see the appearance of [*say the other's name*] in a past life."
4. Concentrate your gaze looking directly into the eye of the subject. You may feel the need to squint and strain your eyes a bit . . . this always precedes change.
    (Stop after ten to fifteen minutes at the most.)
5. The person conducting the exercise then tunes in on the soul of the subject and meditates on what is the life plan of the subject (e.g., "Where did he come from?"). "Why is he in this life? Why did he choose it? What is his life's work? What are the feelings of his soul in this incarnation? What is the therapy being done on his soul by this life's incarnation? What will this life accomplish after he has gone? Will his soul be satisfied?"

(Do not do for more than ten.)

In case you have doubted the tests for seeing into your past incarnations, perhaps you will try it when your mind can accept the exercise. For those "doubters," I shall attempt to explain the theory. You can actually see into past life interchanges with your soul (view yourself at all these levels). In one way or another, when the circumstances are correct, manifestation will occur. We *do not* make the manifestation take place; rather, we *create the circumstances*. We choose the emotion with the attitude for the manifestation to take place. It is simply one way and shows that when circumstances are correct, change will occur. (Science has proven that one piece of steel is not solid mass. Things are *not* as they appear!)

The reason for the word *darkness* in the vocabulary is because the word *light* is in the vocabulary. The difference between positive and negative is: if you are in a dark room and you light a candle in that room, what changed dark to light is the illumination. The room is the same if you take away the candle.

There are two ways of solving a problem—negatively or positively.

If you look at a person beside you and put your hands up in the way of vision, you cannot see the person's face. If you want to see his or her face, what will you do? You will look behind the barrier or remove the barrier. We are conditioned to what we can see and what we can't see through dense opaque objects. The biggest barriers are the unseen.

The reason for darkness is what I am trying to help you learn about so you can master the light. Light by itself is only light, but in contrast to darkness it is illumination.

PAST LIFE REGRESSION, TO BE USED ONLY WITH AN EXPERIENCED THERAPIST OR FRIEND WHO KNOWS YOU WELL

I will give you an exercise that you can work with a friend. It can lead you into an altered state of consciousness. Usually only an experienced therapist, hypnotist, or regressionist should use these exercises to take you into a deep level of the mind. Those of you who are experienced occultists or have many times been in an altered state can utilize this exercise to relax the mind. This deep relaxing technique will give you renewed strength and clarity. Clarification to some unanswered questions that may have troubled you may come out of it.

Now . . . I must give you the how-to's for a safe journey, and balance out all physical tensions. These will take you safely from this incarnation and into another one and back.

1. *Never start* before calling in your spirit guides, saying The Lord's Prayer or the Our Father (three times).
2. Mentally put a blazing white iridescent light around your body and see yourself wrapped in this light from head to toe.
3. Then, set the conditions for the session. Perhaps you wish to explore the lifetime prior to this one or one far back in a time you have lived before. State your needs. If there are people in this life you wish to know about from another incarnation, and you know them in this one, set the conditions for this as well.

4. Always make sure that the person who is taking you into this regression knows when it is time to bring you out of it. Do not stay in altered state of consciousness when you begin to attempt this exercise.
5. Always decide prior to the session that when the regressionist clicks his or her fingers (three times), the person undergoing regression will come out of it.

PAST LIFE REGRESSION:
AN EXERCISE

You can tape this meditation, have someone else tape it, or just remember it to experience a past life.

Put yourself into a state of meditation.

Now that you have completed your deep breathing, I want you to make yourself completely comfortable. Slow down your thoughts . . . think only of the sound of my voice and let yourself be calm and peaceful. I want your eyes closed now . . . keep your full attention on the sound of my voice and use your imagination to feel your body relaxing as I ask you to do so. As the relaxing power is coming into the toes of the left foot, it's moving right on down the ball into the arch, into the heel, right on up to the ankle. Completely relax . . . completely relax. As the relaxing power is moving up the left leg to the knee, it's relaxing all the muscles as it goes and moving up the left leg now to the thigh to the hip, permeating every cell, every atom, and you're relaxing completely . . . relaxing completely. As the relaxing power now moves into the toes of the right foot, moving right on down the ball, into the arch, into the heel, right on up to the ankle, completely relax . . . completely relax. As the relaxing power is moving up the right leg to the knees, it's relaxing all the muscles as it goes, moving on up the right leg now to the thigh, to the hip, permeating every cell, every atom, and you're relaxing completely . . . relaxing completely.

Relaxing power is now coming into the fingers of both of your hands. Feel the fingers of both of your hands relaxing, now your forearms are relaxing and your upper arms are relaxing. Now feel the relaxing power move into the base of your spine, and moving slowly up the spine and into the back of the neck and the shoulder muscles. The back of the neck and shoulder muscles are now becoming loose and limp . . . loose and limp. This completely relaxes and the relaxing power is now moving up the back of the neck and into the scalp . . . relaxing the scalp. Feel yourself relaxing and now draining down into the facial muscles . . . relaxing the facial muscles. Your jaw is relaxed and your throat is relaxed. Your entire body is now relaxed all over in every way, all tension is gone from your body and mind, and I now want you to imagine a golden light coming down from above and entering the top of your head. The light is now filling your body and beginning to manifest around your heart area . . . now feel it. Imagine a big white light emitting from your heart and completely surrounding your body in an aura of protective white light . . . see it . . . feel it and it becomes reality. You are now spiritually protected by an aura of spiritual white light and only the higher masters or your own guides will be able to influence you in any way during this hypnotic session.

Your body will now relax all over in every way, your mind is relaxed and filled with peace. In the background you can hear the soothing beat of the metronome . . . the metronome is saying "sleep . . . sleep . . . sleep."

As you listen to the sound of my voice, pleasant feelings of relaxation are coming over your entire body, and as this feeling of peace and relaxation increases you will find yourself deeper and deeper asleep. Each beat takes you deeper . . . deeper asleep. Go relax . . . go at peace . . . deeper and deeper asleep.

I am now going to count backward from seven to one. As I count backward I want you to use your imagination to see yourself in a situation going down. See yourself in your mind going down with each count you go deeper and deeper asleep. Feel yourself going deeper with each count. Number seven . . . deeper . . . deeper . . . deeper . . . down . . . down . . . down . . . number six . . . deeper . . . deeper . . . deeper . . . down . . . down . . . down . . . number five . . . number four . . . number three . . . number two . . . number one . . .

You are now quite deep and you feel deep. In a moment,

I am going to take you even deeper, but first I want you to think about the word *deep*. Use your imagination and create a scene in your mind that is totally peaceful to you. Let your body and spirit become part of that scene in your mind and imagine that scene. Such a calm relaxed feeling, such a quietness of spirit. Right now you're with yourself, with the world, and with everyone in it. I want you to carry this feeling throughout this session and throughout the rest of this day. All right, now you are very deep in this deep hypnotic sleep but you are going to go even deeper. Much . . . much deeper. I am going to count backward again from seven to one. By the time I get to one, you will be in the deepest possible hypnotic sleep. Number seven . . . deeper . . . deeper . . . deeper . . . down . . . down . . . down . . . number six . . . number five . . . number four . . . number three . . . number two . . . number one . . .

All right, you are now in a deep sleep . . . hypnotic sleep . . . and I am going to give you some suggestions which you will carry out. The first suggestion is that at any time you feel uncomfortable either mentally or physically, you now have the ability to raise your right arm a few inches. This is a self-releasing mechanism and you will be able to count quickly up from one to five. On the count of five you will awaken and feel refreshed. You now have the ability to remove yourself from hypnosis at any time you desire to do so. The next suggestion is that each and every time you are hypnotized you will go deeper than the time before. Each and every time you are hypnotized you will go far deeper . . . far and faster than the time before. This is a suggestion that you will carry out. In the memory banks of your subconscious mind there is a memory of everything that has ever happened to you in this life or any of your past lives. Every thought, every action, every deed is recorded in the memory banks of your own mind. You absolutely have the power and the ability to bring these memories to the surface once again. In a moment, you will actually move backward in time. You will once more open these doors and step into a past life in which you lived at least thirty years. Your own subconscious mind will choose the lifetime that will be of value for you to reexamine at this time. We relive only positive experiences that transpire during this time which would be a happy joyful experience and you relive the events only as an observer. Only an observer, without emotion, as an observer watching a television show.

All right, we are now going to begin to move into your own past life at the age of fifteen. I will count backward from seven to one, and as I do, I want you to feel yourself moving into the past, moving through a tunnel with a light at the end. The light is a door and as you move through it you will see yourself at the age of fifteen in a previous lifetime. You will once again become yourself at the age of fifteen in a previous incarnation. Number seven . . . you're letting go and moving through the tunnel into the past . . . allow it to happen . . . feel it happening. Number six . . . feel yourself moving backward in time, feel the sensation of speed as you move through the tunnel. Number five . . . you're moving on back through the tunnel now toward the light down at the end of the tunnel . . . feel it happening. Number four . . . you're getting closer now and you feel yourself moving backward in time. Number three . . . you're moving backward in time to a previous incarnation at the age of fifteen and you're getting closer now. Number two . . . on the count you will be at the doors of your own past. You will once again be fifteen years of age in a previous lifetime. Number one . . . you are now there.

Let the impressions begin to come in, and I now want you to answer some questions in your mind. Even if the impressions are not yet clear, your mind will know the answer. So, trust your mind, and as you do the impressions will become stronger and stronger. Are you outdoors or indoors? Your mind knows, trust it. Are you male or female? If you are outdoors, I want you to perceive the environment in vivid detail. Are there trees, grass, is it desert? Exactly what kind of environment do you find yourself in now? If you are indoors, what are the walls made of? The floors? See the windows, perceive every detail . . . every detail. Is it night or day? Hot or cold? You absolutely have the power and the ability to let these impressions flow vividly and I want you to look down at your feet, you have this ability to look down at your feet. Sandals, shoes, boots, or are you barefoot, and how are you dressed? You have the ability to step outside of yourself and see how you are dressed. What type of material, what color exactly, how are you dressed? Perceive every detail of what you are receiving. All right, we are now going, so let go of this and you're going to move forward in time.

You are now going to grow up five years and on the count of five you will be twenty years of age in this lifetime we are now examining. Number one . . . we are letting go and moving forward at the age of five years. Number two . . . allow it to happen, you are moving forward in time to the age of twenty. Number three . . . feel it happening. . . . Number four . . . on the next count you will be twenty years of age. Number five . . . you are now twenty years of age. What do you see and what are you doing at this time? Perceive the environment. Are there others there with you? What are their relationships to you? You are twenty years of age and I want to know who is the most important person to you, your mate, your lover, a friend, a relative . . . who is the most important person to you at this time? What is your name?

Trust your mind and allow your name to come through. The first letter of your name is . . . The second letter of your name is . . . The third letter of your name is . . . The fourth letter . . . Now, if there are any additional letters in your name, I want you to realize what they are. See them in your mind. You now know your name. Your name is . . . Now pronounce it in your mind. Your name is . . . All right, I now want to know the year. If the year is important to you in the lifetime we are now experiencing, I want you to see the year. Trust your mind and allow it to come in. The year is . . . ? What country are you in? If your country has a name, I now want you to perceive the name of that country. Now see it in your mind. The name of your country? All right, you now know the most important person to you, the name, the year, and the country you are residing in, and I want you to let go of this and move forward in time once again.

You are now going to age five more years and on the count of five you will be twenty-five years of age. Letting go and moving forward now . . . number one . . . moving forward . . . number two . . . number three . . . number four . . . number five . . . You are now twenty-five years

of age and I want you to perceive every detail of the
environment you find yourself within . . . in vivid, vivid
detail. See the situation in your mind, and I now want you
to answer some additional questions in your mind. What do
you do with your time? If you work, what is your occupation? What do you do with your time? You are now going
to move forward in time once more. I am going to let your
own subconscious mind choose a positive situation that
transpired somewhere between the ages of twenty-five and
thirty and on the count of five you will be there. Letting go
and moving forward in time now to a positive situation that
transpired somewhere between the ages of twenty-five and
thirty.

Moving forward . . . . number one, number two, number
three, number four, number five, you are now there. What
do you see and what are you doing? What is the importance
of this particular situation? I want you to understand the
situation and see it in your mind.

You are now going to return to the present time. On the
count of five, you will be back in the present, remaining in
a deep hypnotic sleep but back in the present time. You will
remember everything that transpired, and on the count of
five you will be back in the present and remain in a deep
hypnotic sleep.

Number one . . . coming back now . . . number two . . .
number three . . . number four . . . number five . . . All
right, in a moment I am going to wake you up. On the
count of five you will open your eyes and be wide awake.
You will awaken feeling good all over, as if you had taken
a nice refreshing nap. You will feel completely revitalized
and full of energy. Your head will be clear, you will be
fully alert, acting with calm self-assurance and feeling good
all over. You will remember absolutely everything that
transpired while in this deep hypnotic sleep. Number one
. . . you're coming up a little . . . feel the lifeblood returning to your arms and legs. Number two . . . coming up
a little more, you feel good all over and glad to be
alive. Number three . . . you're coming on up now . . .
feel a sense of joy and well-being flowing to your body
and mind. Number four . . . in the next count you are

going to open your eyes and be wide awake and feel good all over. Number five . . . wide awake, open your eyes and feel good. Number five . . . wide awake . . . wide awake.

18

Love

Soft, warm, and gentle
    like the dewdrops that fall on Mother Earth
That are kissed and nourished by the sun—
    like the everlasting glow of the embers in a fire
Lost in a sea of indifference

—NEUTRAL

SWEPT AWAY

I was afraid of you
Fear, in not knowing how you came to be or why
When I first came into contact with your soul
I was unnerved—off centered—dead in my tracks
My composure left me, I was switched
In that one split second I was fused with one world
    and another
What was it put into my path, it was time to deal with
It was the remembrance of the tide
Timeless at sea
The waters churning within
Why did I have to cover my imperfections
Why did I run away from myself
Was I playing with the energies or was it playing with me
My eyes have opened, reasoning gone
Does it matter that I was a shell in the sea
Disintegrating into sand
Or is it the tide that counts

LEARNING TO LOVE AND
EXPERIENCING FREE ATTACHMENT

In the beginning there was darkness and through that darkness a voice said, "Let there be light."

God is the center of this experience, the energies of love.

Perhaps nowhere in life is communion with the spirit world more important than in love. Love has been referred to as "that old black magic" and for good reason. Love is nature's most accessible form of alchemy. If we do not love, we cannot survive.

To seek love and the meaning of it is to get in touch with the Divine source. It is important to glorify and amplify love through the use of all we can learn here, and not to destroy it, for love is the key to unity, not only with your lover and fellow man, but with the other world, and with the world that came before and the world that will come after.

The love that grows on the "tree of life" can wither if it is not nourished. We each have within us the sunlight, the rain, and all other nutrients necessary to nurture this tree and keep it growing, spreading its roots deep and its branches high. If we nourish love, it will repay us a thousandfold—it will reenergize us and raise our consciousness to spread beyond our loved one, to the whole human race. Love will shed light on those areas of truth that seem to elude us when we are not loved. We must work at love. We must take responsibility here on Earth and relax our egos and strive to unite with another human being. For, once we have accomplished this, we have achieved the most perfect expression man can accomplish on Earth.

Our characters, therefore, must be developed in ourselves; they cannot be given to us. This need is what the soul must have to mature. It advances by dedicating ourselves to others without rewards.

Love is a motivating force that propels the act of faith and is nourished in a climate of hope. Love is the great longing that conquers our more primitive nature. What's perhaps so magical about love is that it isn't planned. It is biochemical, a need from your unconscious to another's. Love is magical in that it just *is*. When it is there, you know it. It is giving and sharing beyond this superficial place and sharing.

A *true love* is a type that grows. It can exist fully when two individuals have reflected their higher selves; their souls. The meaning of the soul means the sum total of experiences you have had in other lifetimes. Maturing each time around and improving your lovingness to experience unconditional love capacities. Faith and trust sums it up.

Lust or erotic love is a deceptive one. It is experienced when two individuals come together and a spark is ignited. This spark is generated when opposites attract. It is completely sexual. It is not a lasting expression of love, as the fire that is generated in passion lasts only as long as the spark of intimacy survives. Once intimacy has been enhanced, the flame of emotion and attachment dies, the irritation grows, and the source of wonder deteriorates and leaves. This opposite couple is subjugated to the pull of each other's will. Animosities appear, in detriment to the once wonderful relationship they shared. When the physical passions are spent, there are no new conquests or meanings to explore, no new endeavors of enlightenment, no new roads of interest to seek, until finally the abuse of the couple's energies and the problems of coping with emotions such as fear, anxiety, guilt, depression, discouragement, and frustration set in. These defeated lovers might have to pass through a period of self-delusion that for a while can lead to disillusionment, which leads them away from hope and fulfillment.

If you are lucky enough to have found love and feel love, it will radiate from your center, generating and attracting to you all that you desire. Ironically, true love allows you the freedom to detach enough from your lover to develop your own creative potentials and abilities. True love allows you to release new ideas and desires and to stimulate abilities growing from your center. In your aura you will radiate success, poise, and self-assurance.

As you go through life with your true love, you will let go of the incomplete you, the unfinished you. Everything you touch should evolve into harmony with yourself, everything that surrounds you, and every relationship around you. You will find that true love transforms you into a healer automatically—and you will have the power of healing everything you touch. This indeed is the art of cosmic loving.

Love is an attitude that encompasses all other positive emotions. All positive emotion is love. Love is the central core to healing. Our life force is our love energy. As an expression of a human being, love is the highest force. It is harmonious and unifies our existence. Every song is written about an emotion. Most writers write tunes about love as it explains and theorizes, integrates within the whole of our human potential and healing order of life. It must be released and practiced.

Love yourself first without ego and vanity and it will supply and nourish you and everyone around you. It will advance this age as everyone from the past moves into the future of our Earth's creation.

Obviously, total acceptance is the best, hoping beyond hope that something will change. Don't always have an attitude to negotiate a compromise. Don't try to prove we are loved. If we override our own needs and interests, problems become inevitable and unresolvable later on.

Accept what is his or her immediate problem, either inherent, karmic, or self-made, and try to work it through. Be true to your values. Major values cannot be changed. Separate the "biggies" from the "smallies" and have a work plan. Don't live with them and push them aside as the pressures mount up. What are values? It's almost like an attitude that you can't give up without feeling you have suffocated yourself and in doing so have given up a part of you, your character.

STAGE 1

Waiting for the "eureka" experience? The bells ringing and lights flashing may not happen. The enchantment stage of a relationship must go through a period where we see into all of our illusions and perceptions. A quirk that doesn't fit should not be tossed off.

STAGE 2—CONTEMPLATION OF A COMMITMENT

- We're playing for keeps here.
- We pay attention to our own needs.
- You decide what is reality.
- What is need or desire?
- What is want or desire?

AREAS OF POTENTIAL CONFLICT

Don't hope it will change; accept what you see and feel now. Maybe you have to decide to give up some fundamental needs of your own. Am I going to be able to do what I want? Will I be able to do it at my own pace? If he or she sees all of my weaknesses, will he or she still love me? Doubts are your friends! Your relationship with yourself, your relationship with him, matters too.

Another option begins to become plain: ending it or putting off a commitment until the problem can be resolved.

Character is the one quality that we have to develop for ourselves; it cannot be given to us. It is advanced by dedicating ourselves to the soul's needs without any aid. Our individual personality is the means by which we choose to express our character.

A *need* is what the soul must have to mature, while a simple weak want is what the lower self thrives on when making a decision. Determine which of your decisions are based on need and which on want. Why deny a part of yourself that hasn't been made to feel whole or complete yet, unless the partner you have chosen fills in these gaps? Only if you have worked on yourself and are aware of your own inner rhythms and potentials are you working them out and through. We must live them all and forge ahead with *all* of our so-called feelings without the emotional blockage. Bring forth and manifest, live your doubts, as they will become your truths and then the doing becomes effortless!

THE ALCHEMY OF LOVE AND THE SEARCH FOR HAPPINESS

The following was channeled by spirit guides:

Every being shares in this yearning. It is with the arrow of love, from the heart of the Father, with the golden sunshine darting through the flowers in each one of us, we live. When the flashes of joy permeate our inner life from our soul's consciousness, we respond, though our brains do not. Only when the pains of living descend on our minds do we awaken and understand the importance of life. The dreams of our common man's understanding are gone as we have gone way beyond the human mind's comprehension and found our joys in another source of life—giving.

Our God consciousness has lifted us above the planes of physical reality and we live but scenes and figments of a dream. We already know of life's balance, or how to balance and budget the checkbooks of our life. We look back to the disappointments hoping we had learned sooner, but fear has kept us back. Only as soon as we were able to go into the fear of living, did we make our major strides forward.

We have discovered where our endless desires have fit in to our life's scheme of things and changed the art of existence for us. As our dreams grew and were fulfilled, the string of disappointment grew again into a void until the next desire came and went. Some bitter, some sweet, but most just thirst-quenches that gave us double thirst.

Wealth has given us nothing but power to become leaders of men. The wealth through knowledge gained, earns respect, dignity. Knowledge easily learned may be short-lived or far away but knowledge without shortcuts is wisdom. People who strive for happiness for their future existence to make good Karma, may be avoiding our worldly pleasures. Laughter and joy ensure our passage for our present and we then can fulfill our Karma and future. The heartaches and failures lie with ourselves, as God's Universe is surrounded by love and perfection. Misdirected effort to find happiness by the wrong methods might be employed to find the right ones. The majority of us pursue transient forms of happiness. We need to know that unconditional happiness is the birthright of every human being and is necessary to alter and expand our consciousness.

Conditioned happiness is an emotion which must sooner or later subside when those external circumstances change which called it forth. Man *wills* his own path or road individually. Don't look at the view of your life from a mountain top, climb the mountain first or get the help of a guide. Think on that!

How are guides contacted? Change the attitudes of life itself. It is wasting energy trying to alter others who cannot be altered. The wiser way is to alter yourself and your own attitude, understanding and learning how to deal with the realization that man cannot live alone nor be in his own isolated unit of space. We need to give of ourselves, or go on joining with those who can. The unfortunate habit of enthroning one's personality is universal, neither are we the perfect man, but self-centeredness is not to be labeled growth or the understanding of God perfection. Only when we learn to toss all self-oriented things aside, not to seek personal advancement, praise, and comfort, do we balance ourselves toward the welfare of others and gain the insight to the source of happiness. Inner attitudes stem from the heart center and the joys of loving.

Walt Whitman wrote: "No one can acquire for another— not one; No one can grow for another—not one."

Love—is a resting place through which all things grow, flow, and flourish. When the longing for possessing falls away, we live in life's magical glow of light. We bathe in glory, peace, and contentment. Love is our life force, for without it, and put into practice, we die. . . .

SEX AND SEXUAL INTIMACY

To resolve sexual doubts, determine whether the problem is one of attraction or action. If the chemistry isn't there, it isn't good. But that feeling that says, "I *want* this person" can be a bad sign too.

Technique is important to note and watch. Foreplay is therefore a determining factor. Remember, physical attraction, physical affection, and sex are important ingredients in most relationships. Again, use your doubts, to gather information to be able to come to a conclusion about the chemistry. What is in a kiss tells so much. It is the most important part of foreplay and the way you can determine best how you are feeling.

The *brain* is the processor. The brain has to be programmed to be ready for love. Its sensory cells process information more from some parts of the body than from others. The lips, mouth, and tongue hold a large understanding and share the brain's intention. Messages that come to the lips alone come from a sector of the brain larger than the impulses from the whole torso. Now you know why a simple kiss can make you weak, knees buckle, or perhaps even make you understand why you like a friend. It tells all!

About five cranial nerves come together with a good healthy kiss, thereby flooding the brain with complex pleasurable sensations. The act of kissing stimulates the salivary glands—the mouth literally waters to have the experience repeated. Repetition persuades the brain that it's time to send messages the other way. That is, responses of sexual readiness. It is one of the most wonderful aspects of human sexuality.

Fragrance and scent of the partner activate your love centers too and activate the proper brain center and form geometric patterns. Colors and music and love are to be meditated upon too, as the thought forms of patterns and colors and shapes of music are composite parts of the primordial energy that helps one's vibrational force and is transferred through the nervous system and into the psyche. You will know if it's for keeps as it is computed into the psyche, as the soul has to fight for jurisdiction, once having to control the conscious and subconscious mind. The mind will then focus the new vibration against what it has learned from the past. The soul may not be completely in charge as it is still imperfect (character-wise), as there are still some organic problems and the mind still wants to call all of the shots. Therefore, once a partnership has been established, even the correct herbs we take in, liquids, and diet aid true love.

UNIVERSAL LAW STATES

A spiritual union of two is a blending of a compatible harmonious vibration. When the blending has taken place, it is external before becoming internal. Physical attraction plays a vital part.

Harmony is always present when the union exists in love. Purity without restrictions, without commitments, frustration or anguish—based on truth.

Marriage is blessed by God in a physical manner.

Spiritual relationships means that two independent souls own each other. Sharing with each other what we are. Each owns itself totally. There should not be sacrifices. We cannot judge another's truth or deny its validity.

The search for love is not confined to any one class. Everything on this planet thrives on love, whether laborer, poet, or both. Its allure raises our spirit, tantalizes our moods, and helps us to enjoy all other living things. No one is free from the desire

we call love, the yearning for which we say we would go to the
ends of the Earth. If we now break it down again, the yearning
would be the objective. Again, passion and possessing another is
not love. This yearning energy is completeness. "Happiness is
just the thing called love." For happiness is love, love is light,
and light is love. With this great and awesome power, sing,
dance, rejoice!

LOVE:
THE OBJECTIVE IS EXPLAINED

1. This adjective is objective and cannot be broken down further. It is our one basic primordial energy. It is *God*.
2. A couple is selected, prepared, and paired while in spirit prior
   to their incarnation and birth in this existence to find each
   other at the proper astrological time. Therefore, astrological
   timing when they meet is important. This correct matching of
   your energy and vibrations with those of your partner is what
   some call soul mates.

   If we are to experience a few lovers in between, just say
   we needed the karmic experience and feel secure enough with
   our self-esteem, and work for improvement to move on freely
   and happily, and lovingly love thyself. The roots and stems
   from a previous incarnation have to be taken into consideration; there are lessons to be learned.
3. Our physical intelligence helps us to process the necessary
   information to feed into our brain computers. The intellect
   pertains to the priorities and values that are placed on each
   intelligence. In order to change, the old established vibration,
   or lover, must be removed. At that instant, the new vibration
   must be put in or computed for maximum results. Thought
   forms, patterns of pulsations of the brain waves as it is
   sending out and taking in, are vital as the brain is the processor. The mind will then focus on the new vibration against
   what it has known from the past. *The mind* can accumulate
   the vibrations of all persons you have known and *the brain* is
   the processor.

   Chemical, organic, and electrical switches are turned on
   and the psyche will compute whether or not the conscious or
   subconscious mind will have jurisdiction. The nervous system
   is also involved.

4. Fragrances, color, and music do work on this brain computer process and let you know if the chemistry you feel is erotic or a true love feeling. The chemistry must be there to turn you on.

   All this feeds into the psyche both conscious and unconscious, and the true emotions spring from that depth of feeling. The time will be right! Readiness and love are all. The temple area of the body reacts to fragrances and is crucial vibration-wise. It activates the brain centers, as do colors and music.

5. As a part of the above, the use of gems, jewelry, and metals is crucial! Clothing is important not only for colors and adornments but for the fabrics themselves—silk, wool, and so on. The artifacts help to evaluate and understand or perhaps have recall of past lives or otherwise opening the magic doorway of understanding your needs. You will experience a personal intimate revelation of your higher truth from the Universal mind that you have found your counterpart. All these counterparts help to find and evaluate as well as activate your love centers. It also helps the psyche to draw its conclusions about your partner.

QUESTIONS AND ANSWERS:
ON RELEASING ONESELF
AND GIVING ONESELF OVER TO THE
HIGHER SELF AND GOD-KNOWING POWER

Q. How can I cope with my divorce? How can I go it alone and have a peaceful loving divorce?

A. The relationship to yourself is your problem, not your mate's. We come here imperfect and strive for perfection. Fear of leaving a commitment or of failure and fear of not making another mistake must be worked out. Understand, what you search for of knowledge, wisdom, understanding, and truth can always be found. Look inward to discover self-truth. Are you living it? Only you can tap into the well of your resources through resourcefulness. It takes work! Do not fear work. It takes more energy to be unhappy then to be happy.

   Pay attention to your decision-making and manifest action whether you believe it to be right or wrong. If you have

found a physical movement wrong or inadequate, it can be
righted quickly, efficiently, and accurately through the right
action and you'll be back on course.

Look back at your past performance. Look at your track
record with family, lovers, and friends, and see if you like
yourself. If you have doubts, clean up your act. If you again
have doubts, see if it is the person himself you are divorcing
or if your fears of going it alone are bothering you. How
dependent or independent were you? Clear the question up in
your head. *Who* was whose support system? What it boils
down to is, "What specifically are you afraid of?" Is it
losing your freedom to be accountable to another person, to
have that person depend on you?

Next, determine whether the fear is coming from your own
head (based on past experience) or whether there is a real
problem in you. In that case, go for professional help to
decide the real issues. What you don't want is to be vague,
as then you can't get on with your life and begin the new
chapter of growth.

A peaceful divorce occurs when both parties rid themselves of past trauma or perhaps incompatible vibrations. The
peaceful divorce can occur when the past is collected, cleaned
out, and put in your pocket as you are both ready to project
into the future.

Q. How do I become patient, controlling fear, anger, temper,
overcoming procrastination, releasing guilt?
A. A big question!

Doubts are warnings requiring a person to live up to his
responsibilities. Know that first you must be responsible to
you. That takes place by clearing yourself of all negativity
and breaking down the past and letting these deep-rooted
blocks go.

Positivity and optimism defeat discouragement. They attract harmony and peace, and that in turn makes a person
happy. Deserve to be loved and banish all thoughts that
someone else's life or plans are upsetting yours. Resolve all
conflicts by saying affirmations to the effect that everything
that is yours will come to you.

When faced with uncertainty, remain comfortable in those
challenging times until you can work it out. Be motivated to

trust your true feelings and intuitiveness. Go with the facts
and when faced with them tackle them simultaneously. Relax, and the answers will come, thereby setting up no emotional blocks.

Q. How do I live with a straight (nonspiritual) partner or mate
who is good and kind but who I do not feel is living up to his
spiritual obligations?

A. The fantasy of an ideal mate will change and grow as you
both develop through life's experiences. Certainly, some
values must endure. The reality of life is that we must
change; remember, certain lifestyles change, but values are
forever. We all come from different backgrounds but as we
develop we change some of the institutions that our forefa-
thers had. That's what change is all about, perfecting and
preserving our existence by our selective sensitivity. If we do
not ignore the expression of love, our character, our integrity
in truth, then we indeed are spiritual. Acting it out by going
faithfully to a church or temple is not being spiritual. The
fundamental expression for serving another or mankind is.
This does not mean that if we give to a certain charity from
time to time we are spiritual either. Clarity comes from the
soul and the soul determines consciously what indeed is
spiritual.

Free will indeed plays a part, but character is the maturity
of one's soul expression. High standards are part of the
pattern, the ability to forgive is another, selfishness is another. Having the strength to conquer your weaknesses helps
too.

The vows of marriage are like indulging in a wonderful
dream or fantasy. We are overemotional people who think
that what we feel is the gospel or correct. Who are we then
to judge another's thoughts or feelings?

Fidelity and friendship are also a prime requisite. Do you
do anything to hurt each other, or to understand each other's
conflicts? Do you talk them out? Don't ever be a wounded
party. This causes guilt and fear. Talk about the areas of
your separate lives that need change. It isn't spiritual to
rationalize selfishness. Go into and explore your weaknesses
together. Finally, understand the dynamics of your own personal astrological chart. Perhaps your mate who appears to
be nonspiritual is the grounding agent that helps you keep

your head on or from choosing some sect of followers who are not from a God place.

If you determine that your mate's vibrations and love expressions do not match yours, then you're already at this time headed for the divorce court.

Compatibility and understanding can be worked on in many ways. Either a detached professional clinical way, and get counseling, or the way I would recommend: see a competent Astrologer who can pinpoint the star's configurations when you met and do a comparison chart. This will help you to see how you have worked your marriage through. Have you finished with it, and will you continue new growth patterns together with every new cycle of change that ensues?

Lots of luck!

19

Credo—
The Final Conclusions

Blessed she, who sails on the wings of Angels needing to fly
Blessed be he, with the courage of Orion's Belt soaring to go
    into the intergalactic spheres of eternity
Knowing and caring needless of mind, sight and vision
    able to scope the intrinsic cords of light, mind
    and sound . . . separated by only the bliss of oneness
Nothing to do but be sensitive only to the light of the Father
    within
Setting about a motion, a pattern formation dividing two
    worlds of thought and the love of mankind. . . .

Now that you have completed your studies on making your preparations for New Age thinking, healing for yourself and others, and engaged in thinking about the philosophers and doctrines of metaphysics, understanding should begin to seep in. I have tried to explain the alchemical process for instantaneous transformation. I am aware that those who have the willingness and readiness to change from our "traditional past" are ready now to explore further concepts that will include our planet's future as a whole. Otherwise, you would not have picked up this book.

    Self-change always comes first as we must go through our

personal evolution to be a part of a new Universal evolution. The order of our lives must be met with raising our standards, which incorporates the work on our spiritual, physical, and intellectual selves. Believe it or not, life does become simpler as we lend ourselves to the more important issues of life and raise our conscious levels of thought. We cannot remain a lump of clay immune to our changing life-styles. As surely as day turns to night and black to white, those who cling to the "gray" issues surely will not take part in this closing era that will change considerably in the two-thousand-year cycle of unfoldment for Earth's potential improvement.

In life, you have the freedom of opting for pessimism or optimism. No one can force you to do anything you do not want to do, unless you feel an unlimited power in you surging forth investigating our human potential ready and eager to be used.

Growth is a process of development pushing toward the exploration of an inspirational awakening. We are part of an emerging superrace that wishes to explore the adventures of outer-space activity in order to know, in advance, what is to come. We are emerging joyfully through the fog of even remembering our yesterdays to establish a way of life that embodies its collective beliefs and ideals. The wholesale orgy of destruction occurs at the dawning of the resurrecting of a new culture. These times are always led by men who have a direct connection with God and a love of mankind. Some traditions of the past are not so obsolete as we hold on to our value system, but we are challenged now to establish a new berth and rebuild that which is a structural, functional foundation for life needed for the underlying evolution of a new civilization of evolved beings participating. The building blocks are coming alive.

I write this convinced that through crisis, new beginnings are born. The strong individual whose mind is open and wise may not need a guru to help him make his Karma. He can accept in the reincarnation principles that perhaps there are no wrong decisions and be open to these truths, as he can do it all over again if he is dedicated and willing to stick his neck out for a way of life.

It is also my belief that there are many "avatars" among us, reincarnated leaders, clearing the way for our now advancing society. They live in all areas of life and exist in many professions. Some do not yet know who they are. Many incarnated in the fourteenth century, which led to the foundations of many nations. The fifteenth century ended with great voyages in the exploration of Earth. The Renaissance period built a new Europe as well as the eighteenth century, a period of enlightenment, freemasonry, and the revolutionary era. The Industrial Revolution led to world expansion in order to obtain raw materials for industry. The European and American nations failed to meet some tests in the nineteenth century as the old aristocracy and feudal traditions caused much bloodshed. So, I asked the guides what it was all about. Each period of time had its struggles, as did certain civilizations, but why was this century different? We were given many things of wealth, comforts, and power, as the days of Atlantis will attest to. We learned to use the tools of life, including energy, which was contained in crystalized form. Many had strayed from their God-given tools for the utilization and good of mankind. Once it was self-serving, the gift was gone and the race was divided. It led to the devastation and void of a civilization, for it was not deserved any longer. Other centuries began rebuilding again and all mystery was lost from the greatness of our Atlantean bounties. It has taken us a millennium to get back to where we were, only this time on a world scale. A new energy situation begins and many Atlanteans have incarnated again, sharing their old knowledge.

I exist presently in the area of my birth in the United States of America and have been aware of the gatherings here of people from all parts of the globe. My allegiance to the United States is not one of favoritism but of heritage as I can only write as an American, being one. Certainly I am not prejudiced against other nations of people, as I have taken the time to look into my many incarnations, which have been vast. My guides have informed me that most of the master New Age teachers are living in and flocking to this country, and the others who are not, have some tie to the United States either by vocation or by business.

Many souls who have had certain Karmas to work out were born in other areas of the world. Not all have to meet with a mission or with their destinies. Some are working off their Karmic debts in order to grow to conscious thinking. I am told that 1789 saw the beginning of the United States as a strongly organized federal nation, some months later the French Revolution exploded. These two nations represented two ways of dealing with and ending a past history. Although America at the time was full of material achievements, Napoleon's vision of a united Europe was destroyed, as were his personal ambitions.

The choice was made by the hierarchical order from God to make the Americas the new mecca of Atlantis. Presently, we are struggling, the enthusiasm gone. What is a nation without enthusiasm and love for another bent on destruction of fellow men?

The masters were sent down again, born as regular men and women, not quite sure of their identities, only a feeling of a strong sense of duty to aid in a decaying planet's situation. They come from nowhere and everywhere. The United States, having been the bread basket of the world, was picked to have a strong link with the destiny of the world, as were the masters here to serve it.

Crystals destroyed Atlantis some ninety-four thousand years ago and this form of energy continues to be on the rise with those now aware of their marvelous properties. Obviously, we have stepped over the bridge of our past in this present. We have come to the same cycle again, so we must reexamine our past in order not to let history repeat itself. The Atlanteans were the Children of God who asked to be reborn to raise a growing planet to the Stars of Achievement.

The Earth's karmic destiny was met in 1986 and the years to come in the future should bring us through the trials and purifications to make us indeed an esoteric society. The ones with not so good intentions will enable us to face our limitless expectations. The spiritual leaders will come together before the political ones as we master the system of values. America and Russia will align with God's allies in other countries for a planet that is now in need responding to her destiny. Read on to "The Spirit's Voice" as I received the message about the plan for humanity. Hopefully, the prophecies added at the conclusion will give hope that doom and gloom has no place among the survivors of destiny.

I am indeed joyfully awaiting as I live to observe the days ahead!

THE SPIRIT'S VOICE
ON OUR NATION'S HISTORY,
THE UNITED STATES OF AMERICA

(Leading up to why the United States was picked as the chosen spot of the Golden Age)
(This chapter was channeled.)

Europe was to be the continent picked for the Age of Enlightenment by the Hierarchy or the White Brotherhood. In 1794, Robespierre fell from power in the French government and Napoleon Bonaparte took over in France to make it a monarchy. A red letter day in the history of Europe was in 1795 when royalism again was crushed and Napoleon paved his way to power. He concentrated supreme power on one person, himself.

The original plan from above (the White Brotherhood or Spirit Hierarchy) called for France to spearhead the unification of Europe and Napoleon was to be the George Washington. One theory is that Napoleon was an occultist. He could frequently leave his physical body and fly astrally over enemy lines, enabling him to obtain firsthand information. It was this ability that enabled him to devise twelve basic formations that were even used in part during World War II. His military campaigns inspired many commanders who sought the secret of his success. His genius at making war lay in his ability to exploit his enemies' weaknesses. On the European front, Napoleon was aware of his occult powers, and by his nature was unafraid to take chances. Aware of his shrewdness and his powers with the state of confusion with France at that time, he was empowered by terrestrial guidance as a being so very evolved and strong enough to stand up to any opposition.

This ultimately caused his defeat in battle. His exile to Elba was his doom and downfall. The craw in his weakness was his emotional state, as he couldn't handle all of the energy given to him. His pitfalls were his ego nature and negative strength, and therefore he fell mentally and emotionally. Actually, some people believed that he was insane before he eventually succumbed to cancer. His own ego got in the way of his God-given duties as he was physically opened and attuned by spirit for the job to unify all of Europe. That continent was picked by the Brotherhood to be the source of pre–Age of Enlightenment, and Europe was the global choice and physical place picked on Earth for this task from the God source. The dark side of his nature got in the way as he attached himself to the entities of the dark side.

One of Napoleon's earliest campaigns was in northern Italy. After winning his battle his first major official act was to hold free public elections. This was a major deed as there had never been free elections in that part of the world. The aristocracy of Europe feared him because he was the son of a peasant, and here he defeated a monarchy and gave a subjugated people a voice in their own destiny by allowing them to vote. The act of voting was all-important to these people, for voting meant that they had to think. Thinking involves thoughts, thought forms, hopes, ideals, goals, faith, trust, expectation, stress, risk, rewards, self-ishness, and altruism. People suddenly realized that they knew very little of the difficulties of their countrymen because most of them could not read or write. They had limited vocabularies, which meant it was very difficult to form new thought forms and ideas.

He started his political life by using his powers wisely. The monarchy of Europe was aware of this and so they feared and hated Napoleon. His strength and abilities were frightening to them. The psychic energies that were given to him were eventu-ally taken away by the power of the light, as he abused his powers by negative use, which led to his defeat, exile, and eventual death. The French Revolution covered the period of 1789–1795. It ended absolute monarchy in France. While this was happening in Europe, the Americas began to be of interest to the Hierarchy, who switched their focus to bring forth the New Age concepts to America in order to raise the consciousness of the planet. Just as in France, patriots in America also decided that freedom from rule by an absolute power must end. It was with this in mind that the original Declaration of Independence and the Bill of Rights was written.

The Bill of Rights became law in 1791. These first Ten Amendments to the Constitution of the United States guaranteed basic liberties to the American people. George Washington was called "the Father of His Country" and became the first presi-dent of the United States. He laid the cornerstone of the Capitol of the United States. George was also an occultist and was very much in tune with supernatural powers, as were Thomas Jefferson and Benjamin Franklin. Franklin was very aware of the Laws of the Universe at that time.

During the War of 1812, the British forces took some prisoners and held them aboard a warship in Chesapeake Bay. Two Americans received permission from Secretary of State James Monroe to communicate with the British in an effort to have these persons released. One of the men was Francis Scott Key. They were both from Washington, D.C. These men boarded the warship just as the vessel was preparing to bombard Fort McHenry, which protected the city of Baltimore. The bombardment started on September 13, 1814, and continued all day and all night. Key and his friends knew Fort McHenry had little defense. When the morning came they did not know who had won the battle because the haze and smoke were so thick. Suddenly in a break in the mist, Key saw that the American flag was still there and was inspired and awed by it all. He wanted to express his feelings and therefore wrote the words of the song in a few minutes which we call the national anthem. How the song became famous is history, but basically, as guidance has said, Key was a very metaphysical person and his song was channeled and written to serve two purposes:

"The Star Spangled Banner" was brought forth from the creator as a Declaration of Intent for a new spiritual center, called for a new nation of realization to upgrade the quality of the planet Earth.

At the point of creating a new home, with our God-given creative potential we stand for a United Peoples Under God . . . the color and forms on our flag symbolize our free world, to enable us to become as evolved as some of the other planets in other solar systems.

My guides have expressed to me the deep meaning of our national anthem, "The Star Spangled Banner" basically being the antithesis of America, the cornerstone of the New Age. Following is the metaphysical interpretation.

Oh! say, can you see, by the dawn's early light,
See the lights on the levels and planes of our existence opening, declaring that it has begun, the nation under one.

From the light of dawn, the beginning of a time that awakens a budding Universe and peoples of Earth to prepare for a change that incorporates new knowledge coming forth, stabilizing us by the light of the Father to shine on our ways and paths illuminating us by new insight.

What so proudly we hailed at the twilight's last gleaming?
We Hail the creator. The Lords of Karma, the Lords of the Universe, the Cosmic Ripening and Oneness that has burst us into activity. We thank thee.

The end of the day, at the end of the segment or cycle we rise above to the experience, sigh with pleasure that our work is done for the day with hopes of tomorrow.

Whose broad stripes and bright stars, thro' the perilous fight
The geometrics—planets—are for us as symbols of the Universe given as our keys, points to light the road and pave the path as we cling to God's shoulders eternally as we get lifted by his light. It gives us color by the interaction of opposing forces to see our many ways.

Our perilous fight geared us for the survival of mankind, a fight for learning while we are here on a soul's journey. We fight to learn our lessons from our spirit guidance here in this world, seeking the true story of creation within, to experience and raise our consciousness here on this planet.

O'er the ramparts we watched were so gallantly gleaming
The trumpets of Gabriel blast with the sounds and echoes of God's truths but we harken to hear the sounds of our higher selves bound into space igniting as well as consuming our beings—firing justice and truths in us.

How proud we are for our achievements through our pain as we prepare the path for growth. The stream of life, the sea of experience shooting us forward in a blaze of glory.

And the rockets' red glare, the bombs bursting 'n air,
The rockets are our safety valves within us. The preservation of harmony instead of anger.

Gave proof thro' the night that our flag was still there
As we give our purposeful loving thoughts to the Universe, we get answers to our questions by our deeds, which come through by the symbolism of what our flag stands for (spiritual). That we have taken a stand.

A bomb's energy (human way) acts as a detonating device to speed up the time segments of change for mankind.

Oh! Say, does the Star Spangled Banner yet wave

The number of man represents a star-shaped form with five points at each end. It exists as a banner of hope blowing in the wind of glory. The force of this energy moves us ahead with humility for peace as we stand tall despite all our opposition and thrive to carry on and continue with our mission.

O'er the land of the free and the home of the brave

The land America was chosen to be a nation of free souls, free spirit, free to express truth, integrity with character, striving struggle free from negative opposition. We are conditioning ourselves only to love. We are home. Our consciousness has been raised on earth as we are to become another evolved planet in the sky. In due time, many souls that have been going through their Karmic experiences on earth have finally worked all Karma through and there will be no more new souls incarnating on earth to work out our karmic lessons. It is done.

Home is where the Father is. The brave all knowing, we return to the source.

MEANING OF COLORS
OF THE FLAG—THE RED, WHITE, AND BLUE
IN CODE DESCRIBED IN COLOR
AND NUMEROLOGY

Red is the primordial energy (Base Chakra).

White is the embodiment of all the spiritual energies (highest point).

Blue is spiritual intelligence (color of the soul).

RED + WHITE = PINK—the color of spiritual love
RED + BLUE = PURPLE—the color of spiritual wisdom
FIRST CHAKRA—red
SEVENTH CHAKRA—white
FIFTH CHAKRA—blue
$1 + 7 + 5 = 13 / 1 + 3 = 4$ (4) is the number of Earth (land)

Red and white stripes are the *rays* of life energy.

The blue box pertains to a spiritual (land) country being illuminated by spiritual stars (white).

Five-pointed star in flag of United States symbolizes the Union of the states of consciousness.

The illuminated bright white stars symbolize the number of man (five) as in numerology.

The rectangular and triangular shapes are our geometrics of the Universe.

MAN STRETCHED OUT, ARMS OPEN

Washington, Jefferson, Franklin, Key, and others were all fighting in their own way to establish a front for unification while being directed by a higher force, as they witnessed the bloodshed and the battles that went on around them.

The American flag had 13 stars when Washington became

president in 1789 and Betsy Ross was commissioned to sew the colors of the flag of our united nation. The number of stars in the flag, which was originally 13 and represented the 13 colonies, breaks down to the numerological number of Earth. In numerology, $1 + 3 = 4$ (See illustration p. 336); 4 is the number of Earth. Today, 50 states ($5 + 0 = 5$) symbolizes the number for mankind and man on Earth.

All of the early events in the history of the United States were controlled by the power of the God force that was switched from Europe to the United States of America in order to form a new free land. The Light Brotherhood had to start a new frontier to be opened and discovered this United States of America. It was easier to go to a backward land, as the Americas were, because the government had to be started from scratch, with no old regimes or power. This new frontier was to be the melting pot of humanity, the upsurge of growth and change, having new energies to perfect Earth. The enlightenment that was to come of this New Age was to clear out old corruption and power, focusing on higher levels of achievement, thereby establishing new law and order to the globe and the occupants of "terra" (our Earth).

The Confederacy of the United States was brought together to complete the energies started in the other parts of the world to unify the states and levels of consciousness in mankind today. The binding together, producing new boundaries of unified states, makes it possible for a body of souls to be a part of a united nation, undivided.

The Civil War was the war between the North and the South. Each side wore a different color uniform to show their differences of opinion. The colors gave them different vibrations and energies in order to work out their differences and conflicts. The North represented the new style of thinking that had come into being of a new nation under way, while the South was symbolic, the side that represented the old way of government from Europe, the aristocracy. The pain and tears of war are needed for our human destiny so we can accelerate our process of growth and fulfillment. The price of war is dear and we have to be willing to stand up to what we believe in, as individuals, to be able to make alliances for peace above all for one God, one country united. Abraham Lincoln, too, as a great American had a destiny. His purpose was to raise the consciousness of the poor, the weak, and the illiterate. Perhaps his needs were to exemplify love for all men as they are created equally, given certain rights and opportunities whatever color, creed, or human differences they are born to as a people under one God, one nation. He was selected by the Hierarchy to be the forerunner of that time to open the minds of the weak, the uneducated, as well as the pompous, working with a developed egotistic society of bureaucrats to show there is no color, no line, no difference between men. He was educated astrally from spirit. Through his sleep and dream states he became aware of the powers of these two worlds of thought. He found he was not completely alone and was guided by a great power. He was weakened by his own doubt, not truly believing his visions totally and accepting them as the source of truth about his life's mission and destiny from those inner voices' promptings.

This put much pressure on his mind and soul. His physical and emotional concerns depleted him as well, by caring so much for the masses of people he was to lead. He is considered very much like our prophet Edgar Cayce, by allowing the breakdown of his physical health from those worldly pressures he should have been aware of and dealt with. In allowing anything but his positive purpose to come through, his opponents changed his brilliant destiny. He then became their "prey," hunted down by an assassin. He was a caring man with the belief, good or bad, that everyone deserves a chance for their freedom. However, Mr. Lincoln did not learn the lessons of discernment that allowed officials in high public office in the federal government to lead the people unjustly. They spoke as friends and worked against him. He, for the most part unassuming and unaware, could not surmount the pressure and when the realization came it was too late! Through the sadness of his assassination, however, the achievement of his goals and breakthroughs was complete. He rests in the hearts and minds of the world and is considered one of the great leaders of our immediate time.

The United States today is complete as a nation of good thinkers intelligently working toward world peace. At present we are eager to get on with the task of joining in brotherhood with other countries of the world to perfect the quality of life, a least some of us are. The cost of human error for greed, destruction, and power has driven us backward, as history will attest to, taking us away from our original purpose.

The year 1776, George Washington's time, was the beginning

of understanding what it's all about. To reorganize a new nation was where it was at, with individuals filled with love to perfect and create a new world, unafraid to leave behind our tortuous legacies of old, willing to die and sacrifice for life. Good Karma results in the capacity to generate joy and enlightenment for our souls' elevation. Those who intentionally create havoc for power and greed are from the dark aspects of lower worlds and are unable to reach for the heavens. The Age of Aquarius was at our feet then, to begin to generate the seeds enabling us to grow into a privileged society called the "Golden Age," as we move toward the year 2000 over the next twenty to thirty years for this to happen. We had to learn how to change our mistakes and our karmic destiny woven from the past. We on this human level tend to repeat our mistakes and have gone through many trials and purifications over the last two hundred years. In balancing our Karma, we have to balance both our finances and checkbooks as a nation, mentally and emotionally as well. Those who shift with the value of this balance, by paying back what wrongs they incurred, and put value on the higher things that make our heartbeats as prayer, master the system of value. Everything that we call material will then be understood.

IN CONCLUSION

It was not surprising that France gave America a gift symbolizing their friendship for their democratic ways from the oppressive European past we had rejected. The Statue of Liberty stands in New York Harbor inscribed:

> Give me your tired, your poor,
> Your huddle masses yearning to breathe free,
> The wretched refuse of your teeming shore.
> Send these, the homeless, the tempest-lost to me.

Even from the early 1900s, it was predicted that the world was in for great change. How could we not change with the onslaught of the Industrial Revolution, New York and other great cities becoming the "melting pot" with people coming into the United States from all over the world to help us by bringing their fine skills from an old world to a new land.

Most of the written prophecies deal with the last decade of this century. The predictions say: ''The human race as we know it is about to enter into a great change. It is the earthquake generation.'' Predictions of earthquakes and volcanic erruptions in populated areas, starvation, war, and plagues that will result in a massive scale of deaths were also stated. It is to my understanding that the human race will not only survive but will reach a new peak in its social, political, and philosophical evolution. We as humans are physically and emotionally structured to be able to handle extraordinary amounts of pain.

We strengthen as we grow, while going through our myriad experiences, and our hides get tougher with the softness of love for the sacrifices of our struggles. It is a necessary part of human life not only for our individual growth and attainment but for a nation as well. We need to live in a world of truth and love—that is prosperity.

If you look at old television programs you can see our rate of transition. Notice how the changes of just twenty short years have affected our concepts toward modernizing? Not to mention, the changing directions of man's needs, which must change in order to survive.

All the writings of the famed Nostradamus have revealed our very changing planet projected into the year 2000. We, who are living, are a part of his predictions now and I believe some of his works have been misinterpreted. The gloom and doom of his writings served as a warning to those who live in this time, that we get away with nothing. World collapse, by a negative government's leaders, could possibly cause destruction for all, if we don't make moves to suppress the armaments of war. Nuclear power is an example of the black magic to end it all.

As I have written earlier, we can change the direction of negative energy now. Nostradamus explicitly urged mankind to heed the warnings of science and take atomic power under international control. Those are the events of the great Armageddon, even the forecast of extraterrestrials landing to benefit the people of Earth.

We, like Nostradamus, are tying the past to the present in order to prepare for the future. It is a time in which we can shift our understanding to other dimensions in other solar systems as we will be helped with a new mathematical language and new symbols to guide us from our ancient past to new ways. This is the age in which the human race will achieve fulfillment. The positive aspects of man's curiosity and creativity can come to fruition. It is my belief that restrictions of negative power will be cast away and we will be able to be truly free to realize our full potentials. Maybe this will occur through the fear of Universal death. Those opposed assuredly generate bad Karma in a lump sum by dreadful sufferings that take many lifetimes to erase. He who has built perfect character has created for himself immunity to the troubles of life.

Certainly, at this writing our nation as well as other nations are paralyzed by the fears of annihilation. The worship of material possessions or the desire to possess another for one's own ends are altering the face of civilization. They are the agents of destiny, the destroyers of humanity bent on aggression, selfishness, and cruelty . . . the power mongers. No nation or race is free of guilt. No one nation has clean hands. The right-hand path, the hand of God, is intervening now through those enlightened ones warning us that we cannot continue on our old treadmill. It is worn out. Habits of selfishness and greed must go. The issues at stake stand from the standpoint of evolution and from our growth of world awareness. Power abused by dictators is produced by destructive humans on the left-hand path. Their destiny is to work as "group souls" who intentionally work briskly on destruction to destroy all that is love. They are highly developed personalities, you might say the Antichrist. That is, the duality of materialism as the Christ on the other side is the spiritual principle. The real problem is with the soul. The soul alone will determine and remain the victor, to lead us out of the conflict of humanity's future as it decides which way it will go or whom to serve. These issues are at stake to all thinking people. If peace at all costs is the answer, we must work by the power of the light and prepare by concentration of this focused energy. We are nose to nose facing Armageddon, which the 1980s has forced us as a people to accept. Awareness is where it is at! All negativity in man must be purged and cleansed to pave the way for our harvest period and the good of mankind. The Universal religion of love is spreading. We must come to the point of choosing sides, or be washed away as in the flood of Noah's time. The ark would not get too far at this point in human history in the raging seas of desperation. Our planet would not be here to start over again.

Planets in this galaxy and solar system are reported to respond to our cries of help as we have been monitored by highly complex computers that help higher intelligences to evaluate individuals and the parts they play in overall planetary development. I have heard they are in human form, look very much like us, and have been watching our pains and struggles for aeons. They are the ETs or extraterrestrials who are within our reach physically and walk among us now in observation as to our planet's past.

Caution has been used to limit the area of these experiences with them to certain individuals or groups of individuals only. These people's vibrations have a higher degree of light and understanding and can communicate these truths without fear. When our consciousness and God-self has been raised, it causes our vibrations to increase to a higher frequency. Our energy system must vibrate to produce certain light and sound frequencies to attune our energies to theirs. The serious students on Earth are their chosen teachers to help others. Our space sisters and brothers have progressed far, far beyond our technology and can be of service to us. They need not the tree of intellect but reach out to us as the branch of a tree that is rooted in love. They exist too within our atmosphere, in space, monitoring our vibrations even through our sleep states. They feel we are not ready as yet for them to expose themselves, as the inhabitants of this planet are still bridled with fear of the unknown. Many people would think that fairy tales are one thing that stir the imagination but "twilight zone" is another. The directive from these confederations of forces is from God to help us put a stop to destroying ourselves and the planet through the pollution of our atmosphere. They believe that we cause our natural disasters by sending out negative thought forms in the atmosphere that have something to do with many of these happenings and stirring up our natural peaceful environment. Nuclear power, bad thoughts, and fear cause the earthquakes, floods, tidal waves, and even chaotic weather conditions. They are intervening in our Earth evolvement now and are watching over our Earth.

They, too, have Karma to dispense with, pulling them closer to perfection and their God-self. A nuclear explosion would produce a reverberation in the atmospheric pressure of Earth. It would affect other solar systems and Universes if Earth were to be blanked out. Many channels around the globe, as well as myself, have come into the open reporting various contacts with some of these higher sources of intelligence. They will not be held back if man continues to slaughter one another. If violence increases, they will intervene. They look like you and me, and many are working among us as our scientists or in the top political positions of governments around the globe. We will not know who they are as yet.

Our space brothers have a veil of secrecy around them. They cannot bring manifestation to help with our woes until our consciousness is complete and negative ions or thought forms have been released from our systems and auras to bring in their light. The sides must be separated into a constructive force or destructive one first.

In the 1980s, for the past seven years crystallized insight, or Christ consciousness, has been upon us. It is a cycle, if you will, to "get it or not" regarding our energy potential. It breathes, it exists, and the flow of human resources is this potential and is our crucial issue. From 1978 to 1980 was the first three-year cycle that the consciousness of those living on the planet had to be raised, as a superrace of new awareness began emerging. From 1981 to 1983, another three-year cycle occurred. It was a tremendous learning period, a surge of change so strong that the race of master teachers had to be awakened from a deep sleep to integrate with the new energy changes. Old traditions and thought systems were breaking down and had to blend with our new understanding of energy sources. From 1984 to 1986, the cycle was to focus on learning self-healing and self-realization and redirection of our thought processes. The last cycle of a "change or die" pattern exists in the last segment of the '80s. This will be a volatile energy period in our lives. Acceleration and understanding of simple truths will take place. Whom we serve, God or the Devil, will be the final analysis. Belief in who we are as souls is at stake. I call this the final conditioning period where we can still make a shift of change without fear and disenchantment but with eager enthusiasm for a new tomorrow. Life being sacred is the special gift we hold in our hands. Yes, the "Star People" and those of the light are integrated with us now in our society and help us to integrate the new ways of thinking. Truth shall flow and false teachings and manmade idolatries will perish. False religions shall be recognized for their sham. Man's heart will be ready to yield to his spiritual instincts. According to the Law of Repetition, everything returns to a past reference or old cycle. We simply have to recognize that the past is not always good for us.

The 1990s are upon us and will be a time when our technology and resourcefulness are like those of the great civilization of Atlantis. It perished by the misuse of power. I believe that many of the souls here now are strong enough to accomplish the tasks that lie ahead and have been reincarnated from that lifetime. Once again, we strive to reach that apex or point of grandness and achievement. It exists now in our immediate future.

Some souls, God or Devil, are to be given the chance once again to come to the fore, generated and combined with some other energies that are awesome. The power of destruction would exhaust us and be fatal to our life continuance and fatal for Earth. If we change the Law of Repetition, we not only learn by our old lessons, we succeed and purify every living thing and make our heaven on Earth.

America, America, God shed his grace on thee
and crowned thy good with brotherhood, from
sea to shining sea.

THOUGHTS TO PONDER ON

Q. Who was Napoleon?

A. A great conqueror and powerful leader who was born in France and was destined to organize Europe.

Q. Why did the spirit forces pick Napoleon as the physical person on Earth to lead Europe?

A. He had the qualities as a great organizer and the ability to change the life of the people at that time in history because of his great strength, which was a powerful quality.

Q. Why was World War II mentioned?

A. As in any battle, history repeats itself. General Patton was an occultist himself (worked consciously with spirits) and was outspoken as he hated to follow orders. Patton worked along the same principles as Napoleon did and devised the same basic formations of war to outwit his opponents in battle.

Q. Why was the French Revolution a focal point in this discussion?

A. France was chosen as the pre–New Age place, and Napoleon, the leader of that new frontier, was picked by the Hierarchy to start with the unification of Europe.

Q. Why did the plan fail?

A. Napoleon was an egomaniac. The energy of the God force was given to him as he was aware, and power from these sources was put into his hands. A human being has the choice of a positive action or a negative action while in a physical body. Knowing all this, Napoleon chose to use his power for the dark side.

Q. What did the White Brotherhood do when Napoleon enjoyed the negative power he had and gave himself to the dark side of his nature?

A. A plan had to be devised to switch the Hierarchy's plans elsewhere, due to Napoleon's downfall that led him away from his original destiny's goals. The Americas was the chosen location. Several explorers, Columbus among one of them, were led to discover the Americas.

Q. Why was George Washington's role in United States history so vital?

A. While Napoleon was involved in his battle emotional and actual, George Washington in another land was already setting up the policies for the government of America. Washington and his cabinet also had a destiny. They were born with a Divine spark of joy in their hearts inspired by the light and were aware that they had a job to do for a new nation under God (1789). Since our historical pattern was not going anywhere it was decreed two hundred years ago to make the United States of America a promised land. This country's Divine destiny would be to lead the world in the final conclusion prior to the New Age, into the pathway of peace and abundance for all. It was symbolized visibly in the great presidential seal on our currency as the New Jerusalem of Space. We have been the greatest producer of wealth, freedom, and a strong leading nation in the free world. This was the beginning.

Q. Why was Abraham Lincoln elected president?

A. Lincoln, too, was a highly evolved spirit and human being His destiny was to do a job for a new country in his time. H was chosen to break down the barriers of class distinction He helped a man build character and courage without takin away initiative and independence.

Q. What role did Francis Scott Key play?

A. To show, as the years progressed, that the Americas wer still in battle. A creative person, a poet filled with remors for humanity's sufferings, he channeled a song we still us today symbolizing respect for one another and to "Pledg Allegiance" to a worthy America.

Q. And Betsy Ross?

A. She, too, was involved with George Washington; as h channeled the symbols of the flag, she designed and sewe them. Involved in the flag are the symbols of the Univers and the deep connection we have with higher intelligenc guiding us. The blue square in our flag symbolizes the sky while the planets in our galaxy are the white stars. Man is th connecting force between both worlds.

Q. Why did France place the Statue of Liberty in New Yo Harbor?

A. It was a symbolic gesture from France to give the Statue c Liberty to America. It carried over as a bridge the connec tions from an old world to the New World. It is ethnicit from our European past to the "melting pot" where thos who belong to serve here in the United States left the heritage from Europe.

Q. Why were the last hundred years so important to our nation history?

A. The early 1900s was a time when our population gre and cultures and new nationalities from all over the glob were attracted to this new land. The labor of those peop caused our Industrial Revolution and creativity to flouris Those born then, chose the hardships that were a part that generation. We now are offspring and part of the secon and third generations to begin the New Age movement.

Q. Why have the 1980s been singled out as a crucial time period in history?

A. Because we are about to make history change. Our changing values are indeed walking a tightrope in the balance of what the past was all about. The rapid increases in eighty short years went from the age of steam and electricity to nuclear power.

Q. Why are the 1980s linked with Atlantis in the present period?

A. Atlantis was a supercolossal civilization. The people then were blessed with abundance and knowledge through finding God. They were taught the use of great energy power through the use of crystals. It has been predicted that "Atlantis will rise." In a sense, it is now, as some souls who existed then are living now in this time. Again, with the knowledge and use of crystals and other things to harness power. The rediscovery of many metals and stones are used for this use. Only this time, are they for healing and raising our consciousness, or do we find Atlantis repeating itself again by negative destruction by our leaders of the world?

Q. Why the reference to God and the Devil in this chapter?

A. The Devil is a term used to describe the negative aspects of life, the strength of darkness caused by the use of misqualified energy. Devils declare war on the soul focused for good deeds and light.

God is the perfected human being, God is light and the principle that is intentional, conscious and deliberate and the part of man working with the collective souls and spirit of the Universe. The total achievement of pure purpose for love . . .

CHANNELINGS AND PROPHECIES

Prophecies serve a definite purpose. They can alert and warn people of what may transpire given certain circumstances so they can prevent events from happening.

Visions unfold as in a dream or a flash of understanding beyond the realm of man's logic. Not all future events in the course of history are predestined. Events that are negative or positive can be changed with human will. Therefore, as man can change by using his free will, so can the times and dates of these predictions.

1980/SPIRITUAL LEVEL

(Note: I have included a review of recent years to set up future developments.)

Our Earth's atmosphere was filled with a feeling of different currents of change, both within ourselves and within our general environment. It affected our feelings and the quality of our lives. People who lived around "energy centers" of change were feeling it the most. New Age thinkers migrated to these spiritual centers. These major centers are: New York, California, Arizona, Virginia, Jerusalem, Hawaii, Scotland/ England, Italy, Tibet, Australia, Switzerland, and Peru as they became power spots of energy.

PHYSICAL/EARTH LEVEL

- A lot of confusion around changes in family life. We were learning to learn the art of patience as family conditions were not the same from old generations.
- Gatherings of spiritual/physical discussion lecture groups became the rage for self-help. A.A. and diet-and-exercise control centers explored new thinking trends as these groups helped us explore the many changes in dealing with our problems.
- The majority of people were still foggy and happy in their leisure life and work conditions, not caring to grow up. Some were becoming more objective to different career choices such as computer technology, electronics, and so on. New business techniques began.
- People were becoming addicted to "legal drugs" such as Valium for relief of stress or tension and nonlegal drugs, and turning to alcohol as well to quiet their confusion.
- Sexual exploits and porno that started in the late 1960s were blown out of proportion, as was this decaying generation. The newsstands were selling these "way out" magazines that affected the youth for carnal gratification.
- Heavy chemical change in the atmosphere; our air was becoming polluted as well as our waters. Environmental experts

plotted out a course for the solution to this problem that would change the quality of our air.

1981/SPIRITUAL LEVEL

The seeds of new thoughts were planted in men's minds from our spirit guides to help us develop the higher rather than the lower self. The teachings began to flow forth, in man's thinking, and people were getting eager for change. Earth was turning on its axis, speeding up our progress as prophets had predicted, and the changes were felt in the oceans' currents as well. Water symbolizes emotions, and we were feeling the negative aspects of life as being unfulfilling. Hidden occult knowledge was coming out into the open, explaining and revealing some mysteries of life. "Seek and ye shall find." Those people who were ready were listening!

1981/1982

- First spiritual teaching wave from New Age teachers, psychologists, analysts, and seers. Heavy period to help sort out our old feelings. New beginnings for some. Spiritual teachers gathering, waiting to be heard.
- Abundant conflict and anger in the air. Our lives' changes were creating these conflicts and inner turmoil and we had to deal with our fears
- People needed to find faith for enlightenment and feel love for others. The churches were full with those who needed a path to find faith from their surging inner turmoil

1982/SPIRITUAL LEVEL

- We began the search for finding one's own path of the heart. To deal with our many issues for understanding our potential. Astrology began its rise in popularity once again to be a tool of self-help. The realizations of seeking balance as well as accepting ourselves. Adjustments were made to rid the inertia of our past and reach the depth of their inner feelings. A clearing time.

- No new thing was clear, as there was a war mentally between spiritual and material values. A chaotic time to learn how to handle the energy of self-change.

1982/1983

- We pushed for career changes and becoming one's own captain, striving to have our new dreams manifested.
- Uranus, the planet of extremes, moved into Scorpio for the next seven years (December 1981 to 1988). Scorpio energy signifies, among other things, death, rebirth, decay, and regeneration, with Uranus transiting it. Many choices will become available to us and made clear with the planets close to Earth's orbit.
- Ominous feelings on the rise, individual helplessness, increased crime, global pollution, poverty, mental illness, and disease. It is clear that if one would change the world, one must first perfect the self. Balance is the keynote!

MUNDANE LEVEL

- The crux is personal attitude. Our emotional responses: anger, fear, passive/aggressive, erotic behavior.
- Shaping up: Emphasis on body weight, skeletal structure (positive alignment, flexibility), nervous system (tension, lethargy, pain, irritability). Digestion/assimilation: chronic upsets or deficiencies. Emotional responses, very important. Touching upon extremes in mental attitude within the physical body itself. (The spas and physical therapy became the rage.)

1983

- The year of growth and development to find oneself in the stream of life, and take a stand for what you believe in. Most important, to find one's truth. Many were seeking capable counselors and teachers who were advanced in their spiritual understanding to help them grow through this time. A trial and error period . . . certainly as we were between old and new.

- President Reagan's attempted assassination caused tension for the country and the people who were concerned for not only themselves but the country's interests as well. We were developing concerns not only for ourselves and our families but as planet inhabitants ourselves and learning to take responsibility and give thought to world issues.
- Personal relationships were changing and it was also a time to think about making commitments. We needed counselors and physicians to help with our intense emotions and genetic personality conflicts. The masses needed more philosophical, psychiatric, and medical help. Divorces were more plentiful.
- Earth crust unstable at this time due to numerous shifts and wobbles on the planet. We have been given by God two thousand years to study the causes of our limits and we approach this time period now.
- The taking of drugs for destructive use was discussed more openly. Major programs for educating and helping drug abusers got under way.

Author's note: Drugs have been known to open doorways into expanding the brain. It can put us out of touch with reality. Some use it for the direction of spiritual focus—as in going into altered states of awareness—but they have been a destructive cause lending itself to mass suicides and deaths. After the awareness has been opened, however, those who didn't need a crutch and the ones who become responsible for themselves finished with their experimentation. Those who do not want to take the responsibility for themselves and instead put their problems upon others to deal with *became the addicts!*

1984

- This year was critical. The dark forces began to emerge. As prophesied three years before, the light of understanding showed the way. We had been seeding, fertilizing, and developing the light that planted and it had started to grow. Occult teachings were beginning to come out into the open and the clandestine meetings were over. The partial truths, dealing with corruption, lies, and disenchantment were not enough anymore. We were threatened by the side of this negative power as they began to gain control to have people revert to the past and not think for themselves.

- Major crisis to put us on the brink of nuclear war. People gathering, coming together (smoking peace pipes) for solar power, and speaking out for world peace. We gathered in strength.
- People weren't the same in learning levels, some still from the old stock and some separating old paths from new, finding speech is silver, silence is golden.
- This year presented three big problems: we were to go through, as prophesied, an economic collapse (1982–1987) to show people that they could not continue in their old ways, nor could the world. Emotions, mental anxieties, and financial balance must be established.
- The world was indeed in stage 1, readying themselves to make a breakthrough in their own thinking and world consciousness. Caring and feeling for others was a part of this change. As 1984 got under way, it came as the harbinger of what is to come in the near future. Change that is eminent will not be put off. There was a need to control the problems of government, environment, food, and inflation. The chill of our old ways was still in the balance and we had to prepare ourselves to come out from old conditioning, old input, and rise above the plane of indifference to understand our material realities and emotional truths.
- A connection was made, interlocking Earth into the solar system to speed up our process (planetary alignment), intensifying the energies to make us go through the changes faster to meet with our spiritual families and pave the way for our destinies. Indeed, 1984 served as the beginning and would make its point through 1987. Those ready for limitless change would be the survivors of this new generation.

1985

- Year of great communication with personal and spiritual needs. Truth teachings were brought forth into the open, at last! Old ancient teachings were reestablished as well as reestablishment of contact with our ancestors from the stars. The first wave of communication came from the Pleiades and second wave of communication from the star Sirius. We were being totally acknowledged from our outer space friends.

- Total change in our living concepts. Political opposition and struggle became more apparent as we became more interested in our world as a whole. A new circle of law was beginning to emerge, some scandal. In 1985, every living being felt some hardship and the need to make various shifts to find what the word *change* is all about. We had come face to face with facts and had to establish our own belief system once again with faith to make the various adjustments in our immediate surroundings. Many were beginning to open their minds to new thinking and new ways and developing this. Old patterns were leaving us. Many had difficulty. Collective family problems and heavy-duty physical problems were the result of our chaotic crunch and our heavy hearts.
- With the acceleration of change, we were moving into emphasizing our cycle of progress with physical and mental movement. We began to leave behind those who were not part of our change. Our physical bodies were changing as well to accommodate our new inner feelings. Stomach problems, lower back problems, acid, and toxic conditions were paving the way for our metaphysical and medical doctors. Therapists, counselors, and teachers, began to emerge to help and complete the understanding of mundane life and the fight for balance. We had to let go of our old conditioning to make the improvement into our spiritual growth. By the middle of this year, time stood still as the masses were paralyzed by confusion. The coming surge of disenchantment was beginning to take root as we began to recognize that all possibilities were not ours any longer. The inner need compelled us to move forward.
- Alcoholics, drug users, and sexual promiscuity were either on the wane or on the rise. The awareness that sex, being synonomous with sin, was overexposed. Porno and the acceleration of AIDS were proof and the last hurrah for sexual thrills.
- Marriage and having children were the "in" thing again. Emphasis on family life.
- This was an uncomfortable period with heavy emphasis on responsibility. Stress climbed to intolerable heights, causing a rash of mental illness as erratic terrorists' behavior had left our nerves jangled. People were reaching out against the injustices of society. Law cases for malpractice were more prominent.

- The end of 1985 was a transition leading to the realization that we must begin to manifest our needs and search for our hearts' desires.
- The reappearance of Halley's Comet in 1985 and the surge of energy that came with it enabled us to make the profound change in our human destiny. As it continued to move closest to Earth's orbit in 1986, it would help us to adjust to our emotional survival and endurance and work or put us out on a raft of emotional confusion.

1986

The veil of occult interest opened wide. Thousands upon thousands of the world's population became actively interested in extrasensory understanding through books, movies, classes, and the media. It was a year of spiritual awakening. Enlightened teachers, counselors, clergymen, and therapists assisted those who were ready to integrate two worlds of thought. It was found that the intellectuals were not the only channels of the teachings. The housewife, laborer, or farmer gave teachings of love, too, as they gathered the flock and shared their knowledge to help them understand this extreme year (change-or-die period). Our lives' problems were coming to a head and tremendous physical movement went into effect by having to switch from our old philosophies to prepare and enfold our human potential.

- Energy spots around the globe were becoming more powerful as a pole shift was under way, processing Earth changes. Our crystal formations in the Earth became alive and active. It stirred up our emotions to get us to act and push us into leaping forward to exploring our spiritual awareness. So many things were going on as we gave thought to expansion and nothing was the same as it was before. Earth was activated by weather conditions as well.
- Before our eyes, we viewed massive erosion of our coastal shorelines. Massive earthquakes were evidence of what was to come. By the end of this year, the build-up of energy in California and other parts of the west coast disappeared as forty years of pressure from volcanoes in the Earth vanished. Scientists were amazed at this miracle: as prophesy had it, California would "go." This miraculous change was due to

the help of our UFO contacts aiding us with their advanced technologies.
- Massive body and health problems were on the rise. Massage therapists, acupuncture, and new healing methods were used.
- Baby boom started and marriage commitments were being made again.
- AIDS, herpes, and cancer reached fear levels. The growing problem of cocaine, LSD, and other psychedelic drugs showed indications of growing out of proportion and we gave our effort to have it stopped.
- Most heads of state started to shift their consciousness and became aware of some government policies in the future that could prove disastrous for the peoples of the world. The leaders, too, were dividing in thought as scandals were breaking out into the open and corruption was seen for what it was. With scandals out in the open, negativity began to ooze.
- People became interested in the energies of crystals, rocks, and gemstones. The literary community was selling more books than before as people took the time to rest, read, and contemplate on their next move.

1987

In this year, the 144,000 spiritual teachers prophesied by God will all have totally awakened from their "dream mind bodies" and will meet with their destinies. The false prophets as well. Those ready for spiritual teachings will not know one from the other. These teachers will become conscious again and fulfill their roles to raise the planet's energy. Their energies will help change the balance of the planet. So, this year's energy will be extreme. The highs as well as the lows. The "messengers" of God will help to assist in this process. Our souls will be "on the table" and we will find that there are no set ways as all ways are true in the light. The words *I love you* will begin to flow more readily.

The year 1987 will complete the final run of Halley's Comet. This energy will speed up man's consciousness and evolutionary process. The movement of this comet, as it travels through the solar system, will speed up our levels of knowledge. The gravitational pull of this energy going past Earth will affect our tides and energies of the moon as well. The energies of the Sun will be glorified and bring on the predictions of polarization of the North and South Poles and create a huge vacuum that will speed up our progress to pave the path for the "findings" of humanity that have been living underneath the Earth's seas and in the Earth's crust. Its effect, our own personal planet serves as a detonating device for those born in air, earth, and fire signs. The Scorpio energies act as a catalyst to upgrade our thinking, unlocking a door to sacred knowledge and sciences of the ancients as it unfolds. Its richness and quality will cause man to be receptive. Its negative aspects will be felt as well, as it will set off volcanoes, earthquakes, and different weather patterns other than what we are used to. Those born within the Virgo sign will be the most vulnerable to the pulling of this kind of energy. The fixed signs of Taurus, Scorpio, and Aquarius will meet their doom if they are not on the proper path. If so, the energies of opposition will be dissipated. It will fade away.

With these shifts of the North and South Poles, the ocean floor will be changing. By the end of this year the Middle East will have giant explosions on their Earth turf. Desert areas starting to get too cold for inhabitants to live. Natural disasters will kill off masses of people.

The planet entered a period of disruption from the negativity of Earth between 1984 and 1986. Volcanic action will begin to itensify, as well as flooding in certain global areas. Vermont area and New Hampshire, Mt. Vermont . . . Parnassus, Mt. Etna (Italy), Japan, can have tidal wave in Hong Kong, Hawaii; waterways in the Gulf of Mexico will have underground seizures in the days to come.

Coastal shores a problem as the land shifts, with water seepage creating flooding. It will weaken our inner structure of Earth beneath the surface, making a shift in land masses. Abundant snowfall and hazardous weather extremes. Special activity of disruption in the Atlantic Ocean region.

Warping of the electromagnetic field around the planet causes earthquakes. Just as the moon has a part in tidal action affecting the tidal energies or the rising and falling of the magnetic energies of the Earth. The pull of the moon is very real action. Particles of energy that enter the field of Earth cause friction and produce a quick build-up of energy together with certain other planets in the solar system and the effect of where their positions are with this build-up releases explosive energy in the form of earthquakes. The whole solar system is moving in the Milky Way Galaxy and the galaxy is moving in the local Universe. Many storms of electrified particles bombard the planet in space. Huge amounts of snowfall on the East Coast.

- End of year to 1988, earthquake activity under Aegean Sea (Greece).
- Family hardships, little ones dying of malnutrition and starvation will be aided.
- By the end of the year the government will experience a whole revelation as corruption will be reaching the fringes of its peak.
- Planet flaunts its build-up of armaments and munitions of destruction. Violence and destruction in Middle East grave and dangerous. Dark side preparing poisonous gases and weapons of death. Those who follow the darkness and plot to enslave humanity shall fall by their own destruction.
- One must not attempt to see sorrow, but perceive great joy in the emerging New Age to maintain the stability of the planet.
- New type of brain surgery discovered.
- The reincarnation process will be clearly understood and that death is associated with painful fear. The idea of separation will show that we do alternately exist in two worlds at the same time. We will learn that in a lifetime when we sleep, we exist in two worlds as well.
- People are in search of answers and are finding them.

More and more of our celebrities in the United States are reaching the general public with their teachings. They will try to lead the way both in governmental positions and preaching that psychic phenomena is no myth. More and more books are coming out to help us enjoy what is beautiful and also to seek laughter as well as tears. Movie stars of prominence will be writing more and more books to communicate as well as satisfy their spiritual changes, to help us grow and to release the guilt of the past. The prophets will help us to look within, meditate to find the truth with a free heart and a free mind.

- The racists are from the dark side, challenging our right to be a soul. The youth will be in difficulty. The "Prince of Darkness" is involved in stirring up more negativity, but the positive side will be gaining in strength. The "wheat" will definitely be separated from the "chaff."

1988

A year of integration with cosmic and Earth laws. The government of the United States is in for a crucial change that began in 1987 and will continue in 1988. We still sit in new law circles. Civil and social law will tumble. The people will not accept bribes for fear of exposure and many old laws will be rejected. Politics and political changes are imminent and will not be put off. The United States will begin its struggle to be a big power once again in the world's eye (as it surfaces as a spiritual power at last).

1988–1992: THE FIVE YEARS OF RECONSTRUCTION

As February and the Ides of March 1988 arrive, earth will undergo the beginnings of four major developments which we cannot ignore:

- Geographical Changes
- Major Political Movement (Heads of Nations Uniting)
- Economic Development
- Spiritual Integration of Our Minds and Bodies

The planet will experience energy escaping from under the crevices of the earth. As the earth rotates on its axis with more speed, it will cause excess steam and vapors to be released from within earth to the outer surface of the planet. We will get warnings! Our underneath sea levels are changing around the globe, causing unusual currents. The altered atmospheric and stratospheric currents will cause scientists and weather technicians around the globe to ponder the meaning of the strange formation of the different currents. The space of energy fields around our galaxy cannot be ignored, as we will see a change around earth's aura. We will be made aware of the geographical rearrangement and shifting of earth's terrain. Land masses will begin to be changed as the erosion of our shores will create broader rivers and deeper oceans.

Volcanic eruptions can be helpful. They can expose the inner earth and lead to the discoveries of new natural resources. We will find that there will not be an energy crisis such as people in our governments would like us to believe. Many thousands of small and large volcanoes will activate beginning in 1988 to past the year 2000 as weather becomes colder and dryer. Droughts and floods will become part of the change.

South America is under siege. Subterranean (underground) areas will experience more mud slides and brackish water. Many will perish as conditions have closed up spring wells and damaged the water supply. An earthquake will start making the land very hot. There will be changes in the structure of land around Argentina. Discoveries of iron, magnesium, onyx, granite, and lead will increase their resources and capitalists will try to profit and get caught in a new scandal. Coffee plants will burn up. Columbian coffee will perish due to intense heat. Chile, Bolivia, Peru, and Columbia will experience hotter than normal patterns in climate due to the underground turmoil and volcanic eruption. Some countries in South America will become extra cold.

We will see deserts around the world sucked into the earth—evaporating as the sands are collapsing into earth. Shrinkage will cause environmental change.

Massive earthquakes in New York and California will affect the ocean floor, gulf stream and the Gulf of Mexico. Mexico will see new eruptions. Louisiana hit by high winds, floods around coastal areas (food shortages, water supplies). Oil explosion in Texas. Fires will burn for a few days, causing dangerous chemicals released into the atmosphere affecting many states.

Problems in mountains near Mt. Rushmore and North Dakota, also Washington State and in waters around Canadian borders as far as Alaska. East coast will experience much flooding too. Baltic Sea and Canary Islands will feel the changes too. The Netherlands will flood.

A lot of crystal formations planted by the Space Brotherhood millions of years ago before and around the time of Atlantis, will upset our earth's crust as it starts to crack and break off in different areas. Some crystals will act as generators of energy to control the flow of the rivers, streams, waters and tides. These changing currents and the reversal of earth's energy patterns and cycles are causing ice packs to form, especially in the areas that are avalanche-prone. Giant glaciers are moving as the bowels of the earth are rumbling. So there is quite a bit of activity underneath sea level *and* above sea level as many of the ice packs are breaking up. If it continues our geographical boundaries will be changed by these natural disasters.

- New fresh water springs in various parts of the globe as well as our discoveries of new underground tunnels will appear. These caves will be germ-free and become non-pollutant areas. We cannot ignore the pollution in our air or in our seas any longer.
- Rebellion and terrorism will be unfashionable as the governmental seats of the world will choose whether they will serve peace or war. Everything will be out in the open and no hidden any longer and we can begin to define goodness.
- Russia and the United States will join forces to discuss the most vital topic of our space age, psychic phenomena and politics. They will sign many peace treaties. We will find that we have misjudged this nation. Although we have viewed them as backward socially and economically, metaphysics and science will bring us together to work out some of our world's problems. We will actively link together our space activities as well. Russia will have water problems and flooding, with difficulties in Siberia as some relay stations of communication will disappear under the snow.
- Mainland China a threat. The government has some light and extreme dark beings in it. Much in the way of changes happening there now as world affairs thicken and corruption cause destruction. Natural disasters as well. Darkness is ignorance and trouble will come from their superstitions, bad government and growing nuclear power, causing many countries to perk up and pay attention.
- Israel is angry at the United States again. Interference with Iran, Iraq, and so on. The United States will have to side with Israel and this will cause another uprising with Arab countries I can see soldiers moving.
United States will be involved in a military and naval loss devastating to the American people if it is not careful. I see ship and sailors, also some civilians, attacked in Persian Gulf Battleships as well as an aircraft carrier may be attacked starting with the letter "N." Could engage in a war. Afghanistan can unite with the forces of Iran. Khomeini can act as th

Anti-Christ. French, English, Scandinavian and Oriental cargo ships will be near the scene. We must hold our balance as the next three years are critical to avoid war (1988–1990) as negativity is imminent and will not be held off. Crises will be escalated. We must watch every move.

Outbreak of hostilities in Cuba.

Love for our fellow man from those filled with love will see barbarianism at its worst. Atrocities will be expressed outwardly. There can be no negotiating with people on a low level of consciousness—war is imminent.

The planet's structure started its changes in 1886 and prophecy has it that there will be a one-hundred year reconstruction period until 1996.

The stock market will go wild again after the election of a new president. The market will fall as our economy shows signs of depression as the publics mistrust for the new president and national leaders. The changes in the market's overall pattern began in 1987 but fear will persist throughout 1991. The commodities market will be powerful with emphasis on gold, platinum, silver and other precious metals. Also, iron and iron ore. Economic struggles over new policies will be in force until 1990.

State of Pennsylvania will become a keypoint in political issues and a Kansas republican will begin to emerge from left field as a discerning politician and will be able to aid in New Age policies on the side of the light. Many changes in governmental positions will change and change again as our economic concerns will be as problematic as our financial flow.

Our ex-President, Jimmy Carter, through his spiritual understanding and prayer work, will aid our new government and gather many people in support for our country's choices and change. He was once a Prince in Atlantis. Warmongers will encourage war to reduce the national debt and economic situation. Mr. Carter will be of help.

The collective will of man, events on this planet, and the progression and advancement of the light as well as the dark side will give us conscious understanding as members of the human race that we can no longer succumb to this darkness. We have understood in these years that we cannot lower our vibrations any longer. Also, that crystals are not a fad, but an energy form of our conscious awakening to facilitate our energies to come into synchronization.

- Planets are moving with the mind of God. We will listen to nature as our answers will come from God.
- Humanity will see and feel a more energetic movement in the air as a way to continue new dreams as enlightened human together as one consciousness.
- Totally powerful masters in 1989 will help to lead the world out of difficulty on the political scene. Global large-scale organizational changes. Mankind and the general public will look to spiritual leaders to act on their behalf. Justice will overrule. Those rooted in love will fulfill their time, taking charge of their destiny. Star People will come alive to serve our bettering society.
- The change of our values is inevitable, collectively and separately. To go through change will bring light and understanding within ourselves. We will be more adaptable to accept the miraculous, the unexpected, and not feel totally defeated. Man's primary problem is not accepting change. We will learn to experience change. Many find it too disturbing, especially when the mind wants security. Those who cannot change will cross over into another dimension from tragedies involving large groups of people on land, air, or sea travels (also some through illness).
- We will be more aware of the Star People who will give us understanding in this New Age. They will enable us to stay open to our intuitive capacities in all professions and help our energy systems through this difficult time. They will help us to be magnetized and grounded to earth changes and crystalization. A source of spiritual input comes from space ships, as many people on this planet can hear their vibrational sound and tone in their ears. This energy will eventually improve the awareness. Those missionaries, the channels and the healers will be attuned by an audio frequency from the ships to aid them in their work for humanity.
- Space ships are hovering around the planet and are doubling in number in these times of human stress. They are here to help us and also cleanse the pollution seeping out all over the planet. These evolved beings will be seen by more and more people. Some people will report landings on building tops as we come closer to 1990 and 1991. Members of the Air Force will experience many sightings, but will they tell their stories? These are friendly people and are here to aid us as our negativities

are destroying the ozone layers of the atmosphere and endangering their planets. We can count on their help to beam us up to their ships in case of an earth disaster or evacuation. Many of us come from those planets from a prior incarnation. The UFO phenomena will attract media and large public gatherings.

- Watch the youth who are feverishly working through all of their negative experiences in these few short years. There will be a breakdown in their behavioral patterns that will cause exceptional havoc with their nervous systems and emotional natures and they will reveal to us that they cannot handle themselves as much as they would like us to believe. The "rose colored glasses" will come off and they will begin paying their dues emotionally, physically, and financially, coming back to us from their "impulsive lives."

- Baby boom and marriage definitely the rage.

- Celebrities will find new areas to explore their creative potential. They will begin to come forward to tell the public more about their private lives and belief in occult sciences. They will become the most visible "dream and truth seekers" for us.

- Many sick people will go into deep depression states, unable to get out of those patterns. Suicide and self-destructive tendencies on the rampage. Our consciousness will turn inward as we will seek more actively to find that inner sea of peace within. It will beat down our pride and greed. We will not be defeated by our circumstances.

- AIDS will reach the panic stage as well. Big breakthroughs in finding effective cures for cancer.

- Science will once again become metaphysics. It will provide the magic we need, as some of our Cosmic Laws will be fully in effect. Magic is the correct use of the spiritual and physical forces of nature that go beyond the conscious understanding of humans for the betterment of the galaxy. White Magic pertains to the level of understanding and the intent of its use. Black Magic has the potential to be totally destructive, but black and white magic exist simultaneously.

- Religion will be challenged. Conservative churches will be in deep crisis. People will want spiritual manifestations instead of archaic Old World thinking. Churches will begin to change their policies. Many of us on Earth will be attuned to a clearer understanding about human life and will begin to understand the power of prayer.

- Everywhere on Earth energy may be overloaded. We must watch our energy sources, cable and satellites. Does it make sense to replace people in job situations with robots that can talk and computers? A problem will arise when a computer goes haywire in banks as well as institutional resources. There will be blackouts as well.
- Art will be as books, symbolic educators, and bring to us a new style of living, feeling, and thinking.
- Ancient sacraments like Noah's Ark will be found in the state of Pennsylvania. Massive discoveries as well in Mexico, Peru, and Argentina.
- Those countries that work in darkness for greed and treachery will lose their hold and power on the weak and find they cannot continue in their wake of destruction nor be isolationists.
- Leaders of China, the United States and Russia will gather for major talks.
- Some areas of Atlantis will be located in the Gulf of Mexico, Saragasso Sea, Canary Islands and the Caribbean.
- Discussion continues about migration on other planets in space shuttles as well as space homes. A large group of space pioneers will be eager to see if they can exist in space and volunteer to do so.
- Planetary harmony on Earth will begin to increase as the seeds of love that have fertilized will be planted.
- The Bureau of Vital Statistics in the United States will establish a new system for birth records. The data will include problems that may have come up in the mother's pregnancy and father's data as well as a list of the doctors who attended the birth. The records will also contain important astrological and medical information.

The Star Children who were born in the 1960s will be the group responsible for the New Age teachings. They will prepare the race as the first forty year cycle begins. Many incoming souls born between the 1980s to mid-1990s will be born with a higher intelligence and sixth sense. They will shape the world with their extrasensory perception.

Earth will find its true function and be fully formed, creating many new things in harmony with everyone else. Earth will join the Sisterhood of Planets.

Scientists will have found that the common cold does not

exist. A change in the body's temperature that produces a vacuum of energy that closes off the respiratory system and nasal passages is due to contact with incompatible vibrations (people and polluted air). It is a chemical disorder that causes the temperature of the body to rise as a barometer and is contagious.

If we change the body's polarity, by redistributing our energy, we can stimulate healthy organisms to counteract the negative ones. Many new discoveries about developing immunity from colds in 1989, but will the public be informed? This information would negatively affect our pharmaceutical industries.

The global cleansing will be completed in its first phase. The awareness and activity coming from our myriad changes will indeed start a chain reaction around the world. Those people who live in enlightened geographical places will definitely be searching and seeking this light force for more answers to their troubled lives. People in all walks of life will find themselves interested in this great reunion, in replenishing our emotional states in peace. Man is now changing his outlook on life to focus on the discovery of self, self-help, self-aid, self-wisdom, self-discipline. Years of martyrdom and negativity produced regrets and influenced the sympathetic nervous system of our life force that feeds on our depressions. As we look back to the year 1914, we will see how far our attitudes and value systems have changed and we will see our first steps to major improvements in human life.

The energies that were released in 1986 are not done yet, since man is still freeing himself from delusions of his own making. With 1988-1992, each person should have a working plan and positive input life, to work out their individual and everyday karmas. The work load shall increase for thinking men but certain changes with the earth's shifts will free us. As we are put through the tests of time, we will feel less constricted as we see where our work has taken us.

1993–2000: THE LAST STAGE, THE CYCLE OF COMPLETION (2010)

- Our plant life will flourish and their colors and hues will take on a different vibrancy. Life will take on some new meanings.
- Starvation and the homeless problem on Earth will begin to be eradicated and will no longer be a threat to our lives.

- Our power companies will reorganize and a new electrical system will be working as these new electrical treatments will help us to communicate around the world faster than before for our service and utility. Most of our nation's power circuits will be hidden underground.
- Mass transportation for people traveling in large cities as well as rural communities will be streamlined. There will be more double-decker highways. Our trains, too, will be using a new type of service for transit.
- The possibility of another state being added to the United States will be discussed and be put to Congress for voting.
- In this year, we will be enlightened in our physical bodies, as this is the year of total balance and harmony within ourselves. Many changes will have already been made as we feel our energies fit like a glove and we are in tune with our life's work. We will see more restoration to our towns and cities, and new kinds of law enforcement agencies.
- Our water supply will become purer and fresher as fresh water springs will be discovered in many places. We will begin to start healing our bodies with pure water.
- New types of buildings will be constructed that use solar energy. The shapes and forms they will take will keep the energies contained within them. Ores and metals used will be pure, and new types of metals for healing will be uncovered as well as used for building material. Gold, now used as a precious metal, will have new uses, especially in medicine.
- Many people will begin to emigrate and adapt to life on other planets. They will live and breed in star ships and understand life in other galaxies. Housed in these star ships, they will develop plant life, refrigeration systems, and work shops, for scientific research and to make medicine. There will be a self-contained unit for family life. We grow from change.
- World government will substantially change. A discussion group will be formed to deal with changes in how governments, are led by presidents, kings, and queens. In this year, we will begin to set up a new political system whereby there will be one seat of power to serve the peoples of the world, with elected officials chosen from various countries. It will consist of a panel of twelve which will aid and facilitate the process of peace.
- Metaphysicians, scientists, and doctors will become one and the same.

- Division of rich and poor will shift. Jobs will require highly skilled people who will be paid well. Unskilled workers will become the minority.
- The entire solar system is a self-contained unit of energy matter and intelligence. Some solar systems are at the end as well as beginning of a totally new level of energy vibration. People on earth must work to be correctly balanced to this new electro-magnetic energy.
- Society will come to grips with the New Age "black plague" of AIDS and it will ease.
- Astrology will once again be a science and a highly skilled occupation. Most people will tune into the stars for the answers to their lives. Time traveling will become part of many lives. Gasoline engines will have already been replaced with new power technology.
- Earth has gone and come through periods of restoration, disintegration, economic and weather catastrophies and conflicts with race and religions, and still it stands. These backward and forward moves have ended. We have more than survived.

*Thank you, Carmen, my power ray. You know where you are through these channeling sessions.

NEW AGE CLASSICS
ENDURING BOOKS FOR OUR TIME AND BEYOND

☐ 27747   **ZEN AND THE ART OF MOTORCYCLE** $5.50
              MAINTENANCE,   Robert M. Pirsig

The fabulous journey of a man in search of himself . . .
"Profoundly important . . . intellectual entertainment of
the highest order."   —New York Times

☐ 26382   **DANCING WU LI MASTERS: An Overview** $4.95
              of the New Physics,   Gary Zukov

"The Bible" for those who are curious about the mind-
expanding discoveries of advanced physics, but who have
no scientific background.

☐ 26299-8   **ENTROPY: A New World View,**   Jeremy Rifkin $4.50

Tells us why our existing world view is crumbling and
what will replace it.

"An appropriate successor to . . . SILENT SPRING, THE
CLOSING CIRCLE and SMALL IS BEAUTIFUL."
           —Minneapolis Tribune

☐ 34584   **THE MIND'S I: Fantasies and Reflections** $13.95
              on Self and Soul,   Douglas R. Hofstadter
              and Daniel C. Dennett

A searching, probing book that delves deeply into the
domain of self and self-consciousness. Co-authored by
the winner of the Pulitzer Prize.

"Invigorating . . . a heavy set of tennis for the brain."
           —Village Voice

☐ 34683   **METAMAGICAL THEMAS: Questing for the** $15.95
              Essence of Mind and Pattern,
              Douglas R. Hofstadter

The national bestseller by the Pulitzer Prize-winning
author of GODEL, ESCHER, BACH.

For your convenience use this page to order.

Bantam Books, Dept. NA10, 414 East Golf Road,
Des Plaines, IL 60016

Please send me _____ copies of the books I have checked. I am
enclosing $_____ (please add $2.00 to cover postage and handling).
Send check or money order—no cash or C.O.D.s please.

Mr/Ms _____

Address_____

City/State _____ Zip _____
                                           NA10—12/88
Please allow four to six weeks for delivery. This offer expires 6/89.
Prices and availability subject to change without notice.

EXPLORE THE SPIRITUAL WORLD WITH
SHIRLEY MacLAINE AND JESS STERN

Check to see which of these fine titles are missing from your bookshelf:

Titles by Jess Stern:

☐ 26085	EDGAR CAYCE: SLEEPING PROPHET	$4.50
☐ 25150	SOULMATES	$3.95
☐ 26057	YOGA, YOUTH, AND REINCARNATION	$3.95

Titles by Shirley MacLaine:

☐ 27557	DANCING IN THE LIGHT,	$4.95
☐ 27370	OUT ON A LIMB	$4.95
☐ 27438	"DON'T FALL OFF THE MOUNTAIN"	$4.95
☐ 26173	YOU CAN GET THERE FROM HERE	$4.50

Look for them in your bookstore or use the coupon below:

- -

Bantam Books, Dept. PW4, 414 East Golf Road, Des Plaines, IL 60016

Please send me the books I have checked above. I am enclosing $_____ (please add $2.00 to cover postage and handling). Send check or money order—no cash or C.O.D.s please.

Mr/Ms _____

Address _____

City/State _____ Zip _____

PW4—1/89

Please allow four to six weeks for delivery. This offer expires 7/89. Prices and availability subject to change without notice.